Greece's 'Odious' Debt

Greece's 'Odious' Debt

The Looting of the Hellenic Republic by the Euro, the Political Elite and the Investment Community

by Jason Manolopoulos

ANTHEM PRESS
LONDON · NEW YORK · DELHI

Anthem Press
An imprint of Wimbledon Publishing Company
www.anthempress.com

This edition first published in UK and USA 2011
by ANTHEM PRESS
75-76 Blackfriars Road, London SE1 8HA, UK
or PO Box 9779, London SW19 7ZG, UK
and
244 Madison Ave. #116, New York, NY 10016, USA

British Library Cataloguing in Publication Data
A catalogue record for this book is available from the British Library.

Library of Congress Cataloging in Publication Data
Manolopoulos, Jason.
Greece's 'odious' debt : the looting of the Hellenic republic by the
euro, the political elite and the investment community /
by Jason Manolopoulos.
p. cm.
Includes bibliographical references and index.
ISBN 978-0-85728-771-7 (pbk. : alk. paper)
1. Financial crises–Greece. 2. Debts, External–Greece.
3. Euro–Greece. 4. Finance–Greece. 5. Greece–Economic policy–21st
century. 6. European Union. I. Title.
HB3807.5.M36 2011
330.9495'076–dc22
                                                2011012810

ISBN-13: 978 0 85728 771 7 (Pbk)
ISBN-10: 0 85728 771 0 (Pbk)

This title is also available as an eBook.

To my parents

CONTENTS

LIST OF FIGURES AND TABLES

FIGURES

TABLES

PREFACE

As the global recession began in 2008, the Greek economy featured high
levels of public debt, a large trade deficit, undiversified industries, an
overextended public sector, militant trade unions, widespread corruption,
uneven payment of taxes, an overvalued currency, consumers expecting
rising living standards and euro membership based on inaccurate data.
Yet in February 2009, the European Union's economics commissioner
Joaquin Almunia observed:

> The Greek economy is in better condition compared with the
> average condition in the eurozone, which is currently in recession.

When the head of one of the most powerful economic institutions
in the West is making a statement so out of line with reality that it
bears comparison with pronouncements on production targets by the
Soviet Union, something is seriously wrong. We have to ask some
very big questions of the institutions that run our affairs, and we
have to ask questions about beliefs and decision making, as well as
analysis and data.

This book tells the story of an international economic crisis in which
a small country played a crucial role. At the time of writing, it is not
clear whether the impact will be cataclysmic, representing the beginning
of the end of the good way of life for Europeans, or whether it will
force a mere adjustment to the living standards of the old continent.
The reasons are micro and macro, national and global. Not a single
constituency emerges well from this story; Greek politicians, Greek
society, trade unions, leaders of the European Union, the IMF, the
world's investment banks – each and every one has scarcely put a foot
right in a collective display of hubris, miscalculation, overambition,
deception, mis-selling, folly and, in some cases, sheer greed in a saga
that has continued for decades.

Here are the headlines of the crisis:

- The single European currency, the euro, consists of 17 dissimilar economies, and has failed to create a unified currency area. The difference between surplus and deficit nations has widened, in a repeat of earlier experiments.
- The dramatic announcement of 9 May 2010, including an unprecedented liquidity package of more than €750 billion and the abandonment of the European Central Bank's independence through bond purchases, confirms that the euro was mis-sold as an enterprise to the continent's citizens.
- The 'peripheral' countries of the eurozone face years of severe austerity measures with an uncertain chance of success, placing strains on their political systems and even on public order.
- The aggregate sovereign debt of Europe is now measured in trillions of euros, at a time when the continent faces a demographic squeeze, with expensive pensions liabilities and an ageing society. The world's rising economies, especially in Asia, are set to eclipse the old continent.
- Greece has been allowed to borrow in excess of €300 billion, despite a largely unreformed economy, overreliance on mid-tech industries, a chronically inefficient and corrupt public sector and an unreformed political infrastructure with immunity for politicians guilty of financial crimes.
- The global economy has been damaged by an orgy of leverage, in which rent-seeking investment banks have turned money into a commodity, creating destabilising investment bubbles and excessive levels of government debt.

This was no act of fate. Nor was it even unprecedented – I will look at some strikingly similar crises from the recent past, and ask why no lessons were learned. The convenient phrase 'in hindsight', which we have often read from policymakers following the near-collapse of the European Monetary Union in 2010, is dishonest; these people were warned, implicitly and explicitly. Their piloting of the single currency, the Exchange Rate Mechanism, was a failure. Instead of learning from this, the EU's leaders built a bigger version of the same, and dismissed reasoned, intelligent critiques of their plan, all widely and publicly aired. The policy errors made in Argentina in the 1990s were repeated, in tragicomic fashion, in Greece in the 2000s. This begs some big questions. We have to stop applying policies that have failed in theory and failed in practice. If medicine had kept pace with economics, we would still be using blood-letting and mercury.

While researching this book, in seeking to cover all significant dimensions – from Greek history to the foundation of the European Union to the contemporary international bond market – I have been struck by the influence of the psychological dimension, and how it is often overlooked. In the investment world, the discipline of behavioural finance is starting to inform us that markets, and the people who shape them, are often not rational, and that an understanding of psychological biases can shed light on how real markets behave. They also affect policymakers and the economists who advise them. These biases appear to contribute to systemic, repeated errors, such as:

- Extrapolation from recent data to project into the future, assuming a level of continuity that is often not present.
- Misdiagnosis, by identifying patterns that do not exist, or exaggerating the level of knowledge held by policymakers.
- Overly confident projections and explanations.
- A tendency to exaggerate the impact of policy intention, and the degree of control of policymakers, as seen in phrases such as 'too big to fail'.

These psychological dynamics are often hidden behind a wall of data, charts and calculations, yet the politically most important indicators are crude. There is an almost exclusive reliance on the headline GDP growth figure as the key measure of economic performance. This is used to sustain some dangerously misleading statements, such as that of Almunia. It fails to distinguish between debt-fuelled spending and sustainable economic development. This is a symptom of a wider problem, which is to confuse data for performance, and regard behavioural economics as no more than an amusing sideline or a fad. This means that high-risk behaviour – whether it is by reckless investment banks, property developers or national politicians – is not taken into consideration in economic analysis or planning. For example, many commentators have asked me why the collapse in confidence in the affordability of Greek government debt was so sudden in the autumn/winter of 2009–2010. To me, a more telling question is: why did the illusion persist for so long that it was safe to lend such vast sums to such a small, dysfunctional economy?

In looking for answers to what supported the dangerous build-up of debt at the time, one comes across vague metaphors rather than reasoned assessments. For example, the single currency was supposed to act as a 'shield' against default; or else it was a 'train' leading inexorably to economic development. Faith in these special qualities, which turned out to be illusory, could be every bit as strong in an investment bank analyst, or a commissioner at the EU, as in a grassroots campaigner for European monetary union.

Most analyses of the eurozone crisis are couched in the formal language of economics. This book addresses that dimension, but also delves deeper. I intend to consider the historical background of the particular decisions made, and the psychology that shaped them. In particular, notable cognitive biases are observable. There may be a tendency to think that the elites are immune from such primal psychological forces. This saga illustrates graphically that they are not. So in addition to the well-known political and institutional actors in the eurozone drama, I would like to introduce a supporting cast. These are the cognitive biases that have influenced policy – and which, in my view, have often diverted it from a rational course. For example, *confirmation bias* refers to the tendency to notice and to emphasise material that confirms your beliefs, and to overlook or downgrade evidence that contradicts them. *Herd behaviour*, or *groupthink*, the tendency to follow the herd, is common in both the investment and political communities. *Illusion of control*, a tendency to overestimate one's degree of influence over external events, is a common trait of central bankers and organisers of currency pegs. *Overconfidence bias*, the tendency to let the wish become the father of the thought, has been common in European Union elites.

These biases have played more than an incidental role. They have helped to shape an avoidable crisis.

We spend much time analysing the fallout of economic crises, and devote insufficient attention to understanding their causes. The process of building high levels of debt is more enjoyable for politicians, their electorates and the banks than reining in such activity.

Future generations will not thank us for the excesses of the current age. They may even start to look up the definition of the 'odious' debt. This is a legal theory, established in the 1920s, which holds that national debt incurred by a government for purposes that do not serve the best interests of the nation should not be enforceable. Such debts are held to be personal debts of the unrepresentative regime that incurred them and not of that country's population. Could the Greek people cite this, given the off-balance-sheet manipulations to the national deficit a decade ago that had the effect of increasing long-term debt costs? Could the Irish, given that they have been handed the bill for fraudulent banking activity which benefited an unrepresentative elite?

And above all, given the decade-long encouragement of borrowing by unelected European Union commissioners and their refusal to impose sanctions for breaching the deficit and debt limits of the Maastricht Treaty, could the future populations of the EU begin to challenge whether they should pay the colossal bill that the older generation has accumulated? The rush to monetary union and the failure to consult and hold referendums may come back to haunt the EU's leaders.

These are extreme scenarios, but the point is that the extreme nature of the current crisis is still not being fully communicated by political leaders to their electorates due to the psychological nature of its creation. New narratives are being told, such as 'we will return to growth swiftly', or 'your sacrifices will not be in vain'. In the final analysis, behavioural economics is neither a trendy concept nor a fad, it is all there is, because behaviour also determines economic outcomes. Understanding this requires a conceptual leap for our political and institutional leaders, and they do not have much time in which to make it.

Chapter 1

FROM BUENOS AIRES TO ATHENS

Keeping books on social aid is capitalistic nonsense. I just use the money for the poor. I can't stop to count it.

—Eva Perón

As the eurozone crisis reached a critical phase in late 2009 and early 2010, one of the accusations most certain to provoke the fury of representatives of the European Union was the comment that 'Greece is like Argentina'.

Why the comparison, and why the anger? There are many parallels. Argentina and Greece appear to have followed a similar trajectory in their recent histories, not just in the past two decades, but in the entire period since the Second World War. Both suffered under military juntas who justified their actions by anti-Communism. Both have a socialist, clientelist ethos in which interest groups have sought, and often received, direct assistance from the state. Elections and parliamentary decision-making returned in 1974 after seven years of dictatorship in the case of Greece, and in 1983 in the case of Argentina. In both cases, military humiliation at the hands of a foreign power was a major factor in the collapse of the regimes.

Both countries have a history of being the most advanced economy in their region, and are conscious of this status. Overseas visitors to Athens and Buenos Aires have the experience of visiting an advanced economy: both have a grand, modern airport, impressive boulevards and shopping malls. Athens in particular, since the infrastructure improvements for the 2004 Olympics, boasts a modern metro and freeways. The contrast with some of the poorer neighbouring countries in, respectively, the Balkans and South America is sharp – though some of these unfashionable nations may be catching up with, or even overtaking, their illustrious neighbours.

More recently, both countries have relinquished monetary flexibility by respectively pegging their currency to the US dollar and joining the euro. Both enjoyed a honeymoon in the early years of the currency regime, with a superficial appearance of economic success, but in both cases there was a progressive underlying loss of competitiveness. Both experiments featured a lack of the sort of structural reforms needed to adapt to life in a strong currency area, with clientelist practices continuing and being facilitated by easy credit arrangements and high levels of government borrowing. The two economies experienced international economic crises, the Asian and credit crisis respectively, followed by governmental debt crises and International Monetary Fund (IMF) intervention. In the case of Argentina, it ended in default and crisis in December 2001.

This is most probably the reason the comparison causes such fury in Brussels. But the Argentine economic crisis predated Greece's crash by ten years: so were no lessons learned? In economics, we are often tempted to envisage what the long-term scenario may look like. In Argentina's experiment with the peg to the dollar, the long term is now. While every national context is unique, the parallels do seem sufficient here to merit further inquiry as a means of understanding some of the dangerous economic dynamics at play in Greece and the rest of the eurozone, and how they might play out in the next few years.

Exchange Rate Stabilisation

Argentina in 1991 and Greece in 2001 effectively entered exchange rate stabilisation programmes. In the case of Greece, of course, the notion was that it was taking part in a full and permanent currency union. The idea, however, that there was economic convergence with the rest of the eurozone as part of an optimal currency area was fiction, as I shall discuss further in chapters 3 and 8. Essentially, it was a currency peg like Argentina's, with an unreformed economy.

Several studies of exchange rate stabilisation programmes have concluded that they tend to be effective at curbing high inflation, but have dangerous side effects, especially when essential reforms are postponed. They should be used as a short-term emergency measure by a government determined to use the breathing space created to reform the public sector and improve the supply-side. In practice, complacency often creeps in, as the economic data in the first couple of years can be flattering. This was certainly the case in Argentina and Greece. A common pattern is

1) real appreciation of the exchange rate
2) investment and consumption boom
3) deterioration of external accounts.[1]

Argentina: Background to the Dollar Peg

In January 1991 the Chilean Lake District enjoyed perfect summer weather. Thousands of tourists, mostly Argentinian but including a few Europeans, enjoyed the stunning views of shimmering lakes, verdant mountain sides and snow-capped volcanoes in the picturesque resorts of Osorno, Puerto Montt and Chiloé Island, enjoying day after day of clear sunshine in a country completing its first year of democracy following the years of the Pinochet dictatorship. On one day towards the end of the month, however, the resorts suddenly became close to deserted. The weather and Chile's politics were unchanged, but the beaches and lakeside hotels became strangely empty. Puzzled, the few remaining North American and European tourists asked the hotel staff what had occurred. The Argentinians, they explained, had had to return home. There had been a plunge in the value of their currency, the austral, and they could not afford to be abroad for a day longer.[2]

Even this shock was not the peak of hyperinflation in the South American country; two years earlier the consumer price index for Buenos Aires had reached more than 5,000 per cent.[3] An estimate of the longer-term impact of hyperinflation was that, by the time the new peso replaced the austral in 1991, one new peso was equal to 100,000,000,000 pre-1983 pesos.[4] The end of the twentieth century and beginning of the twenty-first witnessed a dramatic fall for what had been the most prosperous country of South America, and one of the ten richest nations in the world in the first half of the twentieth century. By the 1980s and 1990s, a stream of Argentinians of Italian descent were returning to Italy to look for work, in a poignant reversal of the journey their entrepreneurial parents and grandparents had made to one of the more promising of the 'New World' countries.

Some Argentinians will confess that by the late twentieth century the economy had developed the dimensions of a dwarf '*con una cabeza gigante pero un cuerpo pequeño*' ('with a giant head but a small body'). The airport and capital city were everything that you would come to expect of an advanced economy, but there was not the backbone of medium-large enterprises and successful business clusters that one finds in the USA, France, Germany or Japan. It had Yankee ambitions for regional leadership based on a Confederate economy – income based primarily on agriculture and commodities.

When Carlos Menem was elected as president of Argentina in 1989 the country had been suffering from hyperinflation, a recurring problem since the return to democracy six years earlier. He initially pursued some crude anti-inflation measures, such as the confiscation of short-term, high-yielding bank deposits and their replacement with long-term bonds, but these had only short-term effects, and by the end of 1990 inflation had returned, accompanied by a plummeting exchange rate that was to prompt the sudden exodus of Argentinian tourists from their summer holiday destinations.

Early in 1991 Menem changed course. Though from a Peronist background characterised by protectionism, he surprised many critics by following many elements of the orthodoxy of the Washington Consensus: major privatisation programmes, an end to tariffs, and anti-inflation monetary policies. The end of January 1991 saw the appointment of Domingo Cavallo as the country's finance minister, who was about to embark on a bold monetary experiment designed to crush inflation. The idea was brutally simple: in a modern version of the Gold Standard, Argentina introduced convertibility: one peso equalled one US dollar. The system, which began in April 1991, required that the central bank kept enough dollars or gold in reserve to back the total amount of pesos that had been printed.

It fitted perfectly with Argentina's psychology of regional leadership and with recent anxieties over the value of the currency. One of the experts Cavallo consulted was Horacio Liendo, who had written a doctoral thesis on social and economic emergencies. In his account of the crisis, Paul Blustein notes that Liendo was struck by the apparent success of the monetary rule that the Argentine government had adopted in the period 1899 to 1929, the 'three most successful decades' in Argentina's history.[5]

There appear to be some cognitive biases at play here. Liendo may have been misled by an apparent correlation between adoption of the Gold Standard and economic development that was no more than a coincidence. It appears to be a case of *confirmation bias* – the tendency to interpret information in a way that confirms one's preconceptions; and *problem of induction* – making an unsafe inference from an apparent correlation. The 'three most successful decades in Argentina's history' that he noted, between 1899 and 1929, may have been created by a combination of rising immigration, increasing agricultural productivity and wars and revolutions in Europe that affected output in the old continent, creating a strong demand for imports from South America. A currency arrangement can bolster a strong economy, but it cannot create one – a narrative fallacy we will encounter again and again in the course of this book. It could have been a spurious correlation.

Clientelism: The Legacy of Peronism and its Hellenic Counterpart

A major contributory factor to the problems in Argentina and Greece is the phenomenon of 'clientelism' – essentially, interest groups within society requesting favours from politicians as *clients*, often with little regard to a reciprocal contribution to the economy. This occurs in all societies, of course, but for different historical reasons interest groups have been particularly influential in these two countries. In the case of Argentina, clientelism is inextricably linked with Peronism. Understanding this Argentine phenomenon is essential to our being able to understand both the hyperinflation of the 1980s and the currency peg that followed in the 1990s, as well as the problems associated with reform during that decade.

Unfortunately, Argentina's image in the West has been distorted by the romantic view of Eva Perón in the sentimental hit musical *Evita*. The reality was more complicated. Juan Domingo Perón was first elected in 1946, on a mixed programme of support for the working poor, protectionism, patriotism and nationalisation. He sought a 'third way' between the USA and USSR at a time of cold war tension. He tried to establish aircraft and car manufacturing through nationalised initiatives. This was hugely ambitious, and he could not achieve in nine years the kind of industrial development that had taken many decades in North America. In effect, the state tried to occupy the role that an entire social class of industrialists and financiers fulfils in an advanced economy.[6]

While Perón's industrial initiatives failed, the practice of subsidies and favours to certain interest groups remained. The thrust of Peronism became disbursing funds, not creating wealth. Under Perón and the dictators, the state exercised control on businesses, requiring start-up permits, import licenses and so on.[7] This encouraged corruption and the establishment of conglomerates.

Perón's concessions to the trade unions in the 1940s created an inflexible labour market in which it was difficult to fire workers. This was long lasting, and President Carlos Menem baulked at reforming many of these measures in the late 1990s, when the IMF urged labour market reform as part of the economic restructuring deemed necessary to ensure that the currency peg to the dollar would be effective.

In an advanced economy, wealth is created by industries that become concentrated into 'clusters' of specialist providers. Some of this wealth may then be used to support certain political movements. With Peronism and other forms of clientelism, the money flows in the opposite direction: politicians seize revenue from whatever sources are available – oil, soya exports, borrowing from capital markets – and give it to favoured interest groups to buy votes.

This inverted dynamic remains ignored by policymakers in Brussels and in the IMF, and such oversight has been an historic error in policies towards Argentina and subsequently Greece. It is a fundamental mistake of analysis caused by looking at headline financial data, rather than the economic dynamics that lie underneath. True economic convergence is essential to the creation of an optimal currency area as a precursor for monetary union, as I shall discuss further in the next chapter.

Peronism's mixture of apparent opposites – a bizarre coalition of social democracy, Communism and fascism – makes it a difficult phenomenon for those in Western Europe or North America to understand – and indeed it subsequently split into left-wing and right-wing factions. It did not create fertile ground for the development of a strong private sector. But worse was to follow. Economic problems, combined with a suspicion towards Perón from the church and the upper class, contributed to the military coup of 1955. Between that date and the fall of junta in 1983 Argentina suffered brutal dictatorships and relative economic decline. In 1950, the country was economically on a par with Australia or Canada. Argentinian GDP per capita was 84 per cent of the average of developed nations; by 1973 the figure was 65 per cent, and by 1987, 43 per cent. Greeks should heed this warning from history – indicators of relative wealth can fall as well as rise. Greece had a GDP per capita of just US$ 11,580 in 2000, soaring to US$ 31,954 in 2008.[8] By 2009, according to figures released by the Organisation for Economic Co-operation and Development (OECD), the Greek GDP per capita was 88 per cent of the eurozone average.[9] This is likely to prove to be Greece's peak for many years to come.

Impact of Peronism on Business

Gerardo Saporosi, an Argentinian businessman who has kept his franchising business going despite all the economic upheavals of the past 15 years, says that the impact of Peronism and dictatorships was disastrous for industry in what had been an entrepreneurial country:

> Argentina was an industrial power at the end of the nineteenth century and the start of the twentieth. In that era, you could regard Argentina as being equivalent to Canada or Australia. It was in the process of becoming a great power – more advanced, for example, than Brazil, Russia, India or China, the famous 'BRIC' powers of today. The process was abruptly halted by the appearance of Peronism, and various right-wing dictatorships that were backward and nationalist. The country closed itself to the world and is still paying for that dearly.
>
> Also, during the 1960s and 1970s, Argentina was, like other countries around the world, a theatre for operations of the Cold War, in that the USA and the USSR launched their exercises in left-wing terrorism and right-wing counterrevolutions. The result: flight of foreign capital and local savings during the last 40 years. Industries could not re-invest at the rate of the depreciation of their assets, and quietly were liquidated. The policy of convertibility of the 1990s finished off those who were left.
>
> The country is very ambitious, and her entrepreneurs as well. However, it is going to be several decades before Argentina receives inward investment at a level necessary to re-start the process of industrialisation. I doubt that the money of the Argentine diaspora living overseas is ever going to return.

Peronism still has an influence. His 18-year physical exile between 1955 and 1973 meant that politicians of different stripes could evoke his name. He won two general elections, the second by a landslide, and was never defeated at the ballot box, giving extra legitimacy to his legacy. He and his wife have a near-mythical status, though he remains a highly divisive figure.

In Greece, we can recognise the familiar hallmarks of Peronism. There is a pattern similar to its policies, and a similarly inverted money-flow: from politicians to such special interest groups as happen to be flavour of the month; rather than an income of wealth generated in a sustainable way from world-class businesses.

Buying Social Peace

Raul Alfonsin, the first Argentine president after the return to democracy in 1983, was head of the Radical Civic Union. As such, he was an opponent of the Peronists, but head of a left-wing party returned to power following dictatorship. His natural inclination was to reward the constituencies that suffered under the junta, in a manner similar to traditional Peronism. Between 1984 and 1989 there were 13 general strikes, in which unions called for higher wages and better working conditions. In turn, business groups and farmers asked for favours. Attempting to meet these demands placed huge strain on public finances; the deficit increased and monetising the debt led to hyperinflation. Between 1975 and 1989 public debt rose from 14 per cent of GDP to 66 per cent, with most of the increase arising under the Alfonsin regime. According to IMF veteran Vito Tanzi, an adviser to successive Argentine governments, Alfonsin showed little interest in or knowledge of economics, and was motivated by purely political calculations.[10] This period of worsening public deficits and hyperinflation featured a significant flight of Argentinian savings. It is estimated that, by the summer of 1990, some $3 billion of Argentine holdings were moved to Uruguayan banks.[11]

The Argentine state, after decades of clientelism and dictatorship, was highly corrupt and dysfunctional, owing to historical forces rooted in Peronism. This meant that there was little social or economic benefit from public expenditure. During the same decade, there was a remarkably similar initiative to buy social peace in Greece, as the left-wing PASOK government of Andreas Papandreou (1981–89) awarded similar favours to trade unions and other interest groups. He also disbursed patronage to party supporters through political appointments to the public sector on a vast scale. In Greece, the 1980s saw the birth of a ruinously wasteful and corrupt public sector.

Argentine Corruption

Clientelism is an exchange of cash for favours, as opposed to cash for honest endeavour. There is therefore a thin line between clientelist, rent-seeking behaviour and bribery. Corruption in Greece at the highest level has been institutionalised for decades. In a similar way, corruption grew in Argentina in the years of Peronism and military rule. One vivid example from the days of the junta is recounted by Vito

Tanzi. A student of his told him that his father had been approached by a high-ranking member of the military, and proposed that he purchase advertising hoardings that were relatively low in price as they faced the opposite way to on coming traffic in a one-way system. Then the official would ensure that the direction of traffic was reversed, and the two would share the huge profits that ensued as the value of the advertising space increased. 'Over future years, I would become progressively more aware of the existence of corruption in Argentina', Tanzi notes.[12]

Corrupt practices continued in the 1990s. Privatisation programmes, nominally intended to improve economic efficiency, can create opportunities for corrupt practices as valuable state-owned assets are sold. In practice, Argentina's privatisations were a mix of good and bad. In Carlos Menem's first term as president, the major utilities and many other enterprises were privatised. In the case of the telephone system, this led to significant investment, modernisation and service improvements, benefiting the entire country. On the other hand, there was the notorious case of Alfredo Yabran, a businessman accused of profiting secretly from privatisation deals and using his contacts with the Menem regime to arrange a monopoly of postal services. Yabran was suspected of being behind the murder of photographer José Luis Cabezas, who had taken the first picture of him to appear in the media. Cabezas later became a figurehead for the freedom of the press, and Yabran apparently committed suicide. It did not help that Yabran had links to the former military regime.[13]

Carlos Menem himself has faced repeated charges and accusations of corruption, which he has consistently denied. In December 2008, the German multinational company Siemens paid an $800 million fine to settle a case with the US Securities and Exchange Commission (SEC) for the payment of hundreds of millions of dollars in slush funds to win contracts around the world. One of the biggest cases in the SEC charges involved Greece, while another concerned paying bribes to Argentine officials to win the national ID card contract under the Menem administration.[14]

Hellenic Peronism

Greece arrived at its own version of Peronism by a different route, but with some recent parallels. While in Argentina the sense of clientelism – the feeling among some interest groups that 'You owe us' – was forged in large part by a single, charismatic leader, a similar sentiment in

Greece has developed from multiple sources over a longer period of time. These dimensions will be considered in greater depth in chapters 3 and 4, which look at how the history of the country, and the tradition of clientelism, have created a highly dysfunctional and inefficient public sector.

Like Argentina, Greece suffered a right-wing military dictatorship for several years. This followed a civil war and the Nazi occupation of the 1940s, during which Greece lost 13 per cent of her population, the largest proportional loss of all the occupied countries of the Second World War.

Accession to the European Union in 1981, and adoption of the single currency in 2001 seemed like a smooth, continuous process out of the nightmares of the mid-twentieth century. After going through the traumas of recent decades, it was natural to focus on the short-term benefits that being in a hard currency area afforded us from 2002 onwards.

In Greece there is a view that the EU is a safe haven – the thinking being: 'We are in the EU, therefore we are too important to fail, if it comes to a crisis, the Europeans will help us – it's our safety net.' This is the problem with free riding: if you have a trust fund to fall back on, you don't work so hard at school. The same applies to the Greek government; they have lacked motivation because they believe they have a safety net. Thus, it is no coincidence that the pace of reform went through a major slowdown after Greece joined the euro.

Impunity of the Ruling Class

Another common point between Greece and Argentina is the difficulty and/or slowness in bringing members of the elite to trial for serious crimes. On 20 April 2010, just as the Greek debt problem was reaching the scale of a crisis, former Argentine dictator Reynaldo Bignone was jailed for 25 years for his role in the torture and murder of political dissidents during the military rule of the late 1970s and early 1980s. For the first time, a former member of the junta made a formal admission of the 'disappeared' (he acknowledged that 8,000 individuals had suffered this fate). Such impunity makes subsequent austerity measures, clampdowns and so on, once democracy is restored, difficult to implement.

For all the faults of the American system, its principle that everyone is equal before the courts is taken completely seriously. The Founding Fathers' insistence that the judiciary is equal to, and independent of, the executive and parliament is respected and has stood the test of time.

Bernie Madoff is in jail. President Nixon faced impeachment. The accountancy scandals and alleged fraud during the subprime crisis have been followed by court action.

Authorities in the USA and Britain have prosecuted individuals and companies for corrupt payments to Greek and Argentine politicians. But to date scarcely any individuals have been jailed or have even faced trial in Greece for corruption or other scandals.

Oligarchical Business Structures

As well as clientelism, there are other differences between countries like Greece and Argentina on the one hand and advanced economies on the other. These two countries both feature conglomerates run by oligarchs. Because there's so much corruption and bureaucracy, you have to be big and have influence with the government and with the lawyers – and also pay them, effectively with bribes. It's not free competition; it's a rigged game, with semi-protected monopolies and so on. The clientelist relationship between interest groups and the state, created through Peronism and similar attitudes in Greece, are fundamentally different from northern Europe. Russia has these features. So does Turkey, Greece and Argentina. The oligarchs often own newspapers and TV stations – and so can influence the politicians and public opinion. They have their own bank, so they can finance themselves. They have an industrial group. They are organisations geared towards fostering close contacts with ruling politicians and buying favours.

Studies highlight how transition economies are more prone to corruption. One study notes how partial economic liberalisation 'has been combined with a continuing powerful state role in the economy, leading to a situation where there are unprecedented opportunities for firms and government officials to collude, resulting in large-scale corruption'.[15]

The 'Cluster': Feature of an Advanced Economy

An advanced economy is quite different from one dominated by oligarchs. Michael Porter's analysis on the characteristics of an advanced economy has highlighted the role of the 'cluster' of specialist businesses.[16] Yet consideration of such factors does not seem to inform decision makers at a macroeconomic level when considering the prospects for economic growth. The characteristics of a strong real economy are usefully grouped into four dimensions on what Porter calls the 'diamond'. These are defined as

- factor conditions, such as skilled labour, natural resources and infrastructure, necessary to compete in a given industry
- demand conditions
- related and supporting industries, that are internationally competitive
- firm strategy, structure and rivalry.

Chapter 2

GETTING LUCKY

To be successful, keep looking tanned, live in an elegant building (even if you're in the cellar), be seen in smart restaurants (even if you only nurse one drink) and if you borrow, borrow big.

—Aristotle Onassis

In 2001, an unreformed Greek economy was accepted in to the fledgling European single currency. The reasons for this were overwhelmingly political, with economic data fudged, as the EU's leaders emphasised establishing as wide an area as possible for monetary union as part of the European movement's drive for full integration. Greece's *annus mirabilis* was 2004: three years into euro membership, the founding country of the Olympics hosted that year's games. Economic growth had continued since entry into the eurozone. To cap a miraculous year, the national football team astonished the sporting world by defeating favourites Portugal in the final of the European Championship to lift the trophy for the first time.

A decade earlier, it seemed that little could go wrong for Argentina. In 1994, there was a robust 5.8 per cent growth in GDP, yet inflation remained subdued at just 4.2 per cent – exceptionally low given the recent history of the country. Privatisations and free-market reforms led the IMF to treat Argentina as a role model for reforming economies: its 'poster child'.

With Argentina, you can see a superficially favourable state of affairs, but a worrying deterioration in the trade balance, with economic growth sucking in imports.

An Undiversified Economy Gets Lucky

The typical early stages of an exchange rate stabilisation programme were enjoyed by both Argentina in the early 1990s and Greece in the

Table 2.1 Key Economic Indicators in Early Years of Currency Peg: Argentina 1991–1995

	GDP growth (%)	Public sector balance (% of GDP)	Public debt (% of GDP)	Trade balance (US$ billion)
1991	10.5	—	34.8	−0.4
1992	10.3	−0.4	28.3	−6.5
1993	6.3	0.1	30.6	−8.0
1994	5.8	−1.4	33.7	−11.1
1995	−2.8	−3.2	36.7	−5.2

Source: IMF database and World Bank, Global Development Finance.
See *IMF and Argentina: Evaluation Report 2004.*

Table 2.2 Key Economic Indicators in Early Years of Membership of the Euro

	GDP growth (%)	Public sector balance (% of GDP)	Public debt (% of GDP)	Trade balance (US$ billion)
2001	4.2	−3.7 (revised to −6.1%)[1]	103.7	−8.4
2002	3.4	−3.8	101.7	−7.9
2003	5.9	−4.6	97.4	−7.3
2004	4.6	−6.9	98.6	−6.4
2005	2.2	−4.5	100.0	−7.9

Sources: OECD, Eurostat, Economist Intelligence Unit.

early 2000s, witnessing real appreciation of the exchange rate and an investment and consumption boom. Growth rates were strong and inflation subdued, despite a largely unreformed economy. By chance, however, the undiversified and low- to mid-tech economies experienced benign global conditions in the early years of the currency regimes.

Argentina

Throughout the 1990s the Argentine economy grew. Liberalisation of trade by the first Menem administration boosted both imports and exports. The economy was overly dependent on the agricultural sector, but Argentine farmers are among the most productive in the world and conditions were favourable for much of the 1990s. An estimated 58 per cent of Argentina's export earnings came from agriculture,[2] and world prices rose by around 40 per cent in the first half of the 1990s. The factors that formed the basis of these favourable conditions can be summarised as follows:

- *Soya exports*: increasing global demand for soya. Argentina is the world's leading producer of soybean oil. Production of soya and soya-based products tripled during the 1990s, to reach 3 million tonnes by volume and US$ 1.2 billion by value, and became the country's leading export earner.[3] World soya prices spiked in 1996, reaching nearly US$ 8 per bushel (see chart below).

- *Wheat and corn*: in the 1990s, Argentina accounted for about 75 per cent of all wheat produced in South America and was the world's fifth-largest exporter, with production at 14.5 million tonnes. It was the fourth-largest corn-growing country in the world, with production at 13.2 million tonnes.[4] Wheat and corn prices rose in the mid-1990s, reaching around US$ 4 and US$ 3 per bushel respectively (see chart below).

- *Exchange rate*: the peso was linked to the dollar, but the dollar was weak for much of the 1990s, helping exports.

Figure 2.1 Mid-1990s Price Spikes in Wheat, Corn and Soyabeans

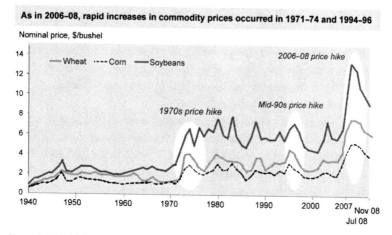

Source: USDA, National Agricultural Statistics Service and World Agricultural Supply and Demand Estimates, 2008.

Greece

With remarkable similarity, Greece enjoyed a lucky period a decade later. Throughout the early 2000s the Greek economy was still significantly reliant on tourism, shipping, agriculture, and then later, real estate. There was insufficient investment in new technologies or developing business clusters in other sectors. But in this period these sectors, especially tourism and shipping, got lucky:

- *Tourism*: the country's largest export earner. It benefited in the early 2000s from the 'Al Qaeda factor': following 9/11, tourism dropped off in Muslim countries and Greece saw its tourist industry rise rapidly from 10 million to 17 million tourists per year.
- *Shipping*: generates thousands of well-paid jobs and demand for high-value financial, legal and technical services. Greece got lucky with the China shipping boom, which paid vast amounts for Greek vessels to transport raw materials.
- *Agriculture*: accounts for 12.5 per cent of Greek employment, compared with an average of just 3.5 per cent in the EU-25 (according to Eurostat 2006 data). This is indicative of a low-value-added economy, but it has attracted EU subsidies.
- *Real estate*: with low euro interest rates, Greece experienced a real estate boom, with house prices more than doubling from 2000 to 2008 (source: Bank of Greece, 2008 annual report).

With such good trading fortune coinciding with the deceptively positive indicators that the early phase of a currency peg can afford, it is possible to see how government leaders could assume that the respective economies were soundly based. In both cases, the early stabilising years, with their flattering growth figures, were the prelude to a ruinous growth in government spending and borrowing.

For individuals, companies and countries alike, it is wisest to invest borrowed money in creating capacity for future earnings. This is something that Argentina in the 1990s and Greece in the 2000s failed to do. The underlying reality is that both countries had deeply ingrained patterns and habits that would make such investment extremely unlikely. While Argentine policymakers made some progress on reform, certainly in the first Menem administration (1989–95), the Greek state remained hugely dysfunctional beneath the apparent shield of the euro. It was completely unreformed in the build-up to entry to monetary union and remained so during the years afterwards.

Borrow, Borrow, Borrow

On the surface, the economic figures were reassuring in the early years of the currency pegs in Argentina and Greece. The ability to borrow, and the willingness of international investors to lend, were in place. In both cases, the freedom to borrow in effectively a hard currency coincided with a desire in the investment community to seek opportunities in government bonds. With unreformed economies, and a state geared towards dispensing favours rather than investing in future capacity, this was a dangerous temptation.

In Argentina government borrowing figures were subdued for a while. Goldman Sachs' paper 'A Bravo New World', published in 1996, declared that: 'For Argentine citizens and for those investors who were willing to believe in the government's promises, the benefits are now becoming apparent.' This reflected widespread confidence in the investment community that the country was truly reformed. But it appeared just as the Argentine government's fiscal position was beginning to deteriorate after Menem's reelection. With such bullishness from the sell-side and nervousness from IMF, which did not want to question its own 'poster child' story – a classic case of both *confirmation bias* and *overconfidence bias* – the spending, and the borrowing, continued. Argentina was awarded 'issuer of the year' in 1998 by the *Latin Finance* magazine.

As late as 1997, the public sector deficit was just 1.6 per cent of GDP. All of this was accounted for by interest payments, and there was actually a slight surplus on a primary basis. But because the borrowing was (effectively) in dollars, it was overvalued with relation to the capacity of the real economy. Secondly, given the stage of the economic cycle, the government should really have been running a healthy surplus at that stage, as a buffer for future risk. An opportunity was missed in the period 1996–98 – boom years when a surplus could have been built up. Policies, attitudes and decisions were heavily procyclical.

Economist Mario Teijeiro, who headed a Buenos Aires-based research institute, sounded the warning. He wrote in 1996 that the government was understating the size of the deficit, for example by excluding factors that were adding to debt, such as bonds to pensioners and suppliers.[5]

Vito Tanzi had warned Menem early in the years of the convertibility experiment that the improvement in public finances had come entirely from the revenue-side. Unless that improvement were accompanied by far greater controls on total public spending, he warned, the danger was that public finances would again become a major concern. He raised concern about higher transfer payments to the provinces, and the cost of higher pensions.[6] The analysis indicated that the economy had 'got lucky', and was highly vulnerable to a change of fortune.

The perverse incentives of benchmarking sent borrowing ever higher. Paul Blustein, author of *And The Money Kept Rolling In (and Out)*, describes the process and how at least one emerging markets veteran, Desmond Lachman of Salomon Smith Barney, predicted an Argentine default long before others – but also that such warnings tended to be in private. Publicly investment banks were more positive, reflecting the conflict of interest given the millions of dollars they earn from arranging bond sales. As an aside, it's worth noting that in an article in January 2010 in the *Financial Times* Lachman publicly warned of an inevitable default for Greece.[7]

The EMBI-Plus index tracks the price and yield of bonds of governments in emerging markets. Each country has a percentage weighting that depends on the amount of bonds already issued. During much of the period 1996–2001, Argentina had the largest weighting, averaging 23.3 per cent. Being underweight in Argentine bonds simply meant that the portfolio held less than the average, and *herd instinct* encourages investors not to be too far from the market norm. This meant that huge amounts were still being lent. Blustein writes: 'The habit of cleaving to the index…virtually forced these investors to lend vast sums to Argentina even if they feared the country was likely to default in the long run.'[8]

Once the bond prices started falling in 2001 some Wall Street institutions made money by taking short positions as bond prices fell, cashing in for a second time. As is now known, the same phenomenon was to occur in Greece.

Argentina was categorised in the mid- to late 1990s as a lower-risk emerging market, while Greece after 2002, owing to its entry in to the eurozone, did not even qualify as 'emerging market' and was categorised as 'developed world'. Just as the subprime crisis had its roots in bundling mortgages of varying quality together, marketing them and getting an investment grade stamp, so was the single currency treated as a hard currency even though its constituent economies were of varying strength. And a monetary union that required *stronger* fiscal and monetary discipline by all participants instead was followed by *weaker* compliance, fed by complacency and *overconfidence bias*.

Exactly as occurred with securitised mortgages prior to the credit crisis, ratings agencies were way behind the curve. Their reactive nature adds hugely to the procyclical nature of investment bubbles and crashes. Not until the first few months of 2010 did the yield on Greek government bonds begin to diverge sharply from German yield. As with all asset bubbles, the story tends to look at its best just before the bursting.

Irrational Exuberance and Procyclical Rhetoric

During the years of the Argentine currency peg, and again in the early to mid-2000s, investment banks were only too happy to believe the rosy scenario of government leaders and the ratings agencies. Far from learning the lessons of Argentina, and the earlier Latin American debt crisis, irrational exuberance reached new heights in the first years of the new millennium, and affected the fledgling European currency.

The euphoria was international, the warnings ignored. In 2005, Paul Krugman in the *New York Times* warned of Alan Greenspan's lax approach to the US fiscal deficit, trade deficit and an impending housing bubble. On an occasion when the then chairman of the Federal Reserve made some cautionary comments, Krugman quipped: 'He's like a man who suggests leaving the barn door ajar, and then – after the horse is gone – delivers a lecture on the importance of keeping your animals properly locked up.'[9] On the matter of public deficit, US governments since 2000 have wanted to enjoy both tax reductions and increased public spending, generating a massive deficit.

For decades, Western economies have run fiat currencies – that is, currencies that consist of currency and credit only, with no link to a convertible commodity such as gold. This makes it easier to create credit expansions. It is popular with politicians, as it can be a shortcut to growth; and it is popular with banks, because they make money on credit-related transactions. The direct losers are savers and those on fixed or low incomes. There is also a greater tendency towards boom and bust with easy credit. This is destabilising enough for an advanced economy with strong business clusters, but it can be devastating for emerging economies. This is discussed further in chapter 8 ('The Washington Consensus').

Greek governments and households in the period 2002–09 were in good company. Encouraged by low interest rates, the governments, corporations and households of several G7 countries were borrowing and spending way beyond their means, supported by a supply industry of inventive euphemisms – leverage, new paradigm, Great Moderation, etc. – that made it sound perfectly safe. The search for yield lowered the risk aversion from 2002 onwards, creating a positive feedback loop elevating all asset prices. Banks lent against these higher asset values, in many countries reducing strict lending criteria, for example on household savings and earnings in a way that enabled individuals to buy houses that many ended up being unable to afford. Key elements of Glass–Steagall were repealed, without deep inquiry as to why it had been required in the first place, a typical example of thinking 'this time it's different'.

It was not simply an Anglo-Saxon problem. Canada and Australia largely avoided the temptations, while many French and German institutions were quite happy to promote Greek borrowing if it meant orders for French and German manufacturers, as discussed further in chapters 3 and 5. European Union leaders, congratulating themselves at having put the euro together, were in no psychological state to discourage the easy borrowing that made GDP indicators in the eurozone periphery look good. Politicians, central bankers, the sell-side and the buy-side all collectively fell for the *overconfidence bias, confirmation bias* and *herd instinct* that sustained the pleasing narrative that Greek bonds were as safe as Germany's and that the underlying economy was robust. All enthusiastically encouraged the borrowing and spending splurge.

Politicians of all stripes, in all countries, may fall for the temptation to 'kick the can down the road' – to buy enough favours in the short term and gamble that the day of reckoning occurs on someone else's watch. Argentina and Greece have simply been more prone to this than many other countries. With similarly opportunistic short-termism, investment banks recouped fees for arranging the loans, and in many cases cashed in as the boom ended by shorting government bonds as the price fell. Although Europe's leaders publicly denounced such speculation, they encouraged the bubble characteristics that made shorting so profitable by arranging fresh debts and calling them a 'bail-out', even beyond the point at which it had become a Ponzi scheme – the Greek government was only able to maintain payments to existing creditors by taking on new ones.

In the bubble economies of the early to mid-2000s, growth was fuelled most obviously by loose lending regimes by the banks and by high private sector borrowing. The overall sentiment was positive and uncritical, with lazy phrases emerging in politicians' speeches and the headlines of the more irrationally exuberant journalists: 'no more boom and bust', 'the Celtic Tiger', 'the Powerhouse of Southeast Europe' and so on are phrases better consigned to history. The old Greek term 'hubris' has better stood the test of time. But in all likelihood there will be new variants of the 'tiger' and the 'powerhouse' emerging as and when debt-fuelled 'growth' reappears in some part or other of the global economy.

Much has been written about private subprime lending and the lack of countercyclical capital buffers by the banks. Incentives for investment bankers and mortgage brokers are heavily procyclical.

But an often-overlooked factor is procyclical rhetoric. This is particularly acute and delusional in the case of housing. The illusion of wealth creation that occurs when vast sums of public and private debt are converted to bricks and mortar seems to have a distorting effect on the judgement, even of intelligent people, based on feelings deep in the human psyche. Government borrowing helps to fuel housing bubbles. All those salaried public sector workers, in the case of Greece enjoying pay rises year-on-year, want somewhere nice to live.

This probably has its roots in the emotional attachment we have to our homes, with their promises of safety, a good style of living and capital gains. In the bubble economies, there has been a marked tendency to describe property price rises in an uncritically positive way. For example, a resumption of an upward trend in property prices is referred to as 'recovery' or 'revival' in the market, even when the increases are taking the cost of the average property well above affordability based on local salary rates – creating bubble properties, in other words. Even after the widespread banking collapses of 2007–08, the subsequent reduction in interest rates and indications of upward movement in house prices in some regions has caused commentators to talk of 'recovery' – as if they had not learned anything, as in all probability they haven't.

Spend, Spend, Spend

For Argentina 1991, read Greece 2001. A borrowed hard currency; a population with a feeling of entitlement, seeking solace after a horrific recent past; easy borrowing terms. Everything was in place for the mother and then the daughter of all spending booms and busts. And with such enthusiastic encouragement from governments, institutional investors and international agencies such as the IMF and the European Union, who was there to apply the brakes? When Argentina in the 1990s and Greece in the 2000s were able to access serious amounts of hard currency on the open markets, the results should have been predictable. In each case, there was a decade-long consumer and public sector spending boom, followed by a cataclysmic economic crash.

While a 'Peronist' president, Carlos Menem appeared to abandon many of the traditional policies, yet the old habits were about to resurface. The shallowness of his free-market reforms, without development of a strong supply-side, which in any case was negatively affected by an overvalued exchange rate, simply meant that income from borrowing and privatisation programmes provided irresistible windfalls for politicians whose deepest instincts were Peronist.

Exactly as would occur with Greece a decade later, the combination of privatisation, borrowing, and a consumer boom helped by a temporarily 'hard' currency meant that, in the first years of the policy, conventional indicators read positive. Goldman Sachs gushed: 'Armed with the belief that most Argentines would rather face unemployment than the well-known cycle of devaluation–inflation–devaluation, President Menem and Finance Minister Domingo Cavallo not only did not renege on their promises, but accelerated their economic reform efforts.'[10]

Reports like this led to a stampede by the sell-side to arrange yet more borrowing, as discussed. But Argentine businessman Gerardo Saporosi remembers this time rather differently:

> Cavallo appeared with the convertibility experiment. It had an instant 'success'. Almost magically, from one day to the next, inflation and chaos disappeared. They had found the 'perfect remedy', and it was going to last ten years. However, few realised that the experiment was going to be disastrous for the national industry, with consequences that we still experience today, ten years after de-activating the convertibility bomb. The correction of the market was pitiless. An economy like Argentina's, which had much lower productivity than that of the USA, had an equivalent currency. You don't have to have a doctorate from Harvard to realise that that was a completely untenable situation, which was going to explode at any moment.
>
> Markets, like nature, don't get it wrong. The type of 'pegged' exchange produced a wave of imports at ridiculous prices. For that reason, the 1990s will be known forever as the decade of the disappearance of the Argentine industry. Unemployment began to rise to extraordinary levels.

Experienced Argentine-observer Walter Molano concurred:

> Exchange rate stabilisation programs are often associated with a strong influx of imported goods. These goods help put downward pressure on the prices of domestic goods, thus helping to suppress the inflation rate. The quick stabilisation of consumer prices

and the real appreciation of the currency provide workers with a rapid increase in real wages. The elimination of the so-called inflation tax often explodes into a consumption boom that attracts further inflows of foreign goods. The pent-up demand for durable goods exacerbates the increase in consumption. Unfortunately, the decline in the inflation rate is not instantaneous. Therefore, there is a lag in the decline in real wages and prices. The result is a real appreciation of the currency and a subsequent dis-equilibrium in the balance of payments.[11]

On the demand-side, Argentine consumers enjoyed enhanced purchasing power, but the supply-side was disappearing. Paraguay, Uruguay and Brazil were better able to attract inward investment. Argentina moved its textile business to Paraguay – just as many Greek textile businesses have transferred to Bulgaria and Turkey since Greece adopted the euro.

In Argentina, towards the end of Menem's presidential term, convertibility's consumer boom was coming to an end. President Menem faced a combination of rising unemployment and the effects of Mexico's Tequila Crisis of 1994, which had a recessionary impact on Argentina.

Menem's reform programme was half-finished. His bid, ultimately successful, for a constitutional amendment to permit his reelection meant that his focus switched to this initiative and to the subsequent 1995 election. Old Peronist instincts to curry short-term favour with key interest groups resurfaced. This may not have been disastrous with a floating currency, but the dollar peg meant that the only adjustment the economy could make to problems of competitiveness was to internal costs, including wages, but this was closed off as Menem ditched labour reform in order to secure union support for his reelection. With unemployment rising, he also baulked at spending cuts that would have curbed the rising deficit, and Peronist-style expenditure continued both by central government and in the provinces.[12] As an example, the IMF noted 'court-ordered compensation payments after the social security reform of the early 1990s and arrears to suppliers'.[13]

With key sectors already privatised, there were reduced opportunities for income from asset sales, so Menem turned to the international bond markets. Rather than scrutinise the risk profile, investment banks saw Argentina as an emerging market with opportunities. Government spending started to rise just as the impetus was being lost in efforts to improve economic efficiency.

A decade later, Greece also enjoyed an unsustainable consumer boom, sucking in imports in the early years of its adoption of the euro. The conditions of the early 2000s gave them an unrepeatable opportunity to consume. Public deficits made the headlines and were the immediate cause of crisis in the eurozone, but the debt was private too. Private households went on a borrowing spree following entry into the single currency, encouraged by much looser lending conditions, contrasted with the previous environment of higher interest rates and tight banking lending regulation.

Greece, it may surprise you to learn, has the highest owner-occupancy rate in all of Europe. During the boom, people bought more than they needed: homes, second homes, holiday homes. The illusion of wealth generated the illusion that all the mortgage repayments could be met.

Another luxury item was cars. During the 2000s, Greece became the highest purchaser per capita of Porsche Cayennes. In 2006, Athens-based freelance journalist Nikos Michaelian reported that sales of SUVs and luxury 4x4 vehicles had doubled in the last five years, despite soaring petrol prices and the shrinking number of parking spaces in Athens, particularly in the city centre. Data from the Association of Motor Vehicle Importers-Representatives (AMVIR) shows that sales of sport utility vehicles in 2005 hit 9,288 compared with 4,010 in 2001.[14] How were all these foreign car purchases financed? Well, as of 2010 there were €8 billion (i.e. over 3.5 per cent of GDP) of car loans outstanding

Figure 2.2 Greek Bank Credit to Households

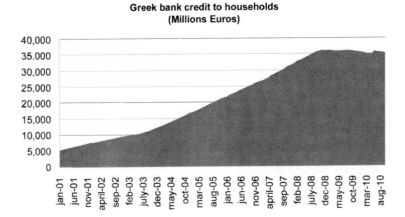

Source: Bank of Greece.

in Greece.[15] Given that Greece has no domestic car industry, this was a direct hit on the current account, with the low euro interest rates enabling outsized spending. Luxury cars and SUVs, overall, do not increase the future productivity of a country, nor its ability to generate free cashflow to pay back borrowed monies. Not surprisingly, with credit frozen, car sales in 2010 were 65.3 per cent lower than in 2008.[16]

Another indication of opulence is the statistic that some 54 per cent of Greek babies are born in private clinics, where the cost ranges from €1,600 to €11,500.[17]

Both Greece and Argentina happened to benefit from external factors that were not related to the performance of their respective economies. They just happened to be in the right place at the right time. These were all classic features of a bubble economy. Instead of curbing the exuberance, local and Western commentators and official agencies such as the European Union and IMF also fell prey to narrative fallacy, using convenient arguments to highlight the economy's apparently excellent performance – in both Argentina and Greece.

The unsustainable spending was not a peculiarity of the consumer and the private sector. With such easy lending terms, the governments of Argentina and Greece had ample opportunity to distribute largesse. In this environment, cost control on major public programmes tends to be weak. In Greece, further incentivised by being the Olympics host in 2004, the infrastructure programmes were huge. By July 2007, the eve of the credit crisis, the *Financial Times* was able to report:

> Low interest rates – the result of euro membership – have fuelled a boom in house-building. Infrastructure improvements carried out for the 2004 Athens Olympics, with financing from the European Union, have modernised the capital's mass transit systems. Funds from the current EU package will help upgrade the highway network, which should accelerate development of a second-home market for Greeks and north Europeans.
>
> Investments in high-end tourist resorts are under way to meet demand for improved services. Ship-owners, having rebased in Athens, are repatriating more of their earnings from the boom in carrying commodities to China and India.
>
> The government is tapping private sector expertise via public–private partnerships. The finance ministry has managed tenders for projects worth €3 billion to build schools, hospitals and offices for local government.[18]

One of the attractions for lower-income countries in joining the European Union has been access to structural development funds to develop infrastructure. In addition to this, and especially in Greece, debt has additionally been used to modernise transport and communications. Across many parts of Europe's peripheries are some of the most modern infrastructures in the world – and also some of the most highly indebted nations, locked in an overvalued currency. An age of mass unemployment coexisting with shiny airports, high-speed trains and new highway networks is beginning across swathes of Europe.

Greece had the added incentive of modernising transport and communications in preparation for the Olympics 'coming home' in 2004. Whenever a city hosts the Olympics, the combination of the pressure of national prestige and a fixed deadline for completion puts the authorities of the city and nation in a weak negotiating position with contractors. In Greece the overspending was eye-watering, set in the context of the endemic waste throughout the public sector.

For all this activity and appearance of wealth, the productive economy of Greece was still structurally reliant on tourism, shipping and agriculture and not unsustainable consumer spending and real estate. It had not industrialised its economy; its main exports remained low-value-added products that previously had remained competitive through devaluations. The Greeks were selling tomatoes to buy Louis Vuitton, and imagining it didn't have to stop one day. Greece was stuck in the middle: between high-tech countries like France and Germany, and low-wage countries like Bulgaria, Romania and Turkey.

The first years of a currency peg can bring about favourable economic indicators, and often a sharply improved situation, especially when the measure has been used to curb hyperinflation, as was the case with Argentina. As we saw earlier, growth figures were favourable, but a widening current account deficit during the period of an overvalued exchange rate pointed to future problems. In both countries, borrowing was used to maintain public spending, in part to favour interest groups. In the latter half of the decade – 1990s in the case of Argentina and 2000s in Greece – both the public finances and current account balance deteriorated, as seen in Table 2.3.

In the case of Argentina, an underlying weakness was exacerbated by the 30 per cent devaluation of the Brazilian real in 1999. Such a sharp effective increase in the price of Argentine exports to its main trading partner had a devastating effect on a country locked into the dollar peg. This, combined with borrowing levels, a stalled labour market and public

Table 2.3 Key Economic Indicators in Later Years of Currency Peg: Argentina 1996–2000

	GDP growth (%)	Public sector balance (% of GDP)	Public debt (% of GDP)	Trade balance (US$ billion)
1996	5.5	−2.9	39.1	−6.8
1997	8.1	−2.1	37.7	−12.2
1998	3.8	−2.1	40.9	−14.5
1999	−3.4	−4.2	47.6	−11.9
2000	−0.8	−3.6	50.9	−8.8
2001	−4.4	−6.2	62.2	−4.5
Greece 2006–2009				
2006	4.5	−2.9	97.8	−9.3
2007	4.5	3.7	95.7	−14.1
2008	2.0	−7.7 (revised)	99.2	−14.0
2009	−2.0	−12.5 (revised)	115.1	−12.0

Sources: OECD, Eurostat, Oxford Economics.[19]

sector reforms helped to bring matters to a head. Argentina experienced debt inflation: with the peso pegged to a hard currency, the exchange rate was disconnected from the real economy. As the dollar appreciated in relative terms, the overvaluation increased and the real cost of the public debt also rose threatening to become unaffordable.

One noteworthy aspect of the data that these charts show is that the trading and fiscal situations are considerably worse for Greece than they were for Argentina. So when European Union leaders say that 'Greece is not like Argentina', many will agree – but for the opposite reason to that intended. Public debt is well over 100 per cent in mid-recession, and is set to continue rising. A report by Oxford Economics, published in February 2010, estimated that the country's real effective exchange rate had been overvalued by around 20 per cent by the end of the decade. The impact of the implied adjustment was therefore huge.[20] If Argentina was a car crash, Greece is a 9/11.

Lessons Learned and Forgotten

Shortly after Greece's entry in to the euro in 2003, the IMF published a paper on the Argentine default. *Lessons from the Crisis in Argentina* by the International Monetary Fund, approved by Timothy Geithner, was published on 8 October 2003. In parts the report's content was understated, bordering on euphemism, with plentiful evidence of our familiar cognitive biases among economic policymakers. In other sections the tone was candid and contrite. The phrase 'in hindsight' recurs. Sadly, it is hindsight that has not been used. Entire sections describing policy errors could apply equally to Greece a decade later.

For example, paragraph 2 reads:

> The events of the crisis, which imposed major hardships on the people of Argentina, are all the more troubling in light of the country's strong past performance. Less than five years earlier, Argentina had been widely hailed as a model of successful economic reform: inflation…was in the low single digits, output growth was impressive, and the economy had successfully weathered the Tequila crisis of the mid-1990s.

There is clear evidence here of the narrative fallacy that economic data tells the full story. There is a failure to analyse the real economy. We see this again and again: the strong headline performance, the convenient story and the scary underlying trends. You could change less than five words of the above passage and this would be applicable for a Greek IMF post-mortem.

On to paragraph 6. Here we read:

> …[E]ven though the interaction between fiscal policy and the currency board arrangement played the central role in Argentina's transformation from an apparent star performer to a crisis country, a combination of other factors, including unfavorable external developments, was also at play. The currency board, although it initially played an essential role in achieving disinflation, was an inherently risky enterprise; it changed over time from being a confidence-enhancing to becoming a confidence-damaging factor… When the economy slid into recession, the currency board became a liability in the context of a build-up of sizeable foreign-currency denominated public debt – signifying the effective fiscal dominance of the policy regime. Not only was the government constrained to carry out a constractionary monetary policy in the midst of a slump, balance sheet vulnerabilities had dramatically raised the cost of exiting the fixed exchange-rate regime.

All one needs to do is to change the words 'currency board' to 'euro', and hey presto, we can accurately describe Greece.

It continues. Paragraph 8:

> Argentina's 1991 Convertibility Plan seemed to herald a new era of high growth and low inflation, to be founded on disciplined macroeconomic policies and market-oriented structural reform. Real GDP growth...rebounded sharply to more than 10 per cent during the first two years of the stabilisation program and more than 5 per cent during 1993–94.

Greece's experience, and the economic indicators, were similarly positive in the first few years of adoption of the euro.

Paragraph 9: here I provide running commentary, with notes in italics:

> Underlying this performance were both existing weaknesses and growing vulnerabilities, particularly in the fiscal area, the external and financial sectors, and the labor market [*in Greece this was the same*]... Fiscal performance, while not conspicuously profligate [*Greece's was a bit higher*]...in terms of headline deficit measures, was repeatedly undermined by off-budget expenditures [*this also occurred in Greece*]... Exports...did not keep pace with sharply rising import demand [*this also occurred in Greece*].

Paragraph 10:

> While the currency board brought significant benefits...it also implied restrictions on the use of monetary policy and the exchange rate as an adjustment tool, putting much of the onus of macroeconomic stabilisation on fiscal policy, and requiring greater nominal flexibility of the economy, especially in the labor market, to absorb external shocks.

Again, this also occurred in Greece.

Paragraph 11:

> ...[P]ublic finances deteriorated in the course of the [decade]. The deterioration was the result of moderate headline deficits... combined with persistent off-budget spending...

Paragraph 13 recommends that:

> A more cautious fiscal stance during this period could have greatly improved the public debt dynamics and likely prevented Argentina's eventual default.

This could also have been applicable in Greece; however the IMF's experiences were not voiced loudly enough, or heard.

In paragraph 14 the IMF acknowledges 'perhaps the most serious misperception', which was:

> ...an overly optimistic view of Argentina's growth potential. Strong growth performance following the macroeconomic stabilisation in the early 1990s, together with structural reforms and low inflation, led most observers – in the IMF, as well as in academia and private markets – to believe that Argentina's potential growth had increased permanently.

This is the same narrative fallacy as we saw later with Greece – belief that the superficially stabilising effects of the early years of a currency peg are symptoms of improved economic performance.

In the same vein, paragraph 15 notes:

> In hindsight, the expansion of Argentina's economy during the 1990s appears to have reflected, in large part, a number of *temporary factors* [my emphasis].[21]

Indeed. And the same with Greece.

Arguably, economists can only ever judge matters 'in hindsight', because they are largely guided by data, and data is historic. The *problem of induction* persuades economists to make *forecasts*, when they should really be analysing risks and considering different scenarios. The tacit assumption that the published 'forecast' is the only – or the most likely – sequence of events is extremely dangerous. There is always a range of possible outcomes, and the fact that one of them happens to be similar to what has gone before does not make it more likely. Yet the lure of forecasting on the basis of extrapolation remains almost irresistible. The ability to borrow vast sums of money and purchase temporary, positive economic data makes this tendency extremely dangerous.

All this collated understanding with the benefit of 'hindsight' counted for little, in terms of a wider understanding of macroeconomic management. It certainly did not influence the judgement of the leaders of the European Union, who, at the point of the publication of this IMF analysis in 2003, had just embarked on an even larger exercise in repeating these mistakes, pretty much to the letter, with the novelty of extending it to several countries. It was just about to happen all over again.

Greece, like Argentina, enjoyed its spending boom – at least in those sectors not hampered by an overvalued exchange rate. The two nations got lucky. As the Argentinian drama of the previous decade illustrates, there are lessons to learn and indications as to how the Greek tale may unfold. The equivalent of the currency peg was the much more ambitious euro project. Greece was not only pegging its currency, it was taking part in the historic drama of the European project, and was about to play a crucial role.

Chapter 3

THE EURO: HARD SELL, OR MIS-SELL?

The euro is not economic at all. It is a completely political step... the historic significance of the euro is to construct a bi-polar economy in the world. The two poles are the dollar and the euro. That is the political meaning of the single European currency. It is a step beyond which there will be others. The euro is just an antipasto.

—Romano Prodi,
President of the European Commission to CNN,
1 January 2002

The foundation of the single European currency in 1999, followed by its completion with the circulation of notes and coins on 1 January 2002, were proud moments for the leaders of the European Union. The presence of 11 founding participants in 1999, followed two years later by the twelfth, Greece, and with the promise that others such as Sweden, Denmark and the UK were waiting in line to join seemed a major step towards the dream of a 'United States of Europe' that many of the continent's politicians had nurtured for decades.

In order to understand the significance of the single currency, and Greece's participation in it, it is essential to understand the nature of the European Union; its foundation, the principles and ambitions of those who guide its affairs, and the sometimes conflicting visions and ambitions of its major powers.

The EU: Origins and Aims

The European Union was born from the ashes of the Second World War. It emerged from postwar initiatives at reconciliation and partnership in Western Europe. Its founding moment was the Schuman Declaration.

On 9 May 1950 the French foreign minister Robert Schuman gave a speech setting out the ideals of European cooperation, based on the principles of economic cooperation and prevention of war. He set out the following objectives for the community:

- To make war between member states 'not only unthinkable, but materially impossible'
- To encourage world peace
- To unify Europe through a step-by-step process, including Eastern Europe – much of which was under Communist control at the time
- To create an international anti-cartel agency
- To create a single market across the community.

He declared: 'Europe will be born from this, a Europe which is solidly united and constructed around a strong framework. It will be a Europe where the standard of living will rise by grouping together production and expanding markets, thus encouraging the lowering of prices.'[1]

In 1951 the six founder countries – France, West Germany, the Netherlands, Belgium, Luxembourg and Italy – formed the European Coal and Steel Community, a supranational body aimed initially, as the name indicates, at pooling natural resources, beginning with those resources most important for armaments industries. The idea was that if a single nation did not have control over coal and steel production it would not be able to wage war against another.

Although the initial level of economic integration was modest, it is clear from the Schuman Declaration that an ideal of a 'United States of Europe' (by implication with a single government and single currency) is consistent with these founding principles. Whether this was always the ultimate goal of the EU, if so what degree of integration this implied, and the extent to which full political and monetary union was necessary were questions that were to cause considerable controversy over the coming decades – especially as the community grew in number from its original 6 members to a total of 27 by the first decade of the new millennium.

The principles of the free market and free movement of people were set out in the 1957 Treaty of Rome, in which the six nations formally founded the European Economic Community. These principles were bolstered by the 1987 Single European Act, which led to the completion of the single market within the European Union (or EC as it was then) by 1 January 1993.

Such measures have greatly assisted trade within Europe, and free trade has been policed by the anti-cartel Competition Commission. By 2002 the EU reported that trade in services had almost doubled since completion of the single market in 1993, from €194 billion to €362 billion. In manufacture, trade had risen from €670 billion to well over €1,000 billion. It also noted that there were still barriers, especially affecting financial services, requiring EU action.[2]

In macro terms, the commitment of Western Europe after the Second World War to a mixed economy, free elections and free trade was an outstanding success. By the end of the century Europe was the third richest area in the world, as measured in terms of GDP per capita, after the USA and Japan. Moreover, the countries that had been in the EEC for longer tended to be far wealthier than more recent entrants to the club – such as the nations of Eastern Europe that had experienced Communist regimes for much of the postwar period, or those in southern Europe (Portugal, Spain, Greece) that had experienced right-wing dictatorships.[3]

At a geopolitical level, an explicit intention of the Common Market, later the European Union, was to tie in Germany's fate with that of France. The two central, large European nations had fought three wars within less than a century, two of which became global and the last resulting in the occupation of France. The sentiment was: never again. In Schuman's words: 'The coming together of the nations of Europe requires the elimination of the age-old opposition of France and Germany.'

In this context, the reported hint by President Nicolas Sarkozy – at the height of the controversy over the Greek deficit in May 2010 – that France could break with Germany, forming closer relations with Spain and Italy, and possibly even withdraw from the euro, was seismic. It was, of course, fiercely denied by the Élysée Palace.

Despite the differing interpretations as to what the 'European project' really is, there is little doubt among true believers: the aim is to create a fully-fledged equivalent of the USA with a single currency, in which the nations become the equivalent of states of the union. In the ambitions of some, rivalry with the superpower of Anglo-Saxon capitalism provides much of the emotional fuel and political impetus.

In order not to upset nationalist sensitivities on the road to monetary and political union, the tendency has been to use euphemism and subterfuge and to complete the project with baby steps, with each treaty taking us a little further than the last, and typically featuring referendum defeats, opt-outs and compromise.

Figure 3.1 Map: GDP per Inhabitant in PPS as Percentage of EU-27 Average (2004)

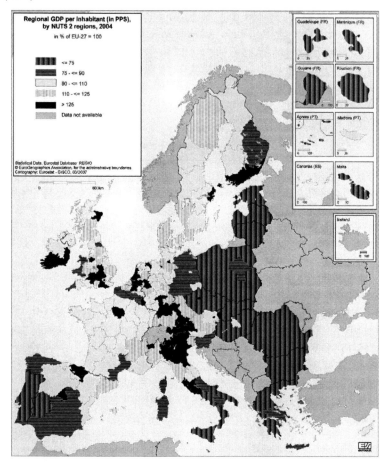

Source: http://europa.eu/abc/keyfigures/qualityoflife/wealthy/index_en.htm#chart10.

At an economic level, the reality was that by the 1970s West Germany had become the powerhouse of Europe. It had transformed its industries after the ruins of war and the allied occupation that followed it, and had become the continent's largest economy and main exporter, prompting British industrialists to mutter: 'We won the war but lost the peace.' This economic renaissance was underpinned, since its independence in 1957, by the mighty Bundesbank, the guardian of the '*ersatz Kaiser*' (see below) the Deutschmark. Though not directly accountable to the electorate, the Bundesbank retained popular support by a population still haunted by the hyperinflation of the 1920s.

Many of the negotiations over the future of the EU since the 1960s and 1970s have involved France and the rest of Europe seeking to harness Germany's economic clout while restraining her ambitions. For the most part, the trade-off has been mutually beneficial.

The Single Currency and the European Project

Monetary union has long been the dream of leaders of the European Union (or EC, or EEC, as it used to be). The concrete proposals that appeared in the Maastricht Treaty in 1991 seemed to come as a shock to some, and enraged eurosceptics around the continent, but it was not a new idea. Schuman had hinted at political and monetary union in 1950, and in the same year the influential French economist Jacques Rueff, a critic of the hegemony of the USA, declared: '*L'Europe se fera par la monnaie ou ne se fera pas*' ['Europe will be made through a common currency, or it will not be made'].

Concrete proposals for a single currency date back to the 1960s. At the time of the 1957 Treaty of Rome capital controls were in place, and the leading economies operated under the Bretton Woods agreement, fixing exchange rates against the US dollar which in turn was linked to gold; there was little practical impetus for a single European currency. A summit at The Hague in 1969 established economic and monetary union as a formal goal, setting an ambitious ten-year plan that was to be upset by the oil price shock and related economic problems of the 1970s. In 1970, the Werner Report set out a three-stage process towards monetary union: irreversible convertibility of currencies, free movement of capital and permanent locking of currencies, potentially leading to a common currency.

In the 1970s, following the breakdown of the Bretton Woods arrangements in 1971, there were currency fluctuations. A long-term trend was the strengthening of the Deutschmark against the franc and the pound sterling. Some companies operating within the EEC, especially larger export-orientated firms from smaller countries such as Belgium or the Netherlands, could gain or lose more profits on exchange rate changes than on the value of trades completed. An attempt to coordinate exchange rates was known as the 'snake', and it ran from 1972–79, based on a fluctuation margin of 2.25 per cent. As it came into being, three new countries joined the EEC: Ireland, the UK and Denmark. Their currencies were initially part of the 'snake', but these, along with the franc and lira, were forced out of the arrangement, so by 1977 it was no more than a greater Deutschmark area, with just Germany, Belgium, the Netherlands, Luxembourg and Denmark participating.

In 1978 the German chancellor Helmut Schmidt and the French president Giscard d'Estaing instigated a new arrangement: the European Monetary System, which was to feature the Exchange Rate Mechanism, limiting exchange rate fluctuations between participating EU states. It came into existence in March 1979. Each currency was to operate within agreed bands, with governments and central banks intervening to protect agreed exchange rate limits.

Almost immediately, however, the system came under pressure. In France, François Mitterrand was elected as president in 1981 on a socialist platform, with Communist Party members in government. Policies of restrictive practices and increased costs to business damaged the French economy, and the Deutschmark continued its long-term rise. Repeated devaluations of the franc, typically couched in euphemistic terms as in part a 'revaluation' of the Deutschmark within the ERM were a feature of the 1980s, until the French government adopted a policy of '*franc fort*'.

Bernard Connolly, a former EU Commission staff member who has become outspokenly sceptical about the European project, acidly commented that the European Monetary System became 'little more than a mechanism for creating sporadic financial market turbulence and retarding inevitable exchange rate movements. It did little or nothing to promote the "convergence" that the Brussels European Council had looked forward to'.[4]

Repeatedly, in the history of initiatives by European politicians to fix or limit exchange rates, we see 'convergence' as an aspiration of their successive experiments. One would imagine that there is little in the way of literature to guide the ingredients of a successful monetary union or currency peg; on each occasion, the EU's leaders seem to be discovering the mechanics of such processes for the first time. In fact, knowledge around an optimal currency area is well established. So before describing what actually happened with the Exchange Rate Mechanism, and then the single currency itself, it is worth summarising the features that appear to characterise a successful single currency area.

An Optimal Currency Area

The essential elements of an optimal currency area, as developed by economists Robert Mundell, Ronald McKinnon and others in the

1960s, are well established.[5] Research would indicate that an optimal currency area possesses the following features:

- *Flexible labour markets*: wages must be able to respond to market conditions; if they rise, there must be at least a commensurate rise in productivity. Mobility of labour is also needed in an optimal currency area, to minimise unemployment and to prevent skills shortages arising in fast-growing industries in thriving areas.
- *Flexible product and financial markets*: an economy has to be capable of generating new jobs and services, through competition, innovation and entrepreneurship. Flexibility in product markets increases the dynamism of economies, making it easier for companies to expand existing markets and create new ones. Capital markets must be liquid and flexible.
- *Integration of participating economic areas*: integration should be in services, labour and capital as well as trade in goods. The more integrated the economies are, the less likely they are to diverge.
- *Diversity*: economies should not be overreliant on particular sectors. The economies of Argentina and then Greece were undiversified but had 'gotten lucky' for a few years. An optimal currency area features advanced, specialist sectors, and some diversity, so that a cyclical downturn in one industry does not seriously affect the whole economy.
- *Strong central government with sound fiscal policies*: fiscal transfers within the currency area can alleviate the impact of an economic shock in one region, such as the natural decline of a certain industry. In the case of a supranational currency area, participating countries should have similar policy attitudes, for example with respect to priorities towards growth, inflation and so on. They also need to be able to cooperate closely with one another.
- *Similarities of inflation rates*: imbalances can arise from persistent differences in national inflation rates. This point is likely to be linked to the degree of integration on the other points.
- *Emphasis on growth*: it helps if the central government has monetary policies orientated towards growth. Within a currency union, a country or region can only restore any lost competitiveness if unit wage costs – that is, labour costs adjusted for productivity improvements – rise by less than those of other member states.[6]

One important operating instruction to add to the above list: they all, or nearly all, need to be in place – three or four is not likely to be enough for a currency to remain strong over extended periods of time. Experience and the literature confirm this. The US dollar works, despite huge economic variety across the states of the union, because there is labour mobility across the country *and* there is strong central government, *and* there is competition *and* an entrepreneurial culture with job creation, and so on. There is a single central bank; and there is an expectation that, if jobs disappear in Michigan, people will move to Arizona.

More recent literature has focused on four key features: the extent of trade; the similarity of shocks and cycles; the degree of labour mobility; and the system of risk sharing, typically through fiscal transfers. It has also been noted that historical data is insufficient to form a judgement on convergence towards an optimal currency area, as the act of joining a currency union will itself have an economic impact.[7]

Literature and experience indicate that it is highly unlikely that formalising a single currency area in itself will affect progress towards achieving the features of the optimal currency area. In chapter 8, as I review the operation of the single currency, I will return to these six characteristics and see how many had been fulfilled – and how far along the road to the destination labelled 'convergence' we had come.

There are, however, difficulties with implementation. For example, some of the criteria are difficult to measure – 'convergence' can have a subjective element. Robert Mundell, one of the pioneers of the optimal currency area theory, emphasised in the early 1960s the importance of labour and capital mobility, and also noted that it is an 'empirical rather than a theoretical question'.[8] There is also a question of priority: is labour market flexibility more important than converged inflation rates, for example? Nonetheless, the literature clearly indicates that a reasonable conclusion of convergence on all, or nearly all, of the above criteria is necessary for a monetary union to function effectively. Economists in the European Commission and European Central Bank (ECB) knew this.

A fairly obvious point about the optimal currency area is that it does not necessarily coincide with national boundaries. For example, in 1990 the Benelux countries plus West Germany were much closer to being an optimal currency area than West Germany plus East Germany, but the latter union went ahead first, and did so using an exchange rate of parity between the Deutschmark and the Ostmark, resulting in a considerable economic burden for the western part of the reunified country.

Pareto's Law Supports Specialist Economies

Complementary to the knowledge on an optimal currency area is the Pareto Principle. It is named after the Italian economist Vilfredo Pareto, and it refers to the manner in which efficient situations are optimal: those in which it is impossible to make one person better off without making one person worse off. It follows from this that countries should specialise where they have a comparative advantage: Germany in heavy machinery and consumer goods, Greece in shipping, services and tourism.

In an optimal currency area, you need to have specialisation. That increases the wealth of everyone. In order to have this, because some sectors will experience a cyclical slump, you must have fiscal transfers to smooth that out. But this facility didn't exist in Europe.

So as well as the principle of whether economic convergence should have occurred before or after European monetary union, there is the additional question of the nature and degree of convergence.

Otmar Issing, a founding member of the ECB board, has made many of the same points as those listed early in the chapter about the key elements required for an optimal currency area. Writing after the adoption of the euro, but before the emerging debt crisis of early 2010, he noted:

> The more the price system (in the widest sense) bears the burden of adjustment, the less important is the loss of the national exchange rate and monetary policy instruments, and the greater the benefit of using a single currency. This benefit increases with the size of the currency area and the economic inter-linkages between the areas forming a monetary union. This applies both to trade in goods and services and to financial market integration.

He reported that studies in the 1990s 'attempted to ascertain which group of countries within Europe might best satisfy the conditions for an optimum currency area. The result was mostly a relatively small group of countries in a kind of "DM-bloc" which, firstly, had tied their exchange rates to the D-Mark for some time and, secondly, whose economy had close linkages to that of Germany'.

Then Issing added: 'This was not shown to be the case for the group of 11 countries. In a word, the euro area that was to be created on 1 January 1999 fell quite a long way short of meeting the conditions for an optimum currency area.'[9]

In the context of subsequent events, this revelation of what was known at the time is quite astonishing. Economic theory did not support the notion of a single currency across as many as 11 European nations in 1999, or 12 (including Greece) by 2001.

ERM, R.I.P.

If theory indicated that only a small number of European economies formed an optimal currency area, what of practical experience? There was also plenty of material here, as the European Community had set in place an experiment. The Exchange Rate Mechanism, successor to the 'snake' and precursor to monetary union, was an arrangement of nominally fixed exchange rates between European currencies.

In September 1992 the British pound was forced out of the ERM, to the horror of the Conservative government but to the delight of the eurosceptics in the same party. The Italian lira left the ERM in the same month, and in November the Spanish peseta and the Portuguese escudo were devalued by 6 per cent against the other currencies. In January 1993 the Irish pound was devalued by 10 per cent. In May the peseta and the escudo were again devalued. In August 1993, the finance ministers took the decision to raise the fluctuation margins to 15 per cent.[10]

A key objective of the Exchange Rate Mechanism – to force or encourage economic convergence as a prelude to a single European currency – had failed completely after 14 years of operation. As the designs for the grand 'Project Euro' were being set out on the drawing board and presented to the parliaments of the continent, the prototype exploded in unexpected fashion. I draw particular attention to the term 'unexpected'. George Soros and other short sellers made fortunes from the collapse of the ERM precisely because there were so few of them anticipating its failure.

This begs some searching questions. Would the stricter requirements of full monetary union be able to achieve the economic convergence that eluded the ERM? Did the European Commission learn the lessons of the failed 1979–93 experiment? Or is the current crisis simply a rerun of the ERM on an altogether more terrible scale?

On what basis was it assumed that the rates at which the entrants to the euro came in were better than those in the ERM? Does locking them in automatically make the exchange rates more suitable? Having failed in theory, and then in practice, this was starting to resemble a political project dressed up as an economic one. The single currency was going to have to be sold to a sceptical public.

(Mis)-Selling the Euro to a Sceptical Public

It was inconvenient, to say the least, that the prototype single currency should fall to pieces in 1992–93 during the period that Europe's leaders agreed the next stage in progress towards monetary union.

The key summit had been held in the Dutch city of Maastricht in December 1991. There could not be a more appropriate place to illustrate some of the practical benefits of a single currency for closely converged economies. Maastricht is a beautiful walled medieval city that lies on the bank of the river Maas (*'Meuse'* in French), in a narrow strip of southern Netherlands, with Germany to the east and Belgium to the west. In the years before the euro, some of the pubs in the city would accept and give change in any one of three currencies. Tills had separate sections, and you could order your drinks in guilders, Deutschmarks or Belgian francs.

The Maastricht Treaty was signed in February 1992, and paved the way to the euro, whose introduction a decade later meant that the multicurrency handling ability of the city's bar staff became an obsolete skill. At this time the differences between northern and southern European economies were considerable, and were easily observable to the tourist. In the early 1990s southern Europe was a cheap place for northern Europeans to visit. A Maastricht citizen who went on holiday in Greece would have some pleasant surprises.

Yet despite the apparent benefits of monetary union, popular support was not overwhelming. Ratifying the Maastricht Treaty was troublesome, and the proposal for monetary union was the most contentious element. The ruling British Conservative Party had become more eurosceptic, signalled by Margaret Thatcher's 'Bruges Speech' in 1988. John Major, successor to Margaret Thatcher and prime minister since 1990, tried to bridge the gap between the two wings of his party. Although he won the April 1992 election, it was with a greatly reduced parliamentary force, though with the help of 'opt-outs' to the more contentious aspects of the legislation, relating to workplace rights and the single currency, the UK Parliament successfully ratified the Maastricht Treaty in 1993.

In Denmark the government submitted the Maastricht Treaty to a referendum in June 1992. The Danish people stunned the rest of the European Union by having the temerity to vote 'No'. Like the UK, the

Danes negotiated opt-outs. Eight years later, in 2000, membership of the euro was put to the voters as a single issue. By a margin of 53.2/46.8 per cent, the Danish people opted to keep the krone.

The Danish vote turned out to be the first of several 'No' votes to European Union treaties in different countries. The precedent to submit a revised form of the treaty to the electorate, which is then approved, was established and has since been repeated.

In France, another country to arrange a referendum on Maastricht, there was the surprise of the '*petit oui*'. A bare majority, just 50.7 per cent of the population of a country that was not only a founding member of the EU, but one half of the celebrated 'Franco-German axis', the engine of European integration, voted in favour.

Only the voters of Denmark, Ireland and France were offered a referendum.

Scepticism to the euro project was widespread in the years leading up to the launch of the new currency. Opinion polls in many countries, notably Germany and Finland, frequently registered opposition. On 9 February 1998, 155 German economists published an open letter called: 'The euro is coming too early.' They protested in particular about insufficient progress having been made in controlling public finances and the lack of reform to labour markets. They declared their commitment to the principle of monetary union, but called clearly both for a delay to the medium term and for strict implementation of convergence criteria.

Four German academics, Wilhelm Hankel, Wilhelm Nölling, Karl Albrecht-Schachtschneider and Joachim Starbatty, made a legal challenge to Germany's entry into the euro in the country's constitutional court. This was on the basis of a ruling in 1993 which held that, once the euro came into force, monetary union would have to satisfy all the conditions of the stabilisation treaty concluded when the single currency was agreed. If it did not, Germany would be obliged to leave. The four were to resume legal action in 2010 over alleged failure to honour the 'no bail-out' rules of the single currency.[11]

In his book *The Birth of the Euro*, Otmar Issing makes passing reference to the fluctuating opinion poll results regarding membership of the euro. Recording the historical significance of the Germans' relationship with the Deutschmark, he emphasises that it was seen as the country's saviour in the postwar years for a population haunted by the wiping out of its wealth in the hyperinflation of the 1920s. The currency was sometimes even referred to as the '*ersatz Kaiser*'. Given this background, he acknowledges that support in his homeland for the conversion of the treasured

Deutschmark to the new euro would be qualified at best. In 1995, only one-third of Germans were in favour of the euro, and 45 per cent were opposed. Even at its peak, at the euro launch in 1999, with reassurances of the robustness of the Stability and Growth Pact pushed to the fore, support only reached 55 per cent. In the largest economy in the eurozone, support for the single currency fluctuated between weak and conditional.

Josef Joffe, editor of *Die Zeit*, has summarised the deal that brought Germany into the euro as being struck by the late François Mitterrand, former French president, and the then German chancellor Helmut Kohl, negotiating over German reunification in 1990: 'Bon, Helmut, this is what we'll do. You get all of Deutschland, and I get half of the Deutschmark.'[12] Even if one takes this quip as satire, there is still little doubt that Germany saw its surrendering of the Deutschmark and of the Bundesbank's control as a price to pay for the rest of the European Union approving German reunification.

Writing in 1995, the former European commissioner Bernard Connolly, who became sceptical of the European project, stated: 'A monetary union cannot survive without a political union, as the Bundesbank has said time without number. But there will not be a political union cohesive enough for everyone to put "Union" interests above national interests. That, too, has been made abundantly clear by the history of the ERM. It follows that the single European currency will certainly be weaker than the Deutschmark and probably weaker than any of the currencies of the Frankenreich bloc presently are.'[13] At the time, he envisaged that the peripheral countries of Greece, Spain, Italy, Ireland and Portugal would be kept out.

I shall return in chapters 7 and 9 to discussion of popular opinion and whether the way in which the euro was presented to the people of Germany, and other participating countries, was a grand case of mis-selling. Of course, while the currency was to some extent sold to the German people, the case didn't have to be made too strongly – for the simple reason that their view was not sought. Neither the Maastricht Treaty nor entry into the single currency was subject to a referendum in Germany.

The German people were promised a greater Deutschmark; the secret deal was for just half, while the lack of convergence towards an optimal currency union meant there was a serious risk it would become less than half. Following the events of 2010, the German people are now being asked to display an act of solidarity towards a grand project the designers of which had not dared ask them to approve.

Convergence First or After: Counting Your Chickens Before they are Hatched

Otmar Issing and others were well aware that the founder members of the single currency fell 'far short' of an optimal currency area. He asserted, however, that the lack of convergence merely meant that the single currency would have a difficult start, and that it was possible to reform *after* its inception. 'Optimists were confident that with a single monetary policy the need for reforms to increase flexibility would become so obvious that policymakers would be bound to react', he noted.[14]

This illustrates the dilemma: with the political momentum to proceed with monetary union facing the economic hurdle that conditions were not ready, which side would win the argument? Political idealism or economic pragmatism?

European leaders displayed classic signs of *cognitive dissonance* – difficulty to accept factual or logical information that contradicts core beliefs – on this point. To put it in more traditional language: the wish is father of the thought. The European project is noble; it *ought* to have brought about economic and political convergence after half a century; therefore the time *ought* to be right for a single currency, and nation-states *ought* to be sufficiently *communautaire* to display the solidarity necessary to make the adjustments necessary for a single currency to function (but we daren't ask them to find out if they are). The first president of the ECB, Wim Duisenberg, commented: 'The euro is much more than just a currency. It is a symbol of European integration in every sense of the word.' When even the president of the central bank puts political idealism ahead of economic pragmatism, the adventure is not getting off to the soundest of starts.

In the 1990s, there were debates continuing within and between institutions and countries. The Germans and Dutch were inclined to the view that there should be fuller economic convergence first, before monetary union. The Italians argued that it was better to proceed with the timetable, with the argument that irreversible union would force convergence. The European Commission wanted full fiscal union, but could not persuade the heads of government. Jacques Delors himself, who as European Commission president had drafted the report that led to the Maastricht Treaty, argued that a single currency should be supported by explicit Europe-wide fiscal coordination.

John Palmer, member of the policy board of the European Policy Centre and for 20 years the European editor of London-based paper the

Guardian, says that the irony is that those most committed to establishing the euro did not have the decisive say on arrangements for the single currency. They argued that there should be fiscal as well as monetary union, but were opposed by the member states, in particular Germany.

> When the Maastricht Treaty was being negotiated, many of those working most intensely on the Stability and Growth Pact and governance arrangements were in no doubt that it should contain a far greater degree of fiscal union, rather than simply relying on the monetary pillar. The majority of the participating governments saw the force of that argument, but it was essentially Germany who thought it was a bridge too far. They thought that they would never be in a position where they would be likely to fall foul. If you recall, [German chancellor Helmut] Kohl had a big battle with the Bundesbank. The Bundesbank were pretty negative [to the single currency] until almost the end. Formally, they said they were in favour, but the thrust of their interventions was to be very critical [in the 1990s].

The end result was a typical EU compromise, or 'fudge'. But there was compromise only on the structure, not on the decision. The 'start' button for the euro was still pressed. In the 1960s, 70s and 80s a fudge rarely had major consequences. Compromise was often a pragmatic way of working through issues. If there are opt-outs or messy compromises on working time rules or fisheries policy, some people may be unhappy, but the consequences do not threaten the very future of the union or the way in which the economy operates. With the euro, the stakes could not have been higher.

Mis-Selling by Metaphor: The Great Train Journey

It has been common to dismiss euroscepticism in the northern countries as being a mixture of national pride, conservatism and prejudice, and to discuss the emergence of a 'two-speed' European Union, with the bulk of countries racing ahead with the benefits of integration while laggards such as Denmark, Sweden and the UK languish on the periphery. But was their resistance to the euro project really xenophobia, or just practical scepticism? Do the benefits of price transparency and a single currency trading area outweigh the loss of national monetary control? Did they – a heretical thought – make the right decision to opt out?

There is nationalism in all countries, but some of the objections to monetary union were practical, based on memories of the ERM. Pressure to keep currencies pegged to the rising Deutschmark meant interest rates were set relatively high. This was held to be partly responsible for the recession which featured high unemployment throughout the industrialised world in the period 1990–92. A 'one-size-fits-all' interest rate is one of the commonest objections to a single currency area extending beyond the optimal region. It was to return as a source of concern (only this time for rates that were seen as too low rather than too high) in the early years of the single currency.

The more xenophobic elements of eurosceptic campaigners, and their ignorance, should not escape criticism, however. They often accuse 'Brussels' of 'imposing' laws, when it is the Council of Ministers that actually decides. They make sweeping generalisations of the supposed laziness and dependence of other populations. Consequentially they constitute a convenient scapegoat, which can make reasoned scepticism to EU proposals difficult.

All manner of false narratives and generalisations are at work.

From the hard line sceptics we hear that the EU is a devious conspiracy designed to destroy the nation-state through subterfuge and move all political power to an unelected elite of central bureaucrats intent on destroying individual liberty.

From the integrationists we hear that the EU was created to prevent war; that it is a project with the goal of greater integration; that to question the mechanics of the next steps towards integration is to be in favour of war and division.

It is unfortunate when some EU leaders give the sceptics and xenophobes ammunition. Consider the following admission:

> Obfuscation and deliberate dissembling have complicated this fundamental debate [about Europe's future]. Some political leaders have concluded that the best way of making progress towards a more federalist outcome is to play 'grandmother's footsteps'. Take a political step forward, and if the electorate does not notice then take the ground gained as the starting point for the next advance. This discredits the EU, and gives voters the impression that it is an elitist conspiracy.

These comments were made not by a eurosceptic but by Chris Patten, a former EU commissioner and supporter of the single currency, writing in the *Financial Times* on 3 June 2010.

In the often polarised atmosphere created by xenophobes and integrationists, it has often been difficult, almost taboo, to criticise the next steps for European integration for fear of being branded nationalistic. Support for the euro became totemic. If you were not enthusiastically in support of the ambitious 1999 starting date, with wide membership, perhaps you were not a true believer. The problem with being a true believer in such an ambitious project is that it can lead to *pseudo certainty*: the belief that by saying it is so, we will make it so, and that any expression of doubt is a sign of bad intention. As the crisis began to threaten the viability of the single currency in early 2010, statements of *pseudo certainty* became more, not less, pronounced. This served only to weaken the credibility of the spokespeople, as I shall discuss further in chapters 7 and 9.

Another by-product of such *herd behaviour*, of thinking in terms of true believers versus back-sliders, is that this leads to a lack of diversity in thinking. Another common feature of the monoculture of the herd is *tunnelling* – concentrating mostly on known parameters, familiar stories and being unprepared for the 'unknown unknown'. The familiar story often becomes solidified to the point that we mistake it for reality. Metaphors and other examples of simplified Platonic forms become accepted as reality. So, rather than engaging in debate, too many enthusiasts for economic and monetary integration saw their movement as a journey. In this context, it felt as though it was already a long time since the Schuman Declaration of 1950 and the Werner Report of 1970.

Their campaign typically took metaphorical shape as a train leaving the station. In 1997, for example, Italy's Europe minister Piero Fassino said: 'The countries that will take part [in the single currency] will be at the heart of Europe and will lead it. The countries that will hold back risk a loss of influence... the [E]uro [E]xpress will be leaving on schedule: It is always preferable to catch a train while you are in time. If you try to catch it at the next station the chances are that it will be crowded, there won't be a seat and you may even miss it altogether.'[15]

It is important to stress the ferocity with which the campaign was sold, and the warnings made. Governments and peoples considering opting out of monetary union were threatened with political irrelevance and economic decline. In 1997, the then EU Commission president Jacques Santer warned that the 'out' countries should think very carefully about the political price they might have to pay for refusing to join what he called a 'winning team'.

Those taking part were promised sunlit uplands as full partners in the world's new economic superpower – the one part of a bipolar world, in Romano Prodi's words, confronting the dollar zone. It is strange how Asia is completely absent from this occidental view of the economic world. In the first decade of the euro's existence, China overtook France, Britain and Germany in terms of economic size, and is now the world's second largest economy.

Fassino's quote represents one of many occasions in the 1990s where the imagery of a rail journey was used to apply pressure on eurosceptics. The choice of the train is revealing. If you are on board, the implication is that you will *inevitably* keep the same pace as the leaders. If you are left at the station, you will *never* catch up. That exclusion is permanent and irrevocable – unlike a road race, where a slow starter may draw level with the leading group by lap 30, or fall behind again if they are off the pace.

Pointing to the obvious inaccuracies of the metaphor to describe the complex matter of European economic integration would run the risk of being described as eurosceptic, or worse. At this point I would like to state my personal position. As I am going to sound sharply critical of EU decisions, policies and institutions in this book, I want to make it clear that I am not a eurosceptic. I agree with the vision of a free-trade European Union, with free movement of people and capital. The completion of the single market has brought huge benefits for businesses and ordinary citizens alike since its completion in 1993. I have no philosophical or nationalistic feelings of opposition to a single currency. The euro is a good thing, done badly; and it has been done very badly.

Catching Up, Fingers Crossed

Central bankers and economics advisers have great difficulty disentangling causes and effects, and of overstating the impact of their decisions. In the last chapter I reported how Horacio Liendo, adviser to Domingo Cavallo, had noted that Argentina's three most successful decades coincided with the adoption of the Gold Standard, and made a conclusion of a simple cause and effect relationship, unrelated to dynamics within the productive economy. Otmar Issing, a founding member of the ECB, makes a similar observation about postwar Germany: 'Without any doubt, a stable currency was to a very large extent the foundation that underpinned the economic reconstruction of Germany after the Second World War.' No mention of the Marshall Plan or the dramatic leaps forward in productivity in the German manufacturing industry that enabled the likes of Bosch, Bayer, BMW, Volkswagen, Audi et al. to take market share from competitors on a huge scale in the postwar years; nor of the peace dividend that Japan and Germany enjoyed through being demilitarised.

Issing does not ignore the 'real' economy, but it is regarded as a supplementary matter, with convergence postponed until after monetary integration. In 2008 he wrote:

> The [Maastricht] Treaty defined the conditions for entry – at least formally – exclusively in *nominal* terms [his emphasis]. Among the 11 founder members there were, nonetheless, considerable differences in living standards and/or productivity. Thus the Treaty ducked the issue of how far a single monetary policy might pose problems for poorer countries in the catching-up process – an integral part of the whole project. With the enlargement of the European Union, and the still greater divergence in living standards between member states, this issue has taken on an extra dimension.[16]

Let's stop a minute. Let's take a look at the *overconfidence bias* and policy contradiction that this statement reveals. The 'catching-up' process for poorer countries is simultaneously integral to the project and absent from its plans. It was just supposed to happen. Fingers crossed. I'll take a more detailed look in the following chapters at exactly what was happening in Greece during this 'catching-up' period.

Arguably, the development of the real economy and improved competitiveness were addressed by the Lisbon agenda set out at the EU summit in Portugal in March 2000. It aimed for radical reform to transform the continent by expanding its research capacity, promoting entrepreneurship and facilitating the take up of information technologies.

Note that this is a full eight years after the Maastricht summit, and was not formally linked to the euro project. In 2004 the Kok Report described limited progress towards the Lisbon agenda, citing 'disappointing delivery' due to 'an overloaded agenda, poor co-ordination and conflicting priorities'. The report complained of a lack of political will by member states.

Convergence: Let's Find Some Criteria

How was convergence supposed to happen? The optimistic view was that liberalisation would encourage improvement of the supply-side. The discipline of removing the ability to carry out a 'competitive devaluation' – a term heavily pejorative in EU circles – ought to force the weaker countries to improve their economic performance. The economic rationale for EMU was that, by ruling out competitive devaluations, it would remove a source of economic instability, and leave countries with no option but to reform their labour markets and open up their economies to greater competition.

In the absence of full integration towards an optimal currency area, the EU did make a serious attempt to ensure fiscal harmonisation, setting convergence criteria for entry into the single currency, which formed the basis for the Stability and Growth Pact that was intended to police discipline within the single currency.

What is interesting about the five convergence criteria in the Maastricht Treaty is the extent to which they betray the tendency towards *illusion of control*, a common and most serious psychological affliction among central bankers. The rules to which participating government members of the European monetary union and their finance ministers pledge to honour do not all lie within the scope of government. These rules are as follows:

- The budget deficit must be kept below 3 per cent of GDP
- Total public debt has to be less than 60 per cent of GDP
- Countries should have an inflation rate within 1.5 per cent of the three EU countries with the lowest rate
- Long-term interest rates must be within 2 per cent of the three lowest interest rates in EU
- Exchange rates must be kept within 'normal' fluctuation margins of Europe's Exchange Rate Mechanism.

These are not policies, they are outcomes; they are the by-products of policies, but also of external events. Central banks and national governments can aim for them, but it is difficult to guarantee them. They can be subject to considerable impact from external shocks – as we have seen following the banking crisis of 2007–09. The volatility of such indicators is evident in the fact that the countries causing concern in the 'convergence' period and the early years of the euro were not Greece,

Spain and Ireland – those most associated with the current crisis – but Italy and Belgium (in the run-up to the euro's launch) and later France and Germany, which broke the rules of the Stability and Growth Pact in the period 2003–04.

No reference is made to the trade balance. At the start of the single currency, the largest trade deficit countries were Portugal and Greece, at around 7 per cent and 3 per cent of GDP respectively.[17] Would the discipline of being in the single currency prompt a huge bout of 'catching up'? In chapter 7, we will discuss whether convergence on trading performance really did occur.

No allowance seems to have been made for the possibility of divergence *after* the single currency launch, in spite of the experience of divergence during the 'fixed' exchange rate system of 1979–93. In reality, adherence to the principles of the Stability and Growth Pact – the successor to the convergence criteria – actually *declined* after monetary union. And nation-states found they could ignore the rules with impunity.

Between 1993 and 1999 there was a lot of converging to do. The European Union's leaders, still committed to the European Union, set a target of 1999 for completing phase three of the Maastricht Treaty. The prototype had failed, but the Treaty committed them to monetary union with the force of law.

What an achievement it would be if they could create the type of convergence in just 6 years that the ERM did not achieve in 14! And if monetary union is complete, unlike the ERM, there will be no escape. Economies will have to converge – won't they?

Goodhart's Law: Or, the Target Becomes the Problem

A problem with setting such targets as those in the Stability and Growth Pact is that the very act of setting them affects the policymaker's decisions. This is a well-established and commonly observed phenomenon. It is sometimes known as Goodhart's Law: it is typically defined to mean that as soon as a government regulates a set of financial assets, these become unreliable as indicators of economic trends, typically because institutions can create new types of asset. Precise measures, accompanied by close scrutiny over short timescales, can create the greatest distortions. It is named after Charles Goodhart, a former chief adviser to the Bank of England. A related observation he made is: 'Any observed statistical regularity will tend to collapse once pressure is placed upon it for control purposes.'[18]

Interested parties who have a personal motive in meeting the outcome will try to meet the number or target instead of honouring the underlying purpose. A paradox here is that data, typically held to be 'hard' information, can be much less accurate than a qualitative description of the underlying dynamics, often supposed to be 'soft' or 'subjective'. Similar observations to Goodhart's Law are the Lucas Critique and Campbell's Law. The Lucas Critique goes further than many other approaches to economics in emphasising the unreliability of historical data and encouraging deeper inquiry into underlying causes. Campbell's Law asserts that quantitative measures in social settings encourage corruption in order to meet the target, rather than honouring the overriding objectives.

A close cousin of Goodhart's Law is a common phenomenon well known in its Spanish translation: '*hecha la ley, hecha la trampa*' – 'as the law is set, so is the loophole'.

The convergence criteria were just statistics: you can hit numbers without having convergence, while maintaining the different structures of the economies. You can put someone in a corset, but it doesn't necessarily make them thin.

Surprise, Surprise: Convergence Achieved in a Mere 18 Months

Judgement on meeting the criteria for entry into the single currency is multidimensional, but the final decision is binary. You are either in or you are out. The EU judged that Greece did not meet the convergence criteria on 3 May 1998 – specifically, that its public sector deficit was excessive. But on 10 November 1999 the European Commission formally announced its recommendation to repeal this ruling. This was upheld by the Council of Ministers later that month. In March 2000, the Greek government formally announced its application to join the third stage of economic and monetary union, and the European Commission and ECB began its analysis of the degree to which the Greek economy converged. It also assessed the progress of the other economy deemed not to have achieved convergence for the first wave of entry on 1 January 1999, which was Sweden.

Two months later, the Commission reported:

> On the basis of the report of the ECB (adopted on 27 April 2000) and of its own 2000 convergence report, the Commission has concluded that Greece fulfils the necessary conditions for the

adoption of the single currency and is proposing a Council decision abrogating Greece's derogation from its obligations regarding the achievement of economic and monetary union. The derogation would be abrogated with effect from 1 January 2001. The report was endorsed by the European Parliament on 18 May.

The Commission recapitulates the main findings about the progress achieved, for each of the two Member States, on the basis of the various criteria mentioned in Article 121(1) of the EC Treaty and indicates that this assessment leads it to conclude that Greece has achieved a high degree of sustainable convergence, justifying the abrogation with effect from 1 January 2001 of its derogation. It notes, on the other hand, that there are no grounds for changing the current status of Sweden.[19]

So what had happened between these dates? The full story is only now beginning to be discussed, a decade later, though key details have been in the public domain for much longer. The Commission's minutes indicate that it was only the public sector deficit expressed as a proportion of GDP that held up Greece's compliance with the convergence criteria. The total public debt was above the 'maximum' of 60 per cent of GDP, but the EU had watered down this requirement through Article 104c(b), which simply required that the debt be in the process of falling and that it should 'approach the reference value (60%) at a satisfactory pace'. This confirms that entry was more political than economic. Entry was seen as a golden prize, with the view that *communautaire* governments should be rewarded with acceptance.

So all the Greek government had to do was reduce the public sector deficit below to 3 per cent. Or appear to.

Fiddled Figures. Big Secret?

With the rules of the convergence criteria and the Stability and Growth Pact public, countries that wanted to join the elite club of European monetary union had clear targets in sight. The act of setting such targets, with a short-term deadline and a pronouncement of an irreversible process, has a tendency to create distortions as people aim for them. Another by-product is that, naturally, all or most energy is spent on meeting the target rather than achieving actual structural and economic convergence.

According to many recent accounts, the 'true' nature of the Greek government's structural deficit did not become clear until after the

October 2009 election, when the incoming PASOK party announced
that the figure was not around 6 per cent of GDP, but was over 12 per
cent. This marked the start of the visible part of the current crisis.

Had the previous Greek governments succeeded in keeping the
fiddled figures secret for almost a decade? Not quite. The miraculous
turnaround, in which Greece went from being an unconverged economy
to a converged one within 18 months, should have raised alarm bells.

Some European Commission officials were indeed suspicious of the
sudden convergence, but the kind of sharing of information that the
European Commission is now calling for – submitting national budgets
to the Commission for approval for example – was not permitted at the
time. John Palmer of the Centre for European Studies, comments:

> There were certain people in Brussels who had grave reservations,
> but did not have the authority – did not have compulsory invigilation
> powers. They could not go in and ask to see the books.
>
> The flavour of it [the debate on Greece's application] was: they
> took very sophisticated banking advice from the investment banks
> about how to present the figures. And to top that, this was a period
> when growth was quite strong. The Greek economy appeared to be
> doing well, and there was a strong desire to reward countries that
> had faithfully committed to the integration process. There was a
> political desire to be helpful.

It is difficult to escape the conclusion that empire building was part
of the agenda: maximising the economic and geographic size of the
eurozone. It enabled the EU's leaders to make favourable comparisons –
on aggregate GDP, population and so on – with the dollar area. This
fits with the geopolitical ambition expressed by Romano Prodi in 2002:
'The two poles are the dollar and the euro. That is the political meaning
of the single European currency.'

There is at least a suspicion that the painstaking work on assessing
true economic convergence and double-checking statistical claims were
much duller agenda items than planning the grand opening of a huge
economic area, and drafting the speeches.

It was actually well known that some countries had hit the targets
with the help of loopholes. This was no secret. *Risk* magazine, for
example, reported the arrangement between Goldman Sachs and the
Greek government in 2003. Moreover, it was based on a blueprint in
Eurostat's 2002 accounting guide, the magazine reported. In 2001 a

report by Italian academic Gustavo Piga for the US Council on Foreign Relations and the International Securities Market Association referred to the arrangements: he called for a 'firm national accounting framework to deal with these window-dressing transactions'. An example was a swap put in place in a 1996 three-year Italian bond.[20] His accusations of eurozone nations performing 'window-dressing' on their public sector deficits were reported in *Risk* in January 2002.

There were open debates between the ministers of finance on this subject at their regular Economic and Financial Affairs Council (Ecofin) meetings. As early as 2000, ministers endorsed the Action Plan on EMU Statistical Requirements. A year later the Ecofin Council approved a list of key European indicators to provide 'a more complete range of variables, higher timeliness and higher frequency of the time series'. Nonetheless, these actions still all took place *after* the fixing of the exchange rates and the assessments of convergence. An Ecofin paper from March 2003 noted that a 'quantum leap' was still needed 'for the European Statistical System to produce macro-economic statistics reaching quality standards comparable...to those of the United States'. Two years later, Ecofin reported some progress, but also noted that the economic indicators provided 'still lag far behind the US indicators and major efforts are still required'.[21]

Generous assumptions appear to have been made as to the real fiscal position that lay behind the incomplete statistics. This is despite the fact that the practice of keeping significant levels of public sector liability off-balance-sheet was already well established. Provincial level deficits had been a major complicating factor in the Argentine debt crisis.

The swap that Goldman Sachs arranged was not unprecedented. It involved cross-currency swaps linked to Greece's outstanding yen and dollar debt. Such arrangements can have a legitimate use in transferring the currency of an obligation to reduce the overall burden. Normally, they are struck at spot prices to 'lock in' a favourable exchange rate. In the case of the Greek–Goldman Sachs deal, they were 'off market' – a weaker level of euro versus dollar or yen was used, resulting in an upfront payment to the Greek government, but subsequent higher interest rates. A deal struck in 2002 is estimated to have created additional credit of $1 billion for the Greek government. So it was a way of borrowing – lucrative for Goldman Sachs, expensive over the longer term to Greek and other eurozone taxpayers – that did not show up in official government borrowing figures. There are similarities with the *megacanje* ('megaswap') arranged by Argentina in 2001, but with the crucial difference that it was secret. When *Risk* magazine broke the story in 2003, both the Greek government and Goldman Sachs declined to comment.

Premature Celebrations

Back in 2002, reservations among many economists, ordinary voters and even within the European Commission itself were put to one side as the formal launch of notes and coins across the 12 economies were celebrated as the clock struck midnight at the start of New Year's Day. The French Indian Ocean island of Réunion was the first to be able to use euros, followed by Greece and Finland on the European mainland. In Athens a pyramid of euros decorated Syntagma Square.

As Western Europe saw in the New Year, there were celebrations outside ECB offices in Frankfurt, outside which a large image of a euro coin was displayed.

The practical rollout – the functioning of ATM machines and so on – went smoothly. Once the risk factors associated with the changeover had passed, the new currency gained value against the dollar. ECB president Wim Duisenberg told a press conference: 'We can already pronounce this unprecedented move a tremendous success. On 1 January at zero hour, the introduction of euro banknotes and coins marked not only the completion of economic and monetary union…but one of the major, if not *the* major, step forward in the history of European integration. I am convinced that 1 January 2002 will appear in the history books in all our countries and beyond as the start of a new era in Europe.'

The optimists, with their faith in 'convergence after', were celebrating. In the next chapter, I will look at the background to Greece's entry into the single currency, rooted in its own unique history, and then describe the actual events that occurred during the 'catching-up' period.

Chapter 4

WESTERN BRANDING, EASTERN LEGACY: A COUNTRY ON A FAULT LINE

'It's too soon to tell' was the famous reply of Chinese Communist leader Zhou Enlai, when asked in the 1970s what he thought had been the impact of the French Revolution nearly two centuries earlier. Doubtless, he was thinking in terms of Marxism's theories of history and revolutions, but he may have inadvertently produced a wise perspective on how a nation's history lives on. The *événements* of 1789 have helped to make France a very different place from Britain or Germany in, for example, the structure of its local government, its particular brand of republican politics, and its general outlook. Doubtless, these influences have helped shape its collective outlook on the European Union and a thousand other matters.

In Greece, our history goes back much further than 1789, and its influence is still being felt. It may be too soon to tell what the impact of Greece's Byzantine past and its subsequent occupation under the Ottoman Empire (1458–1821) is on tax collection, public sector management, military spending, tension in the Aegean region and the fate of the single currency.

Greece's application to join the euro was motivated by the bogus concept of economic convergence and was supported by misleading statistics, as discussed in the previous chapter. It did, however, enjoy excellent branding. Greek philosophy, mythology and language occupy a part in the formation of Western thought. It is not just any part; it is the most elevated. It is spoken of in hushed, reverential tones. In English-speaking countries, for example, Anglo-Saxon words represent the voice of the people. Educated persons are proud of their ability to speak French, and will use terms such as *genre* or *rapprochement*. Those of learning may also know Latin. But only the ultra-elite understand

Greek, part of the study known as 'Classics', which is a term that conveys considerable authority in the English-speaking world.

The deference to Greek culture is understood very broadly in the West. Suppose an Anglo-Saxon politician is facing a tough decision. If he is aiming for the common touch he will refer to being caught 'between a rock and a hard place'. If writing in the *Times Literary Supplement*, he will refer to 'steering a course between Scylla and Charybdis'. In a popular paper, he will warn that 'pride comes before a fall', but in the *Financial Times* or *Harvard Business Review* this will become 'hubris'. Elvis Costello once put the word 'euphemism' into a pop song, and was known as the thinking-man's songwriter afterwards.

The Byron Illusion

Greece held a special place in the hearts of the classically educated Romantic poets of the nineteenth century. Percy Bysshe Shelley wrote:

> But Greece and her foundations are
> Built below the tide of war,
> Based on the crystalline sea
> Of thought and its eternity;
> Her citizens, imperial spirits,
> Rule the present from the past.[1]

There are many other examples. Fellow Romantic poet Lord Byron famously died in the fight for Greek independence. As one commentator in the British paper the *Telegraph* noted, 'there is a wonderful, almost divine irony in the fact that Greece, of all places, turned out to be the Achilles heel of the European Union'.

He added:

> The fact that Greece was allowed to join the euro at all when it clearly did not meet the preconditions for membership can be put down to what I would call the 'Byron Illusion'. When Lord Byron went to fight and die in the nineteenth century Greek War of Independence he went not for a living nation but for a dead idea, an idea nurtured in generations brought up on the Classics... Greeks continued to play on the romance of the ancient past in their application for euro membership, something that seduced Europe's leaders, many of them also educated in the Classics.[2]

While Greece got the flamboyant Byron, the USA was perhaps better served by one of Britain's other intellectual exports, Thomas Paine, who wrote *The Rights of Man*, helping to ensure a nation created through written law.

The branding, however, is deceptive. Greece is not a Western country. It is Orthodox, was part of the Ottoman Empire for over 300 years, prior to which it was part of the Byzantine Empire. We never had a Western-style Reformation, nor the development of a large middle class, nor the emergence of conservative and liberal philanthropy that developed in western and northern Europe and North America. Robert Kaplan in the *New York Times* drew attention to the 'inflexible social order, in which middle classes developed much later than in northern Europe, and which led to economic and political pathologies like statism and autocracy'. He added an accurate summary: '[Modern] Greece is far more the child of Byzantine and Turkish despotism than of Periclean Athens.'[3]

The Byzantine Empire lasted for over one thousand years and left permanent imprints on modern Greece. Whilst we cannot equate the culture of the Byzantine Empire with the Ottoman's despotism, we can see that many of the Byzantine practices in economy continued after the Ottoman era until today, such as the policy of favouring small property holders as protection against Western feudal practices.[4]

The large amount of small business with family-based owners in conjunction with widely dispersed house and land ownership is a significant difference from Western 'cluster based' economies, where acute specialisation and/or economies of scale are essential.

In the Balkans war, my Greek compatriots tended to side with their Orthodox cousins in Serbia. In the 1990s during the years leading up to the single currency, which was intended as the crowning achievement of a European Union dedicated to preventing another mainland war, there actually was a savage conflict in central southern Europe. German and Greek people supported opposing sides. This reflected the same alliances as in the Second World War. This is a detail that didn't figure in the convergence criteria of the Maastricht Treaty.

The Burden

This history, the tag of being the birthplace of civilisation, gives us a proud heritage, but also a burden. The label 'Greek' comes with a weight of history and expectation attached. We have the legacy of being intellectual leaders, but while Greece continues to produce great intellectuals, recent history has been so traumatic, the development of the state and a sense of civic duty so stunted, the involvement of overseas powers so pronounced, that it is difficult to live up to this elevated branding.

History, Grievance and Entitlement

The ancient history of Greece is well known in the West. Knowledge of more recent history is much hazier. I have described how the Greek economy was more of an emerging economy than an advanced one. This is just one of many misunderstandings on the part of European Union leaders. The phenomenon of 'Hellenic Peronism' and its associated entitlement culture has come about through distinct and identifiable historic trends, which I shall attempt to summarise.

Our sense of entitlement has been deepened by more recent events, as well as the cultural legacy. In summary, they can be listed as follows:

1. The notion that we are the creators of civilisation
2. The betrayal by the West in Asia Minor in 1921
3. The Second World War
4. The betrayal over Cyprus in 1974.

1. We are the Creators of Civilisation

We Greeks are acutely conscious of our cultural legacy, and we play to it. The Parthenon towers above the central squares of our capital city, a physical illustration of this towering legacy. There is a feeling, deep down, that the world owes us: we gave you philosophy, democracy, education, geometry. When you play sport, the most celebrated events are the Olympics, featuring the marathon. And if you are someone who likes to keep fit, you go to the gymnasium. We even have the terms 'philhellenic' and 'antihellenic' to describe whether foreigners are 'pro-Greek' or 'anti-Greek', respectively. It is fine to have pride in your nation's heritage; unfortunately, combined with other events in our recent history, it has contributed to a sense of entitlement.

2. Asia Minor Catastrophe

There is a feeling that the West betrayed Greece in 1920–23 in the Asia Minor catastrophe, when Greece lost half of its historic land and suffered huge human losses. British prime minister David Lloyd George had promised territory to Greece in return for support in the fight against the Ottoman Empire. The Treaty of Sèvres, under the terms of the armistice to end the First World War, promised significant territorial gains to Greece, but these were abandoned in the subsequent Treaty of Lausanne in 1923 that followed the Turkish War of Independence.

In the current climate, tension between Turkey and Greece continues, with frequent reports of Turkish infringement of Greek airspace or sea-space. Greek military spending is above the European average as a percentage of GDP (this will be discussed later in this chapter).

3. The Second World War

Winston Churchill expressed his debt to the Greek resistance by declaring: 'Hence we will not say that Greeks fight like heroes, but that heroes fight like Greeks.' He also said: 'If there had not been the virtue and courage of the Greeks, we do not know which the outcome of World War II would had been.' And even Adolf Hitler expressed his admiration of 'the Greek soldier [who] above all, fought with the most courage', addressing the Reichstag on 4 May 1941.[5] Operation Barbarossa was delayed by six weeks, as Greece beat the Italians, therefore allowing the Russian winter to finish off the German army. Josef Stalin said: 'The Russian people will always be grateful to the Greeks for delaying the German army long enough for winter to set in, thereby giving us the precious time we needed to prepare. We will never forget.'

Also, the Greek losses were huge: an estimated 13 per cent of the population perished – more than any other occupied country in percentage terms. There was a famine in the period 1941–42.

The psychological memory is below the surface – but only just, and resentment lingers. In February 2010 Greek deputy prime minister Theodoros Pangalos said: 'They [the Nazis] took away the Greek gold that was in the Bank of Greece, they took away the Greek money and they never gave it back.'

This took the political temperature to fever pitch, at a time when European solidarity needed to be at a maximum for there to be any chance of saving the euro. Not to be outdone, the next month two German Christian Democrat politicians, Josef Schlarmann and Frank Schaeffler, suggested that Greece should sell some of its islands to repay debt, prompting many in Greece to say that 'What they didn't take militarily they will take through economics.'

4. Losing Half of Cyprus in 1974

The Turkish invasion of Cyprus in 1974 led to huge upheaval and caused thousands of Greek Cypriots to become refugees, forced to move to the south of the island. The island remains partitioned.

The Ottoman Legacy

Greece is far from being the only EU country to have been occupied. But the Ottoman occupation was unlike, say, the Spanish occupation of the Netherlands or the Nazi occupation of France, in one important respect: it lasted so long. Its duration was well over three centuries, from the collapse of the Byzantine Empire in the fifteenth century to the birth of the modern era just after the Napoleonic Wars. A whole way of life grew up around survival and resistance. And to paraphrase Zhou Enlai, it probably is too early to tell what the long-term significance is, especially with regards to payment of taxes and tension with Turkey.

Under Ottoman rule, it was a point of pride to avoid paying tax. For three centuries, Greeks were expected to pay *haratzi*, which was effectively an Islamic poll tax levied on Christians. They had to carry a receipt certifying their payment of *jizya* at all times, or they could face imprisonment. More sinister still was the practice of *devsirme*, or παιδομάζωμα (*paidomazoma*) in Greek, in which Greek communities were expected to hand over one child in five to the Ottomans for forced conversion to Islam and service in the Janissary infantry of the Ottoman army. In 1705 Greek rebels killed an official who had been sent to Naoussa in Macedonia to secure more conscripts. The rebels were beheaded and their severed heads were displayed in Thessaloniki.[6] Other tales in Greek folklore feature a mother deliberately crippling her child to prevent his being taken as a military conscript. In other cases, families bribed officials to ensure that their children became officers.[7]

The contrast with other European nations is sharp. In most northern EU members, the history of taxation is closely linked with that of bolstering national independence. No one likes paying taxes, but if the trade-off is a credible defence and, in more recent years, a welfare state, there is more popular support. For example, in the UK income tax was introduced initially as a temporary measure in 1798, to help defences against revolutionary France and resistance to Napoleon's forces. Income tax was put on an automated 'pay as you earn' system in 1944 to help finance the war effort against Nazi Germany. So the roots of British taxation lie in defending or extending national sovereignty: paying for HMS Victory and the Spitfires. There is a world of difference between that and the legacy of an occupied country, where taxation was perceived to have no legitimacy. Of course, nearly two centuries have passed since release from the Ottomans, but in that period Greece has only sporadically enjoyed democratic sovereignty. As discussed, it has had kings and its borders determined by foreign powers, further occupation under the Nazis, a civil war and a military dictatorship.

This legacy has a huge impact on how the state operates and how it is perceived. In the Anglo-Saxon world, the state emerged as a protector of certain rights, such as property and contractual rights. This supported societies with a property-owning ruling class. In Greece, the social group that took control after the Ottoman Empire were the former tax collectors: the ruling class saw the state not as a guarantor of property rights, but as a source of income. So even by the nineteenth century the conditions for clientelism were in place. In the late 1880s there were 214 officials for every 10,000 in the population, compared with 126 in Germany and 73 in Great Britain. At the time, French nobleman Arthur Gobinau observed: 'In Greece a whole society seems to be operating on the motto that to the extent that only the state has money, one should take advantage of this fact and work as a civil servant.'[8] In the 125 years since, little has changed – except that, with the scale of EU grants and the expansion of government borrowing in the early 2000s, the scale of the creation of fake jobs in the public sector and other examples of largesse have grown exponentially.

Greece, despite its long history, is a young nation dominated by foreign powers; in the words of commentator Chronis Polychroniou, Greeks are 'late-comers into the modern culture of constitutional democratic dispositions, civic knowledge and civic education'.[9]

External Interference: A Bavarian King

These grievances underline the extent to which Greece remained a quasi colony even after securing nominal independence from the Ottoman Empire in the nineteenth century. First Great Britain, and later the USA, exerted considerable influence over Greek political affairs in defence of their own regional strategic interests. This was obviously welcomed during the fight against the Axis powers, but its legacy was a stunted sense of national autonomy. This was weakened further by civil war and dictatorship.

Throughout the nineteenth and most of the twentieth centuries, Britain and the USA were the powers behind the throne, literally and figuratively. Great Britain's foreign secretary Palmerston decided, in consultation with the other 'great powers' France and Russia at the Convention of London in 1832, that the country should become a monarchy, following secession from the Ottoman Empire. A Bavarian prince, Otto, or Othon, was declared king.

Democracy is, of course, a Greek word, and in its modern history the practice is well established, with the exceptions of the Nazi occupation and the military dictatorship of 1967–74. Culturally, however, it is a very different type of democracy to the kind you might encounter in northern Europe, especially the Protestant nations. After its independence in 1821, Greece gave full voting rights to almost all male citizens in the 1830s. It was pioneering for the time, but it meant that there was no class struggle accompanying the transformation from feudal to democratic systems, as in Western systems. In the West this struggle allowed the checks and balances to be in place, and further developed over time. Therefore the Greek democratic model was one without true industrialists, without able domestic-based capitalists, filled with ill-trained bureaucrats with complexes and their clan-based supporters, and the custom of seeing the state as an agency to dispense funds in return for favours.

Advanced economies, with their specialist business clusters, are supported by an entire class of investors, merchants and industrialists. Ideally, this class is supported by an incorruptible civil service that builds an infrastructure and invests in human capital.

In Greece, early adoption of universal voting rights, combined with an unreformed clan-based system, led to very close, 'cosy' direct relations between local governments and citizens, who in Greek are referred to as '*pelatiaki*', or customers. This created a form of 'Hellenic Peronism', and created the basis for an entitlement culture and a bloated public sector.

Civil War 1946–1949

Immediately after the Second World War, while the Soviet Union took over most of Eastern Europe, leaving Western Europe to the allies, in Greece the battle between the two forces of capitalism and Communism raged. The Greek resistance was split into left and right wings, supported by different external powers. The pro-Western government, backed by the USA and Great Britain, fought against the Democratic Army of Greece, the military branch of the Greek Communist Party (KKE).

The EAM (Ethniko Apeleftherotiko Metopo), or National Liberation Front, comprised a federation of groups that provided welfare, and had considerable popular backing during the Second World War and the famine. It controlled parts of the country and formed a provisional government in 1944, towards the end of occupation. But it was effectively run by the Communist Party, and was opposed by the official army and police and by anti-Communist politicians. It was also opposed by the bulk of the church, though a few clergy sympathised with the Communists. Right-wing groups intimidated voters at the 1946 elections; the Communist Party abstained. The resultant conservative administration set about destroying the hold that Communists had on trade unions and agricultural cooperatives.

Complicating the matter was the presence in the official army of individuals who had collaborated with the Nazis, and a consequent problem of morale within the ranks. They struggled in fighting a guerrilla war against determined fighters who had proved their patriotic worth during the occupation. However, the government controlled the cities, making it easy for them to detain urban Communist supporters or keep them under surveillance. The result was stalemate. For reasons that are not well understood, Stalin did not send aid to the Communists in Greece, though the fighters did receive some support from Tito in Yugoslavia. Many left-wing fighters were barefoot and their ammunition was rationed. Despite this, the implicit Soviet threat was sufficient to prompt the US government to regard preventing Communist rule in Greece as of strategic importance – not least because of its proximity to the trade routes of the Strait of Constantinople and the Suez Canal, so it stepped in to support the conservative government. In May 1947 President Truman secured the passage through Congress of massive aid to Greece. Under the Truman Doctrine's pledge to defend any nation against totalitarian Communism, the underlying theme was 'whatever it takes'. This pretty much ensured the defeat of the Communists. To this day, there is a strong anti-US sentiment in the Left in Greece, which is often accompanied by anti-corporate and anti-business sentiments. The American aid helped rebuild the infrastructure, increase the size of the merchant fleet and the number of vehicles and modernise agriculture. The Communists continued their defiance for another two years, but they lacked the firepower or international support to take or hold larger towns or cities, so ultimately the resistance was futile.[10]

After the government's victory, the police and army took measures to try to prevent the reemergence of Communist activity. Martial law was used against suspected Communists. At the end of the war, nearly 3,000 people were in prison under sentence of death. The reprisals were not on the scale of Franco in post-civil war Spain, but the suppression of the far-left movements was almost total. The KKE was banned until 1974, along with democracy. In the 1950s, prominent Communist leaders Nikos Beloyannis, Nikos Ploumpidis and several of their followers were executed under the martial code. Others were imprisoned. There was emigration of left-wing activists, especially to Eastern Europe. According to the Committee of Greek Political Refugees in the 1980s, an estimated 50,000 Greek political exiles went abroad, some returning after the return to democracy in 1974.[11]

The postwar era was a period of mass emigration and internal migration from rural to urban areas. Between 1955 and 1971, some 1.5 million people left the Greek countryside: around 900,000 went abroad, and 600,000 went to the larger cities.[12]

While much of Western Europe was benefiting from a new peace and a much better settlement than there had been after the First World War – helped by the Marshall Plan – for Greece conflict and poverty continued. Spain had a brutal civil war; the rest of Western Europe had the Second World War. Greece had both. The subsequent military coup and dictatorship of 1967–74 was prompted by fears in the army among conservatives that Communists could wield influence via elections. There is a direct parallel here with the military coups in South America.

It is in this context that the buying of social peace by George Papandreou in the 1980s needs to be understood.

What is the modern legacy? Because the Communists lost, we do not know how repressive they would have been in government. They could argue that the election in 1946 was unfair, and that they only lost the subsequent civil war because of imperialist intervention by the US. They had fought heroically against the Nazi occupation, and subsequently against the military dictators, so they do not have the almost universally negative image that the movement has in most Western countries. The official Communist Party continues to receive a respectable number of votes in national elections (around 7 per cent in 2009, for example). The only comparable situation in the European Union is that of France, where the Communists played a leading role in the Resistance at a time when many conservatives sided with the Nazis. They subsequently enjoyed an electoral dividend, often securing over 10 per cent of the vote in national elections for several decades after the war. Unlike France, however, Greek Communists continued to enjoy significant support after the fall of the Berlin Wall.

In Greece the extreme anti-corporate, anti-profit attitudes of the Communist movement continue to influence the culture and policy positions of a militant trade union movement. This has a lingering effect in the frequently abortive or half-hearted efforts to create a flexible labour market. This liberalisation is essential for effective adjustment of prices under the free-market European Union, and especially within the single currency.

The Regime of the Colonels

Like Argentina, Greece suffered under a dictatorship at a similar time in the recent past. In Argentina it lasted from 1973 to 1983; in Greece from 1967 to 1974.

The seven-year 'regime of the colonels' began with the 1967 coup d'état, which followed indications that the centre-left party of George Papandreou, the Centre Union, would fall short of a majority in the 28 May elections and form a coalition with the United Democratic Left, suspected of being a cover for the banned Communist Party.

A readable account of the years of dictatorship can be found in *A Man* by renowned Italian journalist Oriana Fallaci. The volume is a biography of resistance leader Alexandros Panagoulis, who had attempted to assassinate the military leader George Papadopoulos in 1968. Panagoulis was sentenced to death by the junta. This was not carried out owing to international pressure, though he was brutally tortured in prison.

After the restoration of democracy Panagoulis became an MP, though he died in a highly suspicious car accident in 1976, shortly before files of the junta's military police that he possessed were to be made public. The files reportedly included evidence of collaboration between mainstream politicians and the junta, and have never surfaced. His short time in parliament was characterised by repeated accusations of this nature.

As the biography shows, the forms of torture used were particularly cruel. This has had the damaging and perverse effect of making Communism more popular. Again there are similarities with South America; for example, many Chilean resistance leaders were granted exile from Pinochet's regime in East Germany by Erich Honecker, giving a benign impression of Eastern European Communism in the minds of many voters in the Cono Sur region. Almost the only reason that there has remained an element of popular support for Marxism in the late twentieth and early twenty-first centuries is the history of violent, criminal acts committed by anti-Communist military regimes.

The dictatorship was also deeply conservative (with a small 'c'), banning miniskirts, ordering church parades on Sundays and so on. Historian David H. Close writes: 'Its policies were opposed in every sphere to the requirements of modernisation: in political organisation, economic policy, education, industrial relations and gender relations.'

He also notes: 'It was too dependent on foreign investment and US backing to try creating an ultra-nationalist movement as fascist parties had done. In these two respects...it resembled the contemporary military dictatorships in two other countries that could be described as economically semi-peripheral to the advanced industrialised countries: Chile and Argentina.'[13]

Protests continued throughout the dictatorship. A student named Kostas Georgakis immolated himself in Matteoti Square in September 1970. He shouted anti-junta protests such as 'Long live free Greece' and 'Down with the tyrants' as he ran away from street cleaners trying to extinguish the flames. He died a few hours after the incident. It was the year after Jan Palach, a Czech student, made the same sacrifice in a protest against the Soviet-backed regime. Both cases served to generate international interest and support, and there are monuments to both young men in their respective countries.

In 1973 the crew of an Hellenic Navy ship, the *Velos*, refused to return to Greece after NATO exercises as a protest against the regime. The captain Nicholaos Pappas defended his actions on the basis of NATO's founding principles to defend sovereign democracy and associated freedoms. The Athens Polytechnic uprising in late 1973 had major repercussions. It led to a hardening of the junta's line, ending its limited liberalisation policy, and then an internal coup. But the new hard line leader Dimitrios Ioannides' further attempted coup in 1974 against Archbishop Makarios of Cyprus prompted the Turkish invasion and the collapse of the military regime. There was to be a curiously similar collapse of the Argentine junta after its military defeat in the Malvinas islands eight years later.

The fact that the military regimes in Argentina and Greece were both right-wing caused one additional lasting factor: it meant that the Communist movement, with its overtly strong commitment to entitlement culture and hostility to the private sector, appeared heroic and retained some popular backing as the people suffered persecution by the regime.

There followed in Greece a period known as the '*metapolitefsi*', referring to the transition from dictatorship to democracy. In the elections of November 1974, Konstantinos Karamanlis, heading his newly formed New Democracy party, won a clear majority. In a plebiscite at the same time people voted to end the monarchy, and so the third Hellenic Republic began.

The Geographic Legacy and a Modern Arms Race

The Aegean Sea is a fault line between political tectonic plates. Greece lies directly between the former Yugoslavia and the Middle East, two of the most violent regions in recent world history. It is the border country with Turkey, which for years has had its application to join the EU blocked, almost certainly because its population is largely Muslim. The eagerness with which Greece was embraced by the European Union and into the single currency shows a keen philhellenism in Western European capitals. This was also a powerful factor in Western support for secession from the Ottoman Empire in the early nineteenth century. Of course, the rivalry between Greece and Troy goes back even further, as celebrated in the universally known epic poems of Homer.

What few in the West seem to appreciate, however, is that this tension continues today. Frequently, Turkish warships are seen in or near to Greek waters, her aircraft in Greek airspace. The invasion of Cyprus was only a generation ago. At the time, many Greek people feared an attempted invasion of other islands and the mainland. Defence spending by modern Greece is the highest, as a proportion of GDP, of any country in the European Union. According to a list published by the US Central Intelligence Agency, the figure stands at 4.6 per cent, twenty-fourth in the world – on a par with China, just ahead of the USA. Next on the European list is Cyprus (3.8 per cent), then France (2.6 per cent). What's striking about this ranking is the extent to which Greece's neighbours feature so strongly. Turkey's spend is actually higher than Greece's (5.6 per cent), while Macedonia, Armenia, and Bosnia and Herzegovina are also heavy spenders. Not all high spenders are hostile to Greece, but this list indicates that much of the world's military hardware is located in this relatively small and volatile geographic area.[14]

Given that both Greece and her military rival Turkey are NATO members, this begs questions of the leadership of Western countries, and of a military alliance which has as its founding principle the concept that an attack on one member represents an attack on all. Yet this arms race between two NATO members is almost invisible in the West. To take an example, on 19 July 2010, following months of rumbling concern over incursions of Greek territorial waters, the *Kathimerini* website ran the following report:

> Greece has raised concerns with Turkey for a second time about the activities of a Turkish marine research ship near Greek territorial waters. Just days after the Piri Reis was spotted between Rhodes and Kastelorizo, prompting an official complaint from the Foreign Ministry to Ankara, Alternate Foreign Minister Dimitris Droutsas expressed Greece's worries about the vessel's activities to Turkish Foreign Minister Ahmet Davutoglu... The ship...is not in Greek territorial waters but is sailing above what Greece considers to be its continental shelf, where Athens claims rights to potential undersea mineral and fossil fuel deposits.[15]

Yet the very next day, in a major report in the *Financial Times* on the rise of Turkey as a regional political power, the tension with Greece was referred to in the past tense! It stated: '[Turkish foreign minister] Ahmet Davutoglu has clocked up more than 100 international trips as he hyperactively pursues his vision of Turkey as a rising regional power... Mr Davutoglu has sought to mediate in conflicts from the Balkans to Baghdad and has used Ankara's fast-growing economic clout to further new friendships, whether with emerging powers including Russia and Brazil or with formerly antagonistic neighbours such as Syria, Iraq and Greece.'[16]

It is one of the unexplained areas of radio silence that you come across from time to time in the Western media: an ongoing, potentially dangerous story that is almost ignored by the reporters and news editors. Occasionally the BBC carries a piece in the Europe section of its website. For example, in May 2010 it reported in a podcast: 'Turkey disputes the extent of Greece's airspace and territorial waters and probes the defences, sometimes several times a day. These dog fights over the Aegean, incredibly between countries that are supposed to be NATO allies, is a huge drain on Greece's finances.'[17] This is a rare exception; generally this arms race and continuing tension receives scant coverage in the more influential capitals of NATO members.

Additionally, other European countries, principally France and Germany, have benefited commercially from arms sales in the Aegean.

During 2010 talks continued between the Greek government and French company DCNS over the purchase of six frigates, at a combined estimated cost of €2.5 billion. In June 2008 French president Nicolas Sarkozy visited Athens to confirm a defence and security agreement with Greece. As well as discussing the potential frigate sale, on the agenda was a revamp of 20 of the Greek air force's Mirage jets, built by French company Dassault.

Rafale International, the joint venture that comprises Dassault, Thales and Snecma, announced in March 2008 the opening of an Athens office, and its intention to see the Rafale Omnirole established as the 'natural continuity of the French supply source to answer the needs of Hellenic Air Force'. This followed the delivery in November 2007 of 15 Mirage 2000-5 aircraft to Greece.[18]

In the same month the Stockholm International Peace Research Institute (SIPRI) singled out the Aegean in an announcement on world regions causing concern. It noted: 'Greece remains among the top five largest recipients of major conventional weapons for 2005–09, but has fallen from third place in 2000–04.'

Only China, India, South Korea and the United Arab Emirates bought more arms than Greece in the five-year period ending 2009. Of these, each of the top three have a considerably greater population and GDP than Greece, indicating that Greece is in the top two when adjusted for national wealth and head of population.[19]

SIPRI does not have precise figures on actual purchase prices. This is a complicated assessment, as many armaments are bought on credit, and information on interest rates is not always available. Instead, the rankings are based on an assessment of the market value of aggregate weapons bought. The following ranking shows figures that are the SIPRI Trend Indicator Values, in US $ millions, at 1990 prices:

Table 4.1 Armaments Imports 2004–2009

	US $ millions
China	13972
India	10625
S. Korea	8073
UAE	7760
Greece	6143

Source: www.sipri.org/databases/armstransfers.

The GDP and population figures are as follows:

Table 4.2 GDP and Population Figures

	GDP	Population
China	$4.33 trn	1.33 bn
India	$1.16 trn	1.17 bn
S. Korea	$929 bn	48.6 m
UAE	$199 bn	4.9 m
Greece	$356 bn	10.7 m

Figures for 2008. GDP figures in US$, from World Bank. Population figures from CIA World Fact Book.

Adjusted for size of economy, therefore, the list of highest military importers 2004–09 becomes:

Table 4.3 Value of Weapons Imports 2004–2009/ GDP × 100, Top Five Importers by Aggregate Value

	(%)
UAE	3.9
Greece	1.7
India	0.92
S. Korea	0.87
China	0.32

Source: www.sipri.org.

And adjusted for size of population, the list is:

Table 4.4 Value of Military Imports 2004–2009 per Head of Population, Top Five Importers by Aggregate Value

	(US$)
UAE	1.58
Greece	0.57
India	0.16
S. Korea	0.01
China	0.009

Source: www.sipri.org.

Siemon Wezeman, researcher at SIPRI, gives another indication of the distorted scale of Greek weapons spending:

> The Greek navy is the same size as the Dutch, Danish and Norwegian navies *combined* in terms of the number of ships. We do find it surprising [how much Greece spends on armaments]. It is a lot of money – both Turkey and especially Greece. It is one of the very few countries that have substantial numbers of aircraft, and a large navy. They keep on buying while the rest of the navies are being reduced.

SIPRI's annual report published in March 2010 showed that Germany is the world's third largest exporter of arms, after the USA and Russia. Its top two customers are Turkey (14 per cent of its sales) and Greece (13 per cent), so its suppliers profit handsomely from both sides of the Aegean arms race.[20] As an example, in 2003 the Greek government announced a contract for 170 Leopard tanks from German company Krauss Maffei Wegmann.

Much of the lending to Greece in the boom years was by large northern European banks. These institutions, some of them based in France and Germany, were loaning billions of euros to the Greek government, much of which was being spent on arms purchases from the likes of Dassault and Krauss Maffei Wegmann. The role of French and German banks in making loans to assist the Greek purchase of French and German manufactured goods, for both civil and military uses, is a major element in the entire saga of the ballooning Greek public sector deficit.

The furore that has erupted since early 2010 over the scale of the Greek public sector deficit has prompted significant intervention by the European Union, supported by the IMF. It is primarily the EU's responsibility to take the lead. But it may be that a decisive role could and should be played by another Brussels-based Western international alliance: NATO. It could oversee a controlled programme of disarmament between its members on opposite sides of the Aegean Sea, while offering guarantees on national security to both.

Geography and Geopolitics

Greece has a geography suited for shipping and trade, but less so for agricultural and industrial development. This has hampered economic development, helped concentrate power in a few wealthy families, and is an essential feature of the history to comprehend alongside the dependence on foreign powers, internal divisions and political violence. An analysis of this dimension appears in an article published by Stratfor Global Intelligence in June 2010. It notes:

> Lack of large areas of arable land combined with poor overland transportation also complicate capital formation... Countries that have low capital growth and considerable infrastructural costs usually tend to develop a very uneven distribution of wealth. The reason is simple: Those who have access to capital get to build and control vital infrastructure and thereby make the decisions both in public and working life. In countries that have to import capital, this becomes even more pronounced, since those who control industries and businesses that bring in foreign cash have more control than those who control fixed infrastructure, which can always be nationalised.

This has significant effects on political developments: 'When such uneven distribution of wealth is entrenched in a society, a serious labour–capital (or, in the European context, a Left–Right) split emerges. This is why Greece is politically similar to Latin American countries, which face the same infrastructural and capital problems, right down to periods of military rule and an ongoing and vicious labour–capital split.'

With the fall of the Berlin Wall, Greece ceased to become important to the West, according to this analysis:

> It did everything it could to retain its membership in the first-world club, borrowing enormous sums of money to spend on the most sophisticated military equipment available and producing erroneous financial records to get into the eurozone.
>
> Ultimately, Greece needs to find a way to become useful again to one or more great powers – unlikely, unless a great-power conflict returns to the Balkans – or to sue for lasting peace with Turkey and begin learning how to live within its geopolitical means.

Stratfor's conclusion is doom-laden and I find it difficult to contradict. Noting the austerity strings attached to the €110 billion 'bail-out' package, this is 'grafted onto Greece's regionalised social geography, vicious left–right split and history of political and social violence'. Some form of default or restructuring of the huge debt is inevitable, it advises. In conclusion:

> It is only a question of when, not if, the Europeans pull the plug on Athens – which most likely will be at the first opportunity, when Greece does not present a systemic risk to the rest of Europe. At that point, without access to international capital or more bail-out money, Greece could face a total collapse of political control and social violence not seen since the military junta of the 1970s. Greece, therefore, finds itself in a very unfamiliar situation. For the first time since the 1820s, it is truly alone.[21]

I think that there are policy options for Greece, and I discuss these in the final chapter, but I agree that the so-called 'bail-out' is anything but, that a default or restructuring of debt is inevitable, and that the political risks are high – and underestimated in Brussels.

Joining the EU: The Largesse Begins

As well as 1974, with the end of the dictatorship, the beginning of '*metapolitefsi*', and the division of Cyprus, another key date in recent history is 1981, when Greece joined the European Union. The nightmares of the mid-twentieth century were coming to an end. The symbol of maturation of democracy, entry into the EU (or EC as it was) heralded a new era. In the same year, George Papandreou became prime minister of the elected PASOK (socialist) government.

The surnames Papandreou and Karamanlis recur in the modern history of Greece, indicating a dynastic aspect to political leadership. The concept of '*soi*', or clan, is very much alive in the political elite. While you can observe this in other countries, it is particularly strong in Greece. In the USA, for example, the Kennedy, Bush and Clinton families have some dynastic features, but it is more likely that an outsider such as Barack Obama can rise to the most senior executive position.

The current prime minister at the time of writing, George Papandreou, is the son of Andreas Papandreou and grandson of George Papandreou senior, prime minister from 1944–45 and again for two short terms in the 1960s. Kostas Karamanlis, prime minister from 2004–09 and still the head of the New Democracy party, is the nephew of Konstantinos Karamanlis, founder of the party and prime minister for four terms. Since 1981 Greek politics has been heavily shaped by populist messages put forward by charismatic leaders, rather than movements based on social class or ideology. Moves towards mass membership parties have been limited.[22]

The period 1974–90 saw periods of weakness for the drachma. The oil price shock and collapse of the Bretton Woods currency exchange system in the early 1970s caused problems of inflation and a weak currency. The drachma was not part of the Exchange Rate Mechanism that ran from 1979–93. Two devaluations, of 15.5 per cent and 15 per cent respectively, took place in 1983 and 1985. In the 1990s a policy of a strong drachma was adopted, combined with a tougher stance on inflation. These policies were supported by both major ruling parties as part of the preparation for entry into the single European currency.[23]

With George Papandreou coming to power at the same time as accession to the European Community, his government was able to take advantage of many of the grants and agricultural subsidies to which a poorer country in the EU became eligible. This enabled him to begin to reward some of the social groups who had suffered under the Axis occupation, civil war and military dictatorship. In 1981, George Papandreou's PASOK party had opposed membership of the European Economic Community and of NATO. It was a populist programme that succeeded in creating a sense of Greeks, or 'the people', as having been wronged by outside forces, namely the authoritarian right, foreign intervention, US imperialism and its associated privileged groups. There was an anti-Western ethos. In common with most populists, however, Papandreou senior was opportunistic. In office after the 1981 election victory, his government dropped opposition to the EEC (now EU) and NATO.[24]

This of course enabled Greece, as a poorer country, to avail itself of generous EU development funds, and later cheap borrowing through membership of the single currency. From the 1980s onwards, Hellenic Peronism – buying social peace – began in earnest. This continued and morphed into a positive orgy of borrowing and spending after entry into the euro in 2001. If all the largesse had been spent on welfare, education and infrastructure, the effects might not have been so damaging. Unfortunately, a disproportionately high amount, by European standards, has gone on military hardware, administrative waste, corruption and sham jobs dished out to party supporters. The public sector only grew in inefficiency, bureaucracy and overstaffing and the government effectively became subordinate to the parties rather than to the nation. The populist path was followed almost entirely by all governments from 1981 onwards. A direct effect of this was the divergence from the input of risk taking and the output of profit. Risk taking became a less frowned upon activity in a society conditioned to recurring benefits and cushy state jobs. Profit became a dirty word, since it was based on 'connections' rather than entrepreneurism.

Chapter 5

THE LOOTING OF GREECE: SCANDALS, CORRUPTION AND A MONSTROUS PUBLIC SECTOR

Greek economics, in numbers:

- **321:** number of dead individuals aged over 100 and receiving a pension.[1]
- **768,009:** total number of civil servants, according to preliminary results of July 2010 census – the first attempt to assess the number of public sector employees.
- **$11 billion:** final cost of the 2004 Athens Olympics, double the initial budget.
- **€30 million:** bank cash deposits of a single Greek doctor.
- **324:** number of householders in northern Athens declaring for tax purposes that they own a swimming pool; **16,974**: number of residential swimming pools in northern Athens detected by satellite photography.
- **53:** number of years that have passed since Lake Kopais was drained. There is still an office to manage the lake's affairs, staffed by **30** full-time civil servants.

The occupation, trauma of civil war, sense of entitlement, the importance of family and clan (or *soi*), and the desire to '*voleutis*' (to get cosy) have combined to create the modern Greek society and economy. It is a monster, a modern day hydra with seven heads: cronyism, statism, nepotism, clientelism, corruption, closed shops and waste. This is a systemic, cultural dimension of the Greek saga; it is not just a case of a few unconnected scandals.

It is institutionalised. Politicians, for example, have awarded themselves immunity from prosecution. Article 62 of the Constitution grants immunity for members of government: they may not be prosecuted, arrested or imprisoned without the approval of Parliament.[2] Given this flagrant breach for a founding principle of democracy – that no one should be above the law and that the judiciary and parliament should be separate – it could be called into question whether Greece is really a democracy at all. Similarly, in 2003 the Greek supreme court ruled that it was not illegal to give bribes, provided they were given after the actions they were supposed to influence! So 'gratitude gifts' are allowed.[3] No minister has gone to jail in the last 30 years, marking Greece out alone among all of the European Union. Have the Greek ministers been more moral than their European counterparts, or was something else at play? No prizes for guessing correctly.

There is no excuse for European Union leaders, Greek society and politicians ignoring the lax accounting, corruption and public sector waste that occurs in Greece. Much of it was on public record. The EU policy of assuming that probity and efficiency in Greece were on a par with the Netherlands was perfectly avoidable on the basis of information in the public domain.

In order for laws to be upheld, the conduct of the political elite and of society as a whole has to support them. The practice of being 'on the take' is widespread and cultural. Compliance with anti-corruption laws and tax payment has to become the norm, not the exception. In Greece the elite and wider society have undermined those who wish to ensure compliance to the principles of probity and efficiency. Instead they have kept the seven heads of the hydra active and alive.

Cronyism

In all societies there are cliques and elitist circles, but in Greece these are peculiarly intense. The same surnames, through different generations, keep recurring as prime ministers. A lack of meritocracy in the public sector is the result of a long and inappropriate focus on the clan and on personal contacts, rather than on merit.

Benjamin Broome, in his book *Exploring the Greek Mosaic*, records:

> Politics [in Greece]...operates through a system of patronage that is known as *rousfeti*, a word of Arabic origin that means, roughly, 'personal influence'... Almost no politician is elected without the alliances formed through *rousfeti*... As one senior member of the government said: 'In Greece, public employment has always been

done by patronage. Government grants and public works projects have been given to friends.' Traditionally, it has been through *rousfeti* that jobs were arranged for relatives, admission to special schools was secured for the children of supporters, red tape was quickly cut for those to whom a favour was owed, and roads and schools were built in isolated communities of party MPs.[4]

After the return of democracy there was a marked trend towards bureaucratic clientelism, creating parasitic jobs for the political clientele of the ruling elite in return for political favours.[5]

Provision first of European Union aid and later of easy credit facilities within the single currency hugely increased the value of favours to be disbursed. In a blunt admission of waste and excess, Deputy Prime Minister Theodore Pangalos, when asked where the public money had all gone, told Parliament in September 2010: 'We all "ate" the money together',[6] i.e. it has been devoured through public hiring and public mismanagement.

In December 2009 Kerin Hope of the *Financial Times* related the anecdote of a Greek public servant who rarely complains about her workload. At the office where the Greek public sector employee (aged in her 40s) records VAT payments, supervisors take a relaxed view of breaks for coffee and shopping, she says. If a family member falls sick, she stays home. 'I don't feel bad, because there are always plenty of other people around to cover for me', she says. 'Nobody here has too much to do'.

The news report added that: 'Stories of such insouciance in Greece's bloated state sector are creating alarm across Europe.'[7] Indeed they are. But this example is neither isolated nor new. It is a shame that such inefficiency did not 'create alarm across Europe' in the period 1999–2001, when EU officials, desperate to hear a good story, pretended that the Greek economy and public sector were sufficiently converged with the rest of Europe to qualify for entry into the single currency.

The *Athens News* columnist Mark Dragoumis has commented that only 2 per cent of patriotic public officials actually do all the work – a heroic achievement on their part. Even if this is an exaggeration, he is right to point to a 2003 study showing that Greece ranked bottom out of 23 developed countries on public sector efficiency. The top four positions were held by Luxembourg, Japan, the Netherlands and Austria.[8] For all the protests against 'low wages' that the street protestors claim, Dragoumis comments: 'If those employed in Greece's public administration were paid the market price for the services they actually offered, their cost to the budget would be 27 per cent lower than it is today. So Greek taxpayers overpay in return for lousy service.'[9]

In July 2010, Greece's public administration watchdog reported several cases of alleged mismanagement and waste in its sixth annual report on public sector maladministration.

More than 4,000 checks by state inspectors in 2009 on the tax declarations of source of wealth ('*pothen esches*') forms submitted by officials in central and local government led to over 900 officials being indicted to appear before a prosecutor.

One case involved a retired former vice president of an association of Culture Ministry employees who was reported to have had €9 million in his bank account that he was unable to justify according to his income. Another case relates to a department head at the Health Ministry who is alleged to have sat on 19 different committees, all paid positions. Leandros Rakintzis, the head of the watchdog, noted that such committee positions should not be paid.[10] In effect, these committees are just vehicles for phony jobs handed out by one crony to another, and signed off by each other.

Statism

In another example of the hydra, Mark Dragoumis relates a tale of clientelist democracy in his book *Greece on the Couch*. A man goes to visit his MP, asking if he can help him secure a position for his son, who is unqualified and has just completed military service. He would like the post to be located close by. In return, he would pledge his vote and that of his *soi* (clan) to the politician. They meet again after a week and the MP says that there are two possibilities: work as a nightwatchman at a factory owned by a friend of his, or a place on a government training programme. The man was dismayed. 'I did not ask you for *work*. I asked for an appointment!' he shouted, and left the room.[11] I wish I could say that this was satire or exaggeration.

A preference for a 'safe' job in the public sector, and the bureaucratic and fiscal headaches of working in the private sector or setting up your own company, conspire to deprive some of the most entrepreneurial individuals from creating wealth. The desire for '*voleftis*' or 'cosiness' has created a cultural preference for public sector jobs, including not very productive ones; by contrast the term '*kerdoskopoi*' for profit-seeker is pejorative.

Surveys from the 1980s showed that around two-thirds of Greek individuals aspired to work in the public sector, an astonishingly high proportion.[12] Between 1971 and 1981 the productive sector fell as a proportion of the Athens economy from 41.6 per cent to 34.2 per cent, while the state-controlled sectors increased from 23 per cent to 31 per cent.[13] The informal economy continued to grow, with many state employees taking a full and active part in order to supplement their income. This has meant that in practice the modernisation and improved performance of public services has been against the immediate interest of large sections of the middle class.[14]

Year-on-year pay rises without links to productivity and cases of laughable overstaffing (some examples are summarised later in this chapter) have occurred more or less consistently from the 1981 election, through the credit crisis and recession, and even up to 2009 and the eve of the full-scale fiscal crisis. As late as 2008, for example, the Economist Intelligence Unit reported that the Ministry of Economy and Finance had decided to increase public sector salaries by 4.5 per cent and pensions by 5 per cent in 2008, resulting in a rise in the public sector wage bill by an estimated 8.9 per cent as a result of targeted increases for judges, teachers, police officers and hospital workers. In the private sector it accepted the largest trade union – the General Confederation of Greek Labour (GSEE) – and employers' associations agreed wage and salary increases of 3.45 per cent from 1 January 2008, 3 per cent from 1 September 2008 and 5.5 per cent from May 2009.[15]

These agreements were being made even as the public sector deficit began climbing far ahead of Maastricht Treaty limits, and only began to be reversed once the European Central Bank and the European Council of Ministers effectively took over control of the Greek economy in early to mid-2010.

For decades, neither PASOK nor New Democracy governments wanted, or dared, to confront the public sector trade unions. Whether this was caused by genuine sympathy with their aims, fear of widespread disruption such as a general strike, guilt over their own excesses at the public's expense, or the simple desire for an easy life is difficult to tell – it was likely a combination of these factors. In a culture of extreme clientelism and statism, what passes for 'normal' is very different from a country with a more balanced view of the relationship between private and public sectors.

As late as December 2009, when the full, colossal scale of the public debt became apparent, George Papandreou was still talking of a 'dialogue' on pensions – an initiative that included negotiating with Communist-led trade unions whose very purpose is to oppose the concept of dialogue in their campaigns for ever-increasing entitlements – in a context where anything other than cuts would mean national bankruptcy. This, combined with year-on-year increases to pensions and salaries, without any contribution in better public sector productivity that continued right up until 2009, gives the impression that even as crisis hit, Greek politicians had little understanding of its scale or of the measures necessary to prevent it.

The expectation of an endless supply of borrowed funds, without thought of repayment, had become akin to drug addiction. As Valdis Dombrovskis the prime minister of Latvia remarked at the Munich Economic Summit in April 2010: 'Real reform starts when government money stops.'

It is almost impossible to fire people in the Greek public sector. This stems partly from reforms in the 1930s, a time when the civil service was entirely political and would change completely with a change in government. It was needed at the time, but the times have changed. Now there are effectively, and constitutionally, jobs for life in the civil service. And if you cannot fire people, productivity inevitably goes down.

In August 2010, the General Inspector of Public Administration reported on benefits and bonuses for senior civil servants. He found that high-ranking officials were receiving up to 18 different cash benefits. One general manager was receiving 20 commissions; another 17. Some 31 employees of, ironically, an auditing function were getting full overtime benefits; all submitted maximum time-sheets. Some 80 officers were getting postgraduate benefits without having completed postgraduate studies. Or there were the benefits awarded to 'IT specialists' who couldn't even use a computer.[16] Other examples of benefits that I am aware of include port workers who receive an extra benefit to look at ships' propellers, and benefits for some office workers if they have to go upstairs or are on time for their jobs.

These benefits are almost as large in aggregate as the salaries themselves: the most recent figures indicate that the public sector wage bill is €7 billion and the benefit bill €6 billion, taking the total bill to €13 billion.[17]

Civil Service Census Finally Begins

Not until summer 2010 was there an attempt to assess the total number of people working in the hydra, with a formal census of civil service posts. At the start of the census, the *Kathimerini* website noted: 'An ambitious government initiative to conduct an online census of the country's civil servants, believed to number between 700,000 and 1 million and to be a significant burden on the debt-ridden state, yesterday started rather more dynamically than expected, as hundreds of thousands of public sector workers sought to declare themselves on the ministry's website, causing the system to crash. According to ministry sources, the system crashed in the morning after about 200,000 civil servants tried to log on at around the same time... Civil servants have been told that failure to register will result in the suspension of their wages.'[18] A couple of weeks later, a figure of 768,009 was announced.

Early Retirement and Pensions

A considerable source of waste of human capital is the absurdly early retirement of many public sector workers. Retirement arrangements that in other countries would only be available to soldiers – such as entitlement to full pension after 25 years – are available to clerical workers.

With the start of austerity measures from 2010, the government has begun to increase the pension age to 65, including for women, in a phased programme between 2011 and 2013. This formed part of a reform package on social security that was approved by Parliament in July 2010, despite sizeable public protests. The measures will also reduce pension payouts and make it easier for employers to sack staff. Economic pressures and high longevity, however, will continue to put pressure on state and occupational pension schemes and retirement incomes for years to come.

A report by leading economists in 2010 noted: 'Employees in Greece could retire at 58 years with full pension, provided that they had completed 37 years of work. The retirement age of 58 was significantly lower than the OECD average of 63.2 years. Moreover, the average pension was significantly higher than the OECD average: it was 95.7 per cent of an employee's average lifetime earnings (evaluated at the time of retirement by adjusting for economy-wide earnings growth), against an OECD average of 60.8 per cent.'

If Greece's pension system had been left unreformed, the authors add, it would have created an additional deficit of 12.5 per cent of GDP by 2050 (OECD 2009b). This is higher than the level of the entire deficit (including pensions) on average over each of the past three decades. It is also higher than spending on education and health combined.[19]

Table 5.1 Retirement Age and Level of Pensions Prior to 2010 Reform

	Official retirement age	Average pension, % of average lifetime earnings (replacement rate)
Greece	58	95.7
OECD	63.2	60.8

Source: OECD.

Probably no other issue has caused more anger in Germany than the generous retirement provisions in Greece – benefits the German taxpayers feel they are being asked to subsidise. The *Frankfurter Allgemeine Zeitung* summarised a common view in Germany with the acerbic observation: 'The Greeks go onto the streets to protest against the increase of the pension age from 61 to 63… Does that mean that the Germans should in the future extend the working age from 67 to 69, so that the Greeks can enjoy their retirement?'[20]

Here are some other comparisons. The data is from a different source, and the figures differ slightly from the OECD indicators in the table above, but tell the same overall story:

- Years of work to earn a full pension: Greece – 35; Germany – 45
- Proportion of wages as pension: Greece – 80%; Germany – 46%
- Number of pension payments a year: Greece – 14; Germany – 12
- Pension increase 2004: Greece – 3%; Germany – 0%
- Pension increase 2005: Greece – 4%; Germany – 0%
- Pension increase 2006: Greece – 4%; Germany – 0%.[21]

In Greece, with its warm climate and healthy diet, even low-income citizens can live a long time. Attempts to reform pension entitlements have run into fierce opposition in recent years, so the hidden costs of pension liabilities are continuing to rise.

Pensions for Dead People

The Greek state has no automatic way of checking if a pensioner has died. If relatives do not declare it, the state continues to pay the pension. The number of unmarried or divorced daughters of civil servants collecting their dead parents' pensions is estimated to be in the tens of thousands. About 40,000 women benefit from the allowance at an annual cost of around €550 million.[22]

Statism, and its close cousin clientelism, ought to be difficult in a democracy, owing to the existence of budget constraint; the simple reason being that the political benefits of state spending are balanced by the political pain of tax rises. Politicians find ways to circumvent the budget constraint. One way is through borrowing; another is through more generous pensions allowances, passing the cost on to future generations and their elected leaders.

Nepotism

Note the case of 269 individuals hired to the Ministry for Rural Development in a single weekend in August 2009, shortly before the general election. Appointments included 18 of Development Minister Konstantinos Hatzidakis' relatives. Posts included gymnasts, scholars, economists, anthropologists, a shipwright and a nutritional technologist.[23]

At the New Acropolis Museum, opened in June 2009, the majority of the employees are from the Pelopponesian village of Kalamata. Antonis Samaras is from Kalamata, and made these appointments when he was minister of culture in the New Democracy government of 2004–09.

Of course, every nation has its elites and its nepotism, but it is particularly marked in Greece. One study showed that in the post-Second World War period (1945–65) more than a third of all ministers had either their father or another relative in politics.[24]

Clientelism

The precedent established by Andreas Papandreou in the 1980s of largesse directed at interest groups, often intensifying in the run-up to an election, has been followed by PASOK and New Democracy administrations alike.

Farmers, for example, have simply come to expect that as soon as they protest their demands will be met. In January 2009 Greek farmers set up roadblocks and formed protests around the country. They drove tractors onto roads at Kipi, the border crossing with Turkey, and at other points in northern Greece. In total around 4,400 tractors blocked different points across the road from the Athens to Thessaloniki, the second city.

'We decided to cut Greece in two', a farmers' representative told Skai radio. Their demands were for minimum guaranteed prices for agricultural products, a freeze on loan repayments, tax-free fuel and higher pensions. The government responded with a package that included a pledge of €75 million in subsidies to cotton producers, €100 million to wheat producers and €75 million in immediate aid through the state-owned Agricultural Bank of Greece.[25] It looks shocking, but it's not isolated – this is a pattern that has been repeated every January for the past 20 years.

EU figures show that Greek farmers receive a subsidy of €570 per hectare, while the average for the EU is €250, and for Latvia just €70 per hectare.[26] €425 million was granted to farmers in 2008–09 from the Greek government.[27] There is much evidence that the way in which the EU's Common Agricultural Policy worked in Greece created state dependency and failed to encourage productivity improvements. When the value of direct EU subsidies began to decline in the 1990s, farmers took to protesting every winter, with producers of cotton, olive oil and citrus fruits blocking major roads with thousands of tractors for weeks on end. One olive grower admitted: 'It's easier to protest than blame ourselves.'[28]

The established custom of acceding to protests and demands simply encourages the behaviour in the same way that paying ransoms encourages hostage taking.

The roots of clientelism lie in the aftermath of dictatorship, in a similar way to the dynamics in Argentina.

> Andreas Papandreou's strategy in the 1980s, based on much populist rhetoric, was to give the disenfranchised the chance to live like the middle class, greatly assisted by EU aid. But this apparent 'wealth' was not being produced by the country, and New Democracy, in government 2004–09, did little to cut costs and increase revenues.[29]

Buying social peace may have been necessary in the years following the dictatorship, but after three and a half decades, these practices now look out of control and completely unjustified.

Corruption

It is always a sure sign that corruption is institutionalised and culturally acceptable when there is a familiar, colloquial term in use for the act. In Greece, we have two. A *fakelaki* (literal translation: small envelope) is an accepted way of speeding up service in Greece. The term *miza* applies to kickbacks or introduction fees, typically for procurement– say a briefcase full of banknotes or a wire transfer.

More than a million citizens paid a bribe (*fakelaki*) last year for better service in the public sector, according to the latest survey of the Greek department of Transparency International. This means that the immediate monetary cost of *fakelaki* on its own has reached €787 million in 2009, which is €39 million higher than the cost in 2008.[30] This cost does not include the wider economic cost of market distortions, overpayment for contracts and so on.

The problem is not getting better, despite repetitive government initiatives. In 2006 Transparency International reported a new Greek law to increase monitoring and transparency within the judiciary, including a more serious categorisation for the crime of attempting to bribe a judge, and a new code of conduct for police officers. A year earlier it had noted apparent progress in efforts by the General Inspector for Public Administration to clamp down on corruption.[31] The 2009 report noted the ratification in Greece of the Council of Europe's Criminal Law Convention on Corruption and the UN Convention against Corruption.[32]

Yet during this period of legislative activity, corruption actually worsened in relative terms. The Corruptions Perception Index 2009 gave Greece a score of just 3.8 out of 10, lower than the 4.3 registered in 2005. A single successful prosecution of a high-ranking official or minister for the Siemens scandal (summarised later in this chapter), followed by a proportionate sentence, would surely do more to clamp down on corruption levels than the mini-industry of new initiatives.

The Corruptions Perception Index ranking puts Greece on a par with other Balkan and Eastern European states, and far behind the scores for northern European countries such as the Netherlands (8.9), Sweden (9.2) or Denmark (9.3). In the international table, New Zealand and Denmark top the 2009 list for honest dealings, while Greece is seventy-first out of a total of 180, compared with forty-fifth out of 159 in 2005.[33]

If this dimension had featured in the Maastricht convergence criteria, might the decision to admit Greece and exclude Sweden have been different?

A study by the Brookings Institution published in 2010 portrays a similar picture. It found that bribery, patronage and other forms of public corruption are major contributors to Greece's public debt. Its estimate was that the Greek state has been losing the equivalent of at least 8 per cent of its gross domestic product each year to these practices, or more than €20 billion (about $27 billion).

'If Greece had better control of corruption – not to Swedish standards, but even at Spain's level – it would have had a smaller budget deficit by 4 per cent of gross domestic product, on average over the past five years', says Daniel Kaufmann, senior fellow at Brookings and the study's author.[34]

Regulated Professions or Closed Shops

A close cousin of clientelism, the practice of regulated professions has disfigured the labour market and held key sectors back from development.

The extent of regulated professions is considerable. One of Greece's main export industries is tourism, so it is remarkable that it is held back by arcane restrictions on the labour market in these sectors. The cruise industry, which has grown consistently in spite of economic gyrations in the past decade, has scarcely benefited Greece. This is largely owing to restrictions on the use of non-Greek crew operating from ports in the country: the 'cabotage' rules insist that at least 10 per cent of a crew must be Greek. In 2010, the Government's attempts to liberalise the sector were met with industrial action by trade unionists, which included the blockading of the main Athens port of Piraeus in April, preventing tourists from gaining access to the Zenith cruise ship; and again in June, leaving tourists unable to disembark. Law-enforcement agencies did not interfere. This prompted the Celebrity cruise company to abandon plans to use Piraeus as the start and end point for six cruises in 2011, and switch to Turkey, causing an estimated loss of €7.5 million to the Greek economy.[35]

The Council of Greek Tourism Companies has estimated that €1.1 billion a year could be added to the Greek economy by ending the cabotage rules.[36]

Other illustrations of closed shops from among the estimated 70 professions with restrictive practices include the following:

- Greece requires scuba diving instructors and English-language teachers to speak Greek even if they do not need it for their jobs.[37]
- Electricians must have a licence that requires membership of the union, and 5,000 social security stamps. Securing the recognition of a qualification from another EU country can require significant legal costs. British electrician Mike Bennett, based in Crete, told *Athens News* in July 2010 that gaining recognition cost him around

GB £10,000 (c. €12,000), principally spent on legal advice and insurance fees, and took seven months.[38]
- Taxi drivers' licenses: with no new licenses being issued, informal market prices reached €250,000.[39]

The above examples are contrary to EU directives supporting the single market and free movement of labour, and the Greek government, having been given a 'final' deadline of December 2009 to comply, eventually began doing so during the course of 2010.

Obviously a trade like that of an electrician, with stringent health and safety requirements, must be regulated, but a test to EU level and a certificate ought to suffice.

There is a clear link between closed shops and diminished tax revenue, as only licensed workers can officially issue invoices and pay taxes. The British electrician Mike Bennett commented that he is not aware of any other non-Greek EU citizen in his locality to have gone through the process of becoming a licensed worker, despite many working as craftsmen: 'I think I'm the only one. I know lots of electricians and plumbers, but none have licences.' The same news report quoted a Polish electrician who had been working for 13 years in Athens. He was licensed in Poland and had tried 'several times' to have his qualification recognised in Greece, but was rejected each time.

The potential figure of lost tax revenue from unregistered tradesmen during the construction boom of 2000–09, which included many privately-built villas, can only be guessed at.

A bid to reform the closed shop in truck driving prompted a week-long protest in the summer of 2010. It led to the closure of most petrol stations, some shortages in shop supplies and travel delays for tourists. Truckers were protesting against the liberalisation of their trade, their principal grievance being that they had paid thousands of euros for licenses that would become worthless as the sector is opened up.[40]

The strike in summer 2010 was only ended when the PASOK government, in desperation, invoked emergency powers and deployed the army to ensure essential services remained open. After a meeting on Sunday 1 August the union, the Federation of Overland Commercial Transporters, narrowly voted to end the protest and announced a return to work the next day.

The government announced: 'The transport market will open, this reform is necessary for the economy and the citizens and for that reason the legislation will go forward.'[41] At the time of writing, it's not clear whether this marks a significant break with the practices of clientelism and closed shops. As things stand, the government is due to end all restrictive practices, in line with EU legislation. There are around 70 professions in Greece with restrictive practices. Following the changes to truck driver registration, next up for liberalisation are lawyers, pharmacists (who enjoy a guaranteed 35 per cent profit margin) and civil engineers.

Waste and Red Tape

To a large extent, waste and red tape are simply a by-product of all of the above, but such practices become ingrained and behavioural; as such these act as one of the heads of the hydra in their own right. If incompetent officials are appointed without the skills for the job or with little to do, or are not really occupying any valid post at all, pointless bureaucratic procedures are inevitably created in order to give an illusion of industry and to extract economic rents from the rest of society. If, in addition, they expect bribes, there is an inevitable distortion in the prioritising of the tasks of public bodies. Cronyism and closed shops cause further misdirection of energy and resources.

Hundreds of bureaucratic procedures tie business people in knots, causing frustrating and pointless delays and additional costs. To establish a company in Greece, 15 procedures and 38 days are required, compared with an average of 6 and 25 respectively in other countries.[42]

In one example where a company wanted to construct a storage facility, it took 211 days and cost €10,600: one day for the notary; 10 days for the creation of an environmental impact assessment and to secure a fire department licence; 15 days to get the foundation permits; 90 days for the construction permit; and 3 days to obtain a social security code for the workers. One day was needed to get planning permission; 45 days to get connected to electricity; another 45 days for water and sanitation. One day was spent registering with another local authority; 3 days submitting forms to a department for hiring personnel; 88 hours to pay VAT; and 12 days to register the company.[43]

The Costa Navarino development also shows how slow and bureaucratic these procedures can be in Greece. It is a high-end, luxury tourism development of the kind Greece needs if it is to remain competitive with the Middle East and other eastern Mediterranean countries as a holiday destination. After 13 years and 3,000 signatures – from local authorities, planning authorities, environment offices and so on – the late shipping magnate and entrepreneur Vassilis

Konstantakopoulos could finally announce completion of one of the biggest tourist complexes in Greece, a €1.2 billion investment. Even a wealthy and determined entrepreneur like Konstantakopoulos finds it hard going to get basic things done. In another development, the Lorcos Group, looking to make a €2 billion investment in five years, since getting appropriate permits has been required to obtain 500 signatures, and estimates that it will need another 1,500 before it can begin the work.[44]

One important detail in the way in which Greek bureaucracy works is that in many of the procedures you have to appear at the office *in person*. You cannot just send a completed form by email. This adds hugely to costs and to the frustration levels of many entrepreneurs, holding back economic development.

The Scandals

These seven heads of the hydra combine to create recurring, systemic scandals and other dysfunctions. There follow some examples. The scandals included here are a selection, not an exhaustive list. There are hundreds and perhaps thousands of others no more nor less scandalous that could have been included, including amongst others public sector companies ('DEKO'), non-governmental organisations ('MKO') and so on. It is not just a case of the occasional bad apple – this is ingrained behaviour throughout the state and society.

There is an element of randomness in the scandals chosen for publication here, and there is definitely a recency bias. If you were involved in others – bigger or more dramatic – that have been omitted here, please don't be offended, and do feel free to email me details for a future edition. Space only allows for a chosen few.

Olympics

Nearly all cities that host the Olympics have cost overruns. Montreal took around three decades to pay for the 1976 games. London 2012 is likely to cost three or four times the original estimates. Given the finite deadlines and the prestige of the events, contracting agents are inherently in a weak position when it comes to negotiations.

When it comes to busting the budget, however, there is no doubt about the winner of the gold medal: step forward, Athens 2004.

By November 2004, the then finance minister George Alogoskoufis admitted that the cost had reached €9 billion, at least twice the original estimate.[45] Since then, specialist stadiums have been empty or underused, either falling into disuse or costing millions to maintain. The final cost is estimated to be over €12 billion. It is one of the most expensive Olympic Games ever held, and widely viewed as one of the least successful in creating ongoing benefits to the host country.[46]

This being Greece, there was a postscript. In 2010 broadcaster Ioannis Pretenteris reported that the Olympic Village, an agency set up to manage the 2004 Olympic Games athletes' village, had increased its personnel to over 150 full-time staff in the past four years, well after the games had ended. Among the professions hired were graphic designers, communications experts and psychologists. The total wage bill amounted to about €23 million.[47]

JP Morgan Bond Scandal

In 2007 it emerged that four Greek pension funds had significantly overpaid for €280 million of Greek government bonds. The investment bank JP Morgan sold the bonds at 92.95 cents on the euro to North Asset Management, a hedge fund based in London. JP Morgan was more than compensated for this loss by a gain from a corresponding deal with the Greek government, a source told the Bloomberg news agency. It had bought the bonds from Greece at 100 cents on the euro; the bank and government entered into a swap transaction, an agreement to exchange fixed rate payments for those based on floating rates. The same day it bought the bonds, North Asset sold them to HypoVereinsbank, part of UniCredit, for 99.9 cents, which then sold them at 99.95 cents to Athens brokerage Acropolis Axepey, which then sold the bonds to the pension funds at 100 cents on the euro.

JP Morgan has claimed that it made the sale on the understanding that North Asset was a 'buy and hold' investor. JP Morgan subsequently repurchased the bonds at face value.

The then prime minister Kostas Karamanlis fired his labour minister Savvas Tsitouridis over the affair. The Greek securities regulator revoked Acropolis's brokerage licence.[48]

Hospitals

The hospital sector has been sorely damaged by examples of wasted resources. This sector accounts for 10 per cent of GDP. The breadth and depth of the mismanagement are so huge that they warrant a whole book dedicated to them, not a mere mention and paragraph. An example follows below.

One case involves 'transfer pricing' in which, instead of importing products directly from the country of origin, the products pass through other countries, receiving mark-ups on the way. The mere existence of such a practice is a proxy indicator of corruption.

The Greek state was the victim of a fraud that supplied hospitals with materials whose transfer pricing reached 1,000 per cent. Through companies from Cyprus, Greek hospitals got the same materials at prices far higher than the initial ones. Another case concerns blood plasma: some €11.2 million was paid by Greek taxpayers for the construction of new buildings for an analysis facility. Construction began in 2000 and finished in 2002, but it never functioned fully. As a result, Greece must still send huge quantities of plasma abroad.[49]

The prime minister himself, George Papandreou, has admitted that stents for heart operations cost up to five times more in Greece than in Germany. He blamed kickbacks that affect procurement in hospitals.[50]

The Siemens Case

The Siemens case is perhaps the clearest and most shocking example of corruption at the heart of the Greek state. It is also an example of the complicity of major German companies in the creation of the Greek economic crisis.

The sums involved are colossal. Details emerged as a by-product of the terrorist attacks on the USA in September 2001. It was this atrocity that persuaded some of the more secretive banking jurisdictions to cooperate internationally in order to help security forces monitor money laundering by terrorist groups. In early 2003, auditors for a Liechtenstein bank noticed unusual money transfers involving an offshore firm called Martha Overseas Corporation, and learned that this was controlled by Prodromos Mavridis, an executive with Siemens in Greece. Millions of euros were being paid in to this Panama-based account from another offshore firm, Eagle Invest & Finance SA, based in the British Virgin Islands and controlled by Germany-based Siemens executive Reinhard Siekaczek. In March 2005 Swiss prosecutors opened their own investigation after Dresdner Bank submitted a report on money laundering, featuring successive suspicious payments. By 2007 Switzerland had frozen around €200 million in bank accounts that the authorities believed were linked to Siemens, according to a report in the

Wall Street Journal based on access to court documents and interviews with prosecutors.[51]

German heavyweight newspaper *Der Spiegel* commented: 'Investigators into the Siemens scandal have found that the company's Greek branch had an annual slush fund of some €15 million, to pay for "commissions" that helped the German technology giant secure contracts. To secure the €500 million OTE (Greek national telecoms) contract alone, the firm allegedly paid €35 million in *miza* in the late 1990s.'[52]

Corruption is an economic matter as well as a legal and a moral one, as it causes misdirection. The current inquiry by the Greek Parliament into the Siemens affair is considering whether the bribes led the Greek state to be overcharged by €57 million for telecoms equipment.[53] The Chinese telecoms company Huawei bid 50 per cent below Siemens for the OTE contracts, yet was unsuccessful. We can only wonder why.

The former head of Siemens in Greece, Michael Christoforakos, was arrested in Germany in June 2009 after going on the run, as one of seven former Siemens managers 'wanted' by Greek prosecutors in connection with a 1990s contract with OTE.

The US Securities and Exchange Commission imposed a record $1.6 billion fine on Siemens for making payments to officials in several countries to help win contracts. The SEC's director of enforcement Linda Thomsen told a press conference in December 2008: 'Employees obtained large amounts of cash from Siemens cash desks. Employees sometimes carried that cash in suitcases across international borders to pay bribes. Payment authorisations were recorded on Post-it notes that were later removed to avoid leaving any permanent record.' Whilst accepting the fine and that it would pay an independent monitor to oversee the company's behaviour for the next four years, Siemens did not technically admit that the payments were bribes.[54]

Christoforakos, who has joint German and Greek nationality, was set to be extradited to Greece, but this was blocked by the German Constitutional Court in September 2009. In March 2010 he received a ten-month suspended prison sentence from a court in Munich.[55]

Both political parties were involved in the Siemens scandal, and colluded with one another. They used slush funds for elections. This was a huge institutional affair, lasting years. This is an example of proven corruption, not merely alleged. There have been prosecutions, and a record fine. Just not in Greece. A parliamentary investigative committee is currently taking place. Let us see if this will be a turning point. Accusations that investigators have dragged their feet do not augur well.[56]

Ferrostaal and Daimler

Siemens is not the only German company accused of paying 'commissions' to help it secure major Greek contracts. In the case of Ferrostaal the issues of military spending and alleged corruption become intertwined. German prosecutors have begun investigating whether bribes were paid by German company Ferrostaal to Greek officials in connection with a contract to supply the Greek navy with two submarines. The continued high military spending at a time of austerity measures for ordinary employees, combined with apparent breaches of EU competition law as well as the more serious accusations of corrupt payments, prompted MEPs to call for the European Commission to clamp down generally on arms deals within the EU.[57]

The Athens Public Prosecutor has been assisting the German prosecutors over alleged corrupt payments by Ferrostaal, and has indicated that the payments involved could be as much as 5 per cent of the purchase price of €1.8 billion.[58]

The US Justice Department has formally accused German carmaker Daimler of paying bribes to officials in 22 countries. Greece is named on the list. *Kathimerini* reported in March 2010 on allegations that Daimler made corrupt payments to officials in Athens in connection with the purchase of 6,500 army jeeps. Investigations are ongoing.[59]

In summary, *Der Spiegel* noted: 'Greece's rampant corruption is one of the reasons why the country's economy is in such a mess. German companies have taken advantage of the system for years in order to secure lucrative deals.' It added: 'Not a single one of the 450 most important corruption cases in recent years [in Greece] has been concluded before a court of law.'[60]

The EOT: Greek Tourist Organisation

The EOT has been a never-ending source of waste, corruption and scandals. An Athens prosecutor started examining the findings of a probe by state public administration officials regarding the alleged mismanagement of more than €70 million in funding destined for tourism promotion campaigns in 2008 and 2009. Deputy Culture and Tourism Minister Giorgos Nikitiadis said that the case should be sent to Parliament if the prosecutor's probe ends up apportioning blame to politicians.

Critics claim that despite a substantial advertisement budget to promote Greece abroad, there was scant evidence of it being used in major overseas networks, and that the government has refused to publish a full breakdown of how the budget was spent.

This is a long-running saga. In one audit it emerged that 20,000 community holidays – a system in Greece in which the state pays for holidays, intended for people who cannot afford one – worth a total of €1.8 million were given to people who didn't fit the criteria. In 2008–09 some €2.5 million was spent on ties, hats, badges and key rings for the promotion of Greek tourism without any invoices, receipts or order forms. It was not made clear where or how such vast quantities of cheap items were stored, how they were used, or how they came to cost so much.[61]

Three employees were hired in 2009, but never showed up. The EOT has hired 36 law firms, 13 general managers and endless numbers of consultants. 'Consultants' and others hired for vaguely defined 'services' are another way of expropriating funds.[62]

PASOK and the Bank of Crete: The Koskotas Affair

The degree of lawlessness and sense of impunity among Greece's elite that continued even after the dictatorship is indicated in the extraordinary testimony of Giorgios Koskotas, former owner of the Bank of Crete. He was jailed, first in Massachusetts and then in Athens, and charged with embezzling more than $200 million from the Bank of Crete. He was released from prison on 16 March 2001 after serving 12 years of a 25-year sentence for embezzlement, forgery and obstruction of justice felonies.

In the six interviews he gave to *Time* journalist Robert Ajemian, Koskotas claimed that under Andreas Papandreou, PASOK leaders had ordered state-managed corporations to transfer large bank deposits out of major national banks into the Bank of Crete, run by Koskotas at the time. He then arranged for the government deposits to draw a much lower rate of interest. The excess interest was siphoned off and went straight to the politicians. In one year, he told *Time*, around 40 payments, in briefcases stuffed with 5,000 drachma notes, were transferred from the Bank of Crete and handed to a confidant of Papandreou. He claimed that pick-ups occurred weekly and over the year amounted to more than three billion drachmas. In addition, Koskotas also claimed that at the Bank of Crete, half a dozen other PASOK leaders twice a month received briefcases filled with money totalling 1.5 billion drachmas (around $10 million at the time).[63]

Papandreou senior was indicted by Parliament, and faced trial in 1991–92 by a special court arranged by Parliament for the case. He refused to cooperate with the trial, saying the charges were politically motivated. He was acquitted by a 7–6 vote. Andreas Papandreou died in 1996. Two junior ministers were found guilty: the former finance minister Dimitris Tsovolas was found guilty on two charges that related to the settlement of a hotel debt to the state; and former transport minister George Petsos was found guilty of granting an illegal building permit to Mr Koskotas. Tsovolas and Petsos received suspended jail sentences.[64]

800,000 Houses without Planning Permission

One of the symptoms of lawlessness, and of the attachment of the Greek people, is the extent of illegal constructions. This also has an impact on tax collection, not only on property, but also on the unregistered plumbers, electricians and builders working on these buildings (see tax section, later in this chapter).

In a case that reached the courts in August 2010, some 157 allegedly illegal properties were built in the Cycladic islands, with bribes of €15,000–€20,000 paid to officials, according to one property owner, not to inform on the construction.[65]

Other Scandals – A Miscellany

- **Ministry of Agriculture:** a minister, two deputy ministers, the secretary-general and a special secretary at one point in time had 64 phone lines between them! The Secretary of State for Rural Development was Michael Karchimakis. No one knows how much was spent on public relations. As for phones, during the three-year period 2006–08 the bill was approximately €20 million.[66]
- **Police uniforms:** they cost €4,000 each; 1,091 suits for €4 million. More expensive than Armani.[67]
- **ERT:** the national state broadcaster spent €1 million on designing new logos.[68]
- **Non-existent cotton fields:** in May 2010, a *Kathimerini* parliamentary report noted: 'More than 30 farmers were found to have obtained state subsidies for non-existent cotton fields in Skourta – an area known for having non-arable land.'
- **Macedonian Protein:** owned by three offshore companies and with a €250,000 turnover and zero employees, Macedonian Protein managed to get a development grant of €8.5 million under Development Law 3299/04. It was signed by the then minister of development.[69]

- **A 200 square metre hotel with 17 rooms (and a tidy government grant):** in Crete, the head of the municipalties Phanasis Karounsis discovered some monsters. One of the key scandals was the conversion of a 200 square metre building into a hotel 'with 17 rooms' in a central part of Heraklion, with a grant budget of €1.99 million.
- **Kopais Lake Agency:** established in the 1950s to oversee the draining of a lake and the construction of a new road, the agency completed its task in 1957. Head of the audit office Leandros Rakintzis said in 2010: 'Today Kopais has a full-time staff of 30 people. No one knows what they do. Not only that, but every year they advertise for new staff. It has a board, a president and the president of the board has a full-time driver.'
- **Organisation of the Cultural Capital of Europe – Thessaloniki 1997:** when Greece's second-largest city was chosen as the European cultural capital for 1997, the government established an agency to oversee the year's cultural activities. This was still in existence by mid-2010, and claimed still to be finishing work associated with the cultural year programme.
- **Road tolls:** an employee of the Ministry of Public Works apparently spent his working days picking up discarded receipts from toll road booths. He would then give the receipts to his superiors, who paid him cash equal to the amounts shown on them, sometimes as much as €800 ($1100) a day. His bosses then used the receipts to generate bogus travel diaries and claim generous daily travel allowances.[70]
- **Olympic Airways:** labour unions blocked government attempts to sell the debt-ridden Olympic Airways for decades. Family members of employees could fly around the world for free. Olympic was sold in 2008, 'but only after the state lavishly compensated or rehired about 4,600 employees', Reuters reported. Many ex-employees blocked Athens' thoroughfares because they had not received all their severance money.[71]
- **Disability benefits:** in Thessaly, Crete and mainland Greece disability pension rates exceed 18 per cent of total pensions, and there are individual villages with rates of more than 35 per cent. Several cases of clear fraud have been identified, including a blind individual playing backgammon, whilst others have been seen climbing scaffolding or working as taxi drivers or delivery boys.[72]

I would like to reiterate – for those who have not lived or worked in Greece – that the above is quite a small selection of the reports or accusations of bribes, waste, cronyism and so on that are a daily part of Greek public life. The absurd becomes normal; the kleptocracy no more than a pastime.

Tax: A Vicious Circle

Tax avoidance, like protesting, is a national pastime in Greece. Sometimes they even combine. In March 2010 taxi drivers and owners of petrol stations held a 24-hour strike to protest against proposals to require them to give VAT receipts to customers. It is an inaccurate summary to say that tax collection is weak in Greece. In many cases, for some unfortunate individuals, the regime of tax collection is overly zealous. It is more the case that the system is highly erratic and unfair, encouraging widespread evasion. As discussed earlier, tax evasion is a deeply ingrained cultural habit in Greece, dating back to the Ottoman era. One survey indicated that a huge 96 per cent of Greeks would be prepared to bribe an IRS official to reduce their tax debt.[73]

Tax evasion is on such a scale that there are in effect two parallel economies: the formal and the informal one. In mid-2010 a Greek trader based in New York wrote a missive that was widely circulated in trading circles via email. It chronicled the bribes, corruption and the hold on the economy of just 20 oligarchical families, and the rise to wealth of the PASOK oligarchy since the 1981 election win. He also drew attention to the massive assets, untaxed and off balance sheet, held by Greek individuals and companies:

> We Greeks are some of the world's richest people. On the official statistics alone, we are comfortably in the world's top 40 for per capita GDP. But that's peanuts. Lest we forget, that's our declared income. Don't quote me on this apocryphal statistic, but I'm reliably informed that exactly six Greeks declared more than a million euro in income last time anybody counted. And exactly 85 declared more than half a million.

The tax collection agency has reported that doctors, lawyers and businessmen have sent to Swiss accounts up to €15 million each, having only declared revenues of €40,000–80,000.[74]

The *Financial Times* gave a figure of fewer than 5,000 who declare annual incomes of more than €100,000. The same report added that more than 60,000 Greek households have investments in cash and securities of more than €1 million according to estimates by a private Greek bank. There was also a rush of activity in early 2010 among middle-income earners to get their tax affairs in order, in preparation for the expected clampdown.[75]

In April 2010, Finance Minister George Papaconstantinou claimed a higher number were paying tax, but acknowledged that it was far below the number of taxpayers there should be. In an interview with the British newspaper the *Observer*, he said: 'If you look at the actual numbers, you will see that the number of people declaring over €100,000 a year is roughly 15,000. I don't think that there is anyone in this country who believes there are only 15,000 Greeks earning more than €100,000 a year.'[76]

Ilias Plaskovitis, general secretary of the Greek Finance Ministry, told the *New York Times* in 2010: 'There are many people with a house, with a cottage in the country, with two cars and maybe a small boat who claim they are earning €12,000 a year. You cannot heat this house or buy the gas for the car with that kind of income.' The Greek government has set a goal for itself of collecting at least $1.6 billion more than last year. Mr Plaskovitis said that EU officials did not let him use that figure in the deficit reduction projections. 'They said, "Yes, yes, we have heard that before, but it never happens."'[77]

There have been reports of significant transfers of wealth by high-income people out of Greece. This may be more to do with fears around the banking system and a potential default or expulsion from the euro than any desire to avoid taxes. Cash has been moved to bank accounts in Switzerland and Cyprus, while real estate in London has also been popular. In April 2010 Greek buyers accounted for about 6 per cent of all property purchases above £2 million (c. €2.3 million) in the UK capital, according to estate agent Knight Frank.

> 'In the last four to six weeks a lot of money has been moved abroad; I've heard extraordinary figures', financial analyst Kostas Panagopoulos said in a newspaper interview in February 2010. 'People are moving funds either because they don't trust our banking system, want to avoid what they fear will be taxes on deposits or are simply anxious about the future of our economy.'[78]

While tax evasion is common, those who do try to comply sometimes face a torrid time. One successful Greece-based entrepreneur told me in an interview that he wants to stay in the country and pay taxes, but that if he declares all his profits, he will be taxed more than he earns.

Because he is known to the revenue officers, he attracts a lot of attention. In an interview for this book, he says:

> What is really a maze is the tax system. This is a real nightmare. You always have to keep money in a drawer in the office, in case someone from the tax office comes by for a coffee. Because of all the contradicting articles in taxation law, it's impossible to be 100% clean. Do you know that our tax system gets a double digit number of revisions every year? Huge books, hundreds of pages long each one, containing changes or updates are published every single month and the accountants have to keep themselves up to date
>
> So, for $100 profit this year you would have to pay $100 tax, waiting to offset a part of this money next year. That's why we have to lie. We have to distribute our revenues and expenses in such a way that we can survive the tax system. But there is no legal way to do that. You can't tell a client 'can you please pay me next year'.

Doctors

In the land that gave the world the Hippocratic Oath, the principle of 'first do no harm' does not, it seems, extend to safeguarding the public purse. Tax evasion has become endemic in the medical profession.

In May 2010 the finance ministry 'named and shamed' 57 doctors accused of failing to pay tax. It also announced fines of several hundred thousand euros on 11 of them, and warned that it would confiscate the contents of bank accounts belonging to those who owed money to the state.

In August 2010 the head of a tax agency said that a doctor in the DePuy scandal had sent €4 million to Switzerland – a huge multiple of his declared wage.[79] As part of the inquiries into the DePuy scandal, Greek tax authorities opened the accounts of 12 orthopedic doctors and found that during 2001–08 they had bank deposits of €31 million.[80]

In the Greek equivalent of Harley Street there are 151 doctors. A total of 34 of them reported income of *less* than €10,000; 30 doctors declared income of between €10,000–€20,000; some 32 reported the range €20,000–€30,000; a further 19 claimed in the range €30,000–€50,000; 25 doctors gave €50,000–€100,000 and only 11 acknowledged an income of €100,000–€550,000. One doctor prescribed €25,000 worth of drugs per month, receiving 'volume fees'. Other doctors would set up 'joint ventures' with particular pharmacies and lead all their prescriptions to that particular pharmacy.[81]

The Vicious Circle

Tax collection in Greece is a vicious circle. The authorities hound the honest few, and let thousands of high income individuals escape with impunity. The Greek IRS has to start facilitating compliance as well as clamping down on non-compliance.

From mid-2010 onwards, the government has announced moves against the more flagrant non-payment of taxes by higher earners. As well as naming and shaming high-income doctors, proceedings were begun against singer Tolis Voskopoulos, a huge star in Greece, over alleged non-payment of more than €5 million. This caused political problems for the government, as his wife is Angela Gerekou, tourism minister in the PASOK government. She denied knowledge of her husband's tax affairs, but felt compelled to resign.

The government desperately needs some convictions, or payment of arrears, of high-income people. This would encourage compliance, increase revenues, lessen the pressure on the few who do pay and the overly zealous tax officers who pursue them. There needs to be a simpler, fairer system, based on moderate rates, where the expectation is that you pay, and where those who do comply are treated fairly and with dignity. This, however, is a cultural change, not just a technical one. The elite have to drop their culture of impunity.

The Oligarchs and Conglomerates

In a clientelist state, featuring the seven heads of the hydra, an oligarchy is more likely to flourish than specialist clusters of advanced industries. The opaque world of the oligarch typically features a conglomerate, in which a company may have its own bank, newspaper, TV station and industrial firms. In this system, economic power is concentrated in just a few hands; there is not the backbone of medium-sized industries supported by regional banks that you see in Germany or France.

Local Greek oligarchies secured lucrative government contacts from public works, and many based their whole existence on this. Many of these contacts were at overpriced cost levels since there was competition on 'connections' rather than on efficiency, cost or other needed metrics. These businesses focused on building special relationships with the governments, often in conjunction with foreign multinationals rather than on product innovation, for instance. Similarly, controlling media outlets became a prerequisite for effectively running a business, rather than a profit-seeking exercise.

Greece's most famous tycoon of modern times was Aristotle Onassis, who once reportedly quipped: 'Never trust a person who does not accept a bribe.'

The Legacy

The seven-headed monster of the Greek public sector is not just a colourful side show to the hard economic story of the euro and the sovereign debt crisis. It is responsible in its own right for a large part of the crisis: the waste induced by cronyism, corruption and sheer incompetence runs into billions of euros.

This is cultural. Too many Greek politicians consider themselves to be above the law and treat taxpayers' money as if it were their own. This infects wider attitudes towards respect for the law and for public funds. The politicians' sense of outrage should anyone proceed with inquiries, even in a context of *prima facie* evidence of bribery or maladministration on an institutional scale, is palpable. The legacy is multidimensional: leaders have no authority when calling for sacrifice by ordinary citizens, or requiring that taxes be paid, or that local hospitals manage their budgets responsibly, or that doctors treat on the basis of illness rather than *fakelaki*. Their fiscal irresponsibility creates injustice and colossal political risk in multiple ways.

In a radio interview in April 2010, for example, the head of the dockers' union declared: 'Today, the people are being asked to pay yet again for the money that the business people have taken. We don't owe anyone anything. We're not responsible for the debt, and yet we're being asked to pay it back.'

What he failed to volunteer is that the dockers themselves have been beneficiaries of closed shops and other features of the hydra.[82] The more you disagree with his Marxist politics, the angrier you should be that both PASOK and New Democracy governments should have handed him so much ammunition.

Matters such as probity, auditing, efficiency of tax collection, national culture and the nature of public spending were subjects studiously ignored by European Union leaders in assessment of Greece's suitability for entry into the euro. The uselessness of relying purely on aggregate data to make economic judgements is evident here. Not all deficits are the same. Not all growth is the same. Not all borrowing is the same. If some of the colossal amounts of hard currency borrowed by the Greek state in the early 2000s had been spent on actual investment – like, for example, the 15 Institutes of Technology set up in India by the Nehru administration after independence that helped create the country's technology hubs – then there would at least be a platform for growth to pay off the debts.

But after this industrial-scale kleptocracy and waste, what do we have? A modern airport, a metro system, some highways, sports stadiums (some unused), expensive investigations into corruption and fraud that may or may not lead to prosecutions, and enough military hardware to invade a medium-sized country – but to what purpose is a national defence if we have lost control of the national economy?

The Looting of Greece: A Lawless State

There is no place for understatement in this dimension of the Greek saga. The scandals and corruption are not mere footnotes to the tragedy of Greece and the euro, they were part of a lawless, kleptocratic culture that largely wasted the early benefits of EU membership, looted the wealth of the nation for the benefit of an undeserving cadre, and imperilled the single currency.

Greeks of all backgrounds have been responsible: both the upper class with their underreporting of income and the masses with their numerous cushy jobs and overgenerous pensions. There was a tacit collusion amongst all. Greece was a low-tax, low-public service economy, papered over by EU cohesion funds, bond market borrowings and a brain drain of those Greeks who would support meritocracy. This was always an unsustainable Ponzi system. The only question was: what took it so long to blow up?

The EU was acquiescent in this. Successive Greek governments and the planners of the euro, while ignoring such dimensions as national culture, corruption and waste, appeared for ten years to have pulled off an unlikely coup: catapulting a developing nation into the premier division through monetary union, and creating a future global currency. It was all about to go horribly wrong.

Chapter 6

GETTING UNLUCKY – IT ALL BEGINS TO UNRAVEL

It's like déjà-vu, all over again.

—Yogi Berra

As the global recession began in 2008, Greece had high levels of public debt, a large trade deficit, an overextended public sector, militant trade unions, a 'Peronist' entitlement culture, widespread corruption, uneven payment of taxes, complacent EU stewardship, an overvalued currency, consumers expecting rising living standards and euro membership based on inaccurate data.

What Could Possibly Go Wrong?

In 1998, Argentina had faced a similar situation. It had appeared to weather the financial crises of the mid-1990s – the Tequila and Southeast Asia crises and the Russian default – reasonably well; just as Greece seemed initially to be unscathed by the subprime crisis a decade later. But hard-currency-denominated debt was increasing for the South American country in the late 1990s, and competitiveness continued to be harmed by the dollar peg. Moreover, internal reform faltered, and the internal dynamics of clientelism and a rigid labour market hampered recovery. In addition there was a significant amount of off-balance-sheet public sector deficit, incurred by the provinces.

In 1998 and 2008 respectively, the countries were locked into currency regimes which formally ruled out the normal release valve, devaluation. Greece was locked more significantly. A typical devaluation may result in a climb-down by the finance ministry, a couple of ministerial resignations and a risk of inflation. Departure from the eurozone, on the other hand, would mean a constitutional and political crisis for the entire

27-member European Union. International treaties would be broken, as well as promises to the electorate. For the EU's leaders, preserving the euro was an overriding objective; the very thought of a default and the departure of a member state was the absolute last resort – indeed, in the minds of many not even a last resort, but something unthinkable. The Maastricht Treaty which established the euro had no provision for expulsion of a member. The background to this ideological devotion to the single currency as a central part of the European project, despite the incomplete infrastructure to support it, is long and complicated.

Misleading Data: The Turkey Graph

Philosophers are familiar with the tale of the turkey and Thanksgiving Day as a way of illustrating the *problem of induction*, the unpredictability of events and the uselessness of using extrapolations to make forecasts. If you record the health and weight gain of a turkey in the USA on a graph through October and most of November, there is a continuous

Figure 6.1 Turkey Graph

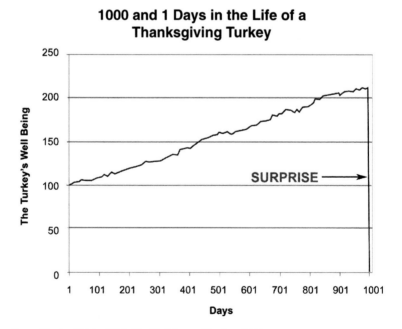

Source: Nassim Nicholas Taleb, The Black Swan, Allen Lane 2007.

improvement. The turkey could reasonably conclude that the human being is benign, and that daily feedings will continue indefinitely. Bertrand Russell discussed this problem, and it was revived by Nassim Nicholas Taleb, in *The Black Swan*, who observed: 'The history of a process over a thousand days tells you nothing about what is to happen next.'[1]

In the early 1990s and early 2000s respectively, Argentina's and Greece's economic graphs resembled those of the turkey.

Data can give misleading impressions, at least where it fails to distinguish between debt-fuelled spending and sustainable economic development. Digging behind the economic growth figures showed that the nature of the growth was unsustainable in Argentina in the 1990s and Greece in the 2000s. Trends in investment, saving and the trade balance were worsening in an unsustainable fashion. It was financed to a dangerous degree by borrowing, and principally external borrowing. Ultimately, this operates like a giant Ponzi scheme: without changed patterns or fundamental reform, the 'growth' can only continue through more borrowing.

The trade balance in Greece, indeed in all the peripheral eurozone countries, deteriorated in the 2000s. This was contrary to the predictions of the euro's architects and had severely destabilising results, as I shall discuss further in the next chapter.

Exactly the same pattern had occurred in Argentina a decade earlier. In this case, the trade deficits were lower, but an overvalued exchange rate, reduced productive base, a largely unreformed internal economy, and increasing reliance on external borrowing to finance 'growth' had led to the same unstable dynamics.

Yet it was this form of Ponzi-style 'growth' that prompted eulogies by the European Commission's economics commissioner Joaquin Almunia, who towards the end of the decade described the Greek economy as 'better than the EU average'. I will further discuss the spectacularly wrong assessments of EU leaders and their disastrous impact in the next chapter.

More sober institutions also understated the risks building up in the Greek economy. In 2007, a report by the Organisation for Economic Co-operation and Development stated: 'Contrary to expectations of a post-Olympics slump, the economy has continued to grow briskly in 2005 and 2006 during a period of substantial fiscal consolidation.' It noted that the public sector deficit had fallen from a peak of 7.75 per cent of GDP in 2004 to an estimated 2.5 per cent in 2006 – though to be fair this was before the sharp revision of government statistics, which did not occur until the end of 2009.[2]

In October 2008, a country report on Greece by the Economist Intelligence Unit, despite noting high wage settlements and a high trade deficit, struck a benign note: GDP growth decelerated from 4 per cent in 2007 to an estimated 2.6 per cent in 2008. The Unit expected GDP growth to slow to 1.4 per cent in 2009 before picking up to 2.1 per cent in 2010.[3]

Great Moderation

As well as *overconfidence bias*, there is a tendency in human nature to assume a certain moderation, especially within economics, and to downplay the possibility of extreme events – or 'black swans' – occurring suddenly within an apparently benign context. We are wired as a species to deal with problems on a human scale. The sums involved in globalised finance mean that errors or overshoots in policy can have repercussions beyond our obvious capacity to cope, but they sometimes create the illusion of moderation in the upward part of the turkey graph.

Economists have referred to the 'Great Moderation' of the late 1990s and early 2000s. The unfortunate phrase was the title of a talk by the current chairman of the US Federal Reserve Ben Bernanke in 2004, made when he was a Federal Reserve governor. He referred to the 'increased depth and sophistication' of financial markets, deregulation, a shift away from manufacturing toward services, and increased openness to trade and international capital flows. To be fair, he acknowledged the role of 'good luck', and warned that there was no guarantee that moderate conditions would continue indefinitely.[4]

He made the assumption, while acknowledging it as 'temporary', that 'monetary policymakers have an accurate understanding of the economy and that they choose policies to promote the best economic performance possible', and that economic shocks were becoming more minor and less frequent. With hindsight, we now know that policymakers did not grasp the scale of the risks accumulating in the securitisation of mortgage assets, in the off-balance-sheet nature of many government debts (particularly in Europe) and in the misleading statistics that lay behind the application of at least one EU member state, Greece, to join the euro. These, and other hidden factors, increased the risk of a 'black swan' while making the conditions more comfortable in the short term. They lay below the surface of the comforting phrase 'the depth and sophistication of financial markets'. The Great Moderation belongs in the same category of economists' phrases as 'This Time It's Different' and 'New Paradigm'. Come to think of it, the term 'sophistication' ought to be a warning sign in the context of investment banking.

The turkey was at its most relaxed and well fed just before the day of the chop.

In both Argentina and Greece, when indicators did head south, they did so rapidly. For Greece the situation was, if anything, worse than Argentina's had been. By the end of 2001 Argentina's public debt to GDP ratio was 62 per cent, having risen from 41 per cent in 1998. At the end of 2009 Greece's was 114 per cent. Argentina's public deficit reached 6.4 per cent GDP in 2001, while Greece's was 12.7 per cent of GDP in 2009. The magnitude of the Greek economic collapse did not become publicly acknowledged until late 2009, when the new PASOK government announced that previous statistics had seriously understated public borrowing requirements. At a stroke, it was doubled to nearly 13 per cent, a key moment in the escalation of the eurozone sovereign debt crisis – though the underlying figures, especially on the trade balance, public sector inefficiency and the external profile of the debt, had been worsening for years. A subsequent calculation by Bank of America Merrill Lynch indicated a breakdown as follows: a cyclical component of around 2.5 per cent of GDP, a core deficit of 6 per cent, and interest expenses at 4.5 per cent of GDP.[5]

Both countries had seen their competitiveness erode by 20 per cent over the previous decade as the exchange rate was inflated. In 2009 Greece had a current account deficit equal to 11.2 per cent of GDP, while Argentina's 2002 current account deficit was only 1.7 per cent of GDP.[6]

The weaknesses and imbalances within the economies – clientelism, a boom that was based on consumption and debt, an uncompetitive exchange rate for industry – meant that vicious spirals set in quickly, and were reinforced by the inability to devalue.

Decades in the Making

The situation in Greece should not have taken commentators by surprise. The planners of the single currency did not consider the supply-side, nor did they dig beneath the apparently favourable public sector borrowing requirements, nor become suspicious over its apparently rapid improvement in 2001, despite the warnings. Three academics who called for a positive response to the crisis that emerged in 2010, arguing that default was not inevitable, also pointed to the systemic,

long-term nature of the problem. Costas Meghir, Dimitri Vayanos and
Nikos Vettas jointly authored a paper that commented as follows:

> Even if Greece's debt were to magically disappear overnight...
> reforms would be needed; or else Greece would find itself with a
> new debt problem again soon.
> When was the public debt accumulated? Debt increased sharply
> during the 1980s, and further increased, at a lower pace, during the
> 1990s and 2000s.
> How did the public debt affect the economy? Debt triggered a
> decrease in productive investment and an increase in consumption.
> Why is Greece heavily indebted to foreigners? Because Greek
> citizens were consuming beyond their means with money that their
> government was borrowing from foreigners.[7]

This neatly summarises the core features of the crisis that was developing
and that the European Union leaders had so complacently overlooked.

Greece could only continue importing more than it was exporting
because it was borrowing from foreigners. During the 1990s, it was
borrowing an average of 4.1 per cent a year. This increased to 10.2 per
cent during the 2000s. External debt increased from 42.7 per cent of
GDP in 2000 to 82.5 per cent in 2009. Transfers from the European
Union were declining as poorer Eastern European countries joined,
and the interest payments were increasing on the rising debt levels.
Domestic savings became insufficient to purchase the bonds issued by
the government, hence the external element of the debt ballooned:
from just over 10 per cent in the early 1990s to around 80 per cent by
2009. Total external debt increased from 42.7 per cent of GDP in 2000
to 82.5 per cent in 2009.[8]

Table 6.2, below, shows the public debt at the end of each decade,
expressed as a percentage of GDP, while Table 6.3 shows the deterioration
of investment and the increase in consumption.

Table 6.1 Greek Government Deficit

Decade	1960–69	1970–79	1980–89	1990–99	2000–09
Government deficit (% of GDP)	0.6	1.2	8.1	8.4	5.9

Source: OECD.

Table 6.2 Greek Government Debt

Year	1980	1990	2000	2009
Government debt (% of GDP)	26	71	101.5	115.1

Source: OECD.

Table 6.3 Consumption and Investment

Decade	1970–79	1980–89	1990–99	2000–09
(% of GDP)				
Consumption	77.2	85.1	90.1	88.8
Investment	30.7	23	20.6	22.6

Source: OECD.

As can been seen, as the deficits ballooned in the 1980s and continued on the same trajectory, the debt explosion that began then essentially piled up for another two decades thereafter.

As noted in the previous chapter, the Greek state had little to show for all this spending, by contrast with examples such as Brazil or India, which had invested more substantially in the future technological capacity of the nation. Had the borrowing financed research and development, or other forms of investment in human capital, there could have been an improved productive base for the economy to support more sustainable forms of growth that could, over time, reduce the public and private sector deficits. One report notes:

> The bulk was spent instead to increase the wage bill in the public sector, i.e., more public servants and higher salaries, and to increase the pension bill, i.e., more pensioners and higher pensions.[9]

Worse, continued high levels of tax evasion and corruption, and inflexible labour markets further suppressed opportunities for high-growth, high added-value businesses. Companies that evade taxes tend to be smaller and low-tech. To make up the shortfall governments increase taxation on larger and more high-tech companies, hampering their profitability. Corruption and its associated bureaucratic hurdles also create extra costs for businesses, as do closed shops.[10] The seven heads of the Greek public sector 'hydra' devoured what potential there might have been for a sustainable way out of the accruing debt problems.

> The recipients of government money increased their consumption in response to their higher incomes... Investment decreased because fewer private savings were available to finance it. Indeed, the government was borrowing by selling bonds to Greek citizens, who were in effect dividing their savings between bonds issued by the government and bonds issued by private firms...since most of the money that the government was raising...was not spent on public infrastructures, the aggregate productive investment by the public and the private sector decreased.[11]

An Inevitable Default?

Argentina had suffered the same sudden slide once confidence began to fall away. Although some observers had warned from 1996 onwards that Argentine government debt was starting to become unsustainable, most took a relaxed view.

Even as late as September 2000, just a year before the default, JP Morgan published a report headed: 'Argentina's debt dynamics: Much ado about not so much'. Reassuring noises also emanated from ABN AMRO. Some of the positive comments came from sell-side firms, which had a conflict of interest as they earn fees from underwriting government bonds. Walter Molano, head of research at BCP Securities, stated in early 1999: 'A full-blown economic crisis may still be a year away, but it seems like the die has been cast.' In December 2000, he explicitly linked the sell-side institutions' conflicts of interest with their muted reports of the pressures that were building:

> Why was the Street so positive on Argentina a year ago, when the Menem government was the picture of complacency? Why did the Street forgive all of Argentina's excessive borrowing between 1997 and 1999? Why did the Street ignore Argentina's lack of fiscal discipline during the past four years? It probably has nothing to do with the fact that Argentina was one of the biggest bond issuers in the world during that same period.[12]

The early reforms of Menem were well handled but not followed through, and highlight some of the problems of convertibility or dollarisation. The

Convertibility Plan coincided with liberalisation of current and capital accounts, allowing capital to enter the country. There was also reform of the labour market, reduction in tariffs, coinciding with the establishment of the Mercosur trading bloc in southern South America.

The Convertibility Plan, though effective in squeezing inflation out of the system, had some negative impacts, especially on the competitiveness of Argentinian companies. Market-based reforms just may have been enough to see the country through in the long term. The Menem administration and the IMF, having downplayed the negative effects of convertibility were now about to squander its gains. All along, however, the narrative fallacy of unmitigated economic progress was continuing in official pronouncements. This pattern is entirely in keeping with long-established research on currency pegs, which note a short-term stabilisation effect, but a risk of longer-term problems, especially where complacency creeps in.

Menem was constitutionally barred from standing for a second term. Instead of consolidating and deepening economic reforms to bolster the real economy, which in any case had been damaged by an overinflated exchange rate, his administration devoted its energies to seeking a constitutional change and reelection.

Unfortunately the IMF still clung to its narrative of the 'poster boy', even more so as the Tequila Crisis in 1995, the Southeast Asia crisis two years later and the Russian default left it with less and less good news to be able to relate. Moreover, superficially at least, Argentina coped with these economic shocks remarkably well.

Buenos Aires and the IMF (Continued)

In chapter 2, quotes from the 2003 IMF post-mortem on Argentina concentrating on aspects of the fiscal position highlighted the almost eerie similarities with the situation in Greece a decade later. The report also covered structural and trading dimensions. For example, it noted the relatively low proportion, just 10 per cent, of the Argentine economy that exports comprised. A comparison with the export growth in neighbouring Chile, helped by a competitive exchange rate (their comment, not mine) is telling.

Similarities with Greece extend to the labour market. For example, in paragraph 26 the IMF note:

> Like any fixed exchange rate system, the currency board required flexible domestic prices and wages to mitigate the impact of

economic shocks on output and employment. Historically, labour regulation in Argentina has been highly protective of individual workers, imposing high barriers to dismissal and guaranteeing generous fringe benefits. In addition, collective bargaining at the industry level greatly reduced wage flexibility.

The IMF could copy and paste this into a report on Greece. We resume in paragraph 74, with my observations in italics:

Argentina's crisis involved vulnerabilities that were already present...during the boom years [*exactly like Greece*] ...key elements were public debt dynamics, constraint on monetary policy imposed by the currency board and weaknesses on the structural side. There was little sense of urgency [*similar to the sense of protection Greece felt once in the euro*].

Paragraph 76:

The currency board [*euro*] turned from being a source of policy credibility to a handicap to adjustment. On the one hand, the currency board was relatively successful in containing the adverse effects of financial market contagion from the Russian default [*in the same way, Greece was insulated in 2008 and 2009*]... In addition... Argentina lost competitiveness under the currency board following the Brazilian devaluation [*Turkey devalued 30 per cent post-credit crisis*]. Finally, by lending credibility to the exchange rate peg, the currency board arrangement allowed Argentina's public sector to continue borrowing excessively [*Yes! Quite!*].

Paragraph 79 reads:

Argentina's story underscores many of the lessons that we have learned from previous crises.

Add Greece to your list, please.
    Paragraph 84 informs us:

Hard pegs are not as hard as often supposed: in extremis a government can unwind a currency board, albeit at considerable cost to the country.

This is a classic case of the *problem of induction* – failing to consider black swan events.

And then later:

> To the extent that a hard peg [*like Euro membership*] does secure credibility, this can be a mixed blessing: the high credibility of Argentina's currency board through 2000 helped enable the country to borrow from the capital markets at spreads that did not fully reflect the risks. This temporarily insulated the country from adverse market reactions to unsustainable policies, and thus ultimately allowed a much bigger disaster to materialise.[13]

We witness here the problem of benchmarking and dancing with your peers; the problems of induction, overlending, procyclical biases, the flawed logic of investors that in the search for yield believed that once in the euro the credit risk of countries is equal. All this occurred with Argentina and subsequently in Greece, almost as a carbon copy.

Athens and the IMF: Complacency Returns

Had the IMF learned its lessons? To an extent, perhaps, but there was a serious understatement of risks in Greece a few years later. In 2009, a full six years after its *mea culpa* on Argentina, the Fund published a report following 'stress tests' in Greece.[14] Even as the severely unbalanced economy reached full-scale Ponzification there was a reference to the 'resilience' of growth, as though the imbalances that the report itself noted were mere details that could iron themselves out. Argentina should have sounded the alert over how misleading a headline growth statistic can be.

On the banking system, it adds:

> Stress tests (conducted jointly by Bank of Greece and IMF staff) suggest that the banking system has enough buffers to weather the expected downturn.

There are hints of *illusion of knowledge* here.

Regarding market risk, the report notes:

> Although trading books are relatively small, high volatility on equity, bond, and foreign exchange markets could generate losses.

Understatement of the year here, I think.

IMF officials used in their 'stress test' an increase in sovereign spreads of +150 basis points – clearly overestimating their predictive abilities as spreads increased to over +1,000 basis points. This ex-post 'unprecedented' volatility in Greek government bonds wiped out the entire Greek banking equity by 6 May 2010. I guess they were a tad overconfident.

They continue:

> The stress tests suggest that profits, capital cushions (including with the government's assistance), and stepped-up provisionings should provide enough resources to absorb foreseen losses. Assuming simultaneous shocks, some institutions may require up to a total of €2.9 billion in new capital (1.2% percent of GDP) – a relatively moderate amount. Banks appear to have enough funds, but need to prepare gradual exit strategies to reduce dependence on ECB facilities.

Well, well, we all know what transpired as of May 2010: the ECB had diluted its collateral requirements and it remained the only lifeline for Greek banks. This report also alluded to the mysterious safety net that the single currency was supposed automatically to confer upon eurozone members, irrespective of the seriousness of the economic fundamentals – something I shall address in the next chapter.

When Taxi Drivers Know the Yields

Ask a cab driver in Berlin or New York what the spreads are between his government's bonds and others, and you are likely to receive a blank look. Those in Buenos Aires and Athens are more likely to be aware. It's always a worrying sign when the yield on government debt appears on the front page and not just in the business section. In May 2010, this phenomenon occurred in Spain for the first time in Europe's sovereign debt crisis, as the yield on the Spanish government's short-term borrowing reached six times the rate of Germany's.[15]

When taxi drivers and retired aunts know what the difference in basis points is between the cost of the country's public borrowing compared with the USA or Germany, your economy has problems. The Spanish term *riesgo-país* (literal translation: 'country-risk') has featured in Argentine headlines frequently in the course of the past two decades.

For much of the 1990s, it was running at around +300 basis points above the US rate: this is elevated, but not ruinously so. Then, as the debt problem started to deteriorate beyond the government's control, it spiked to more than +1,000 in late 1998, not falling below +500 until default in 2001.

Public awareness of spreads is a little litmus test indicating a government's solvency. It's also a neat illustration of the interrelationship between the economic gods in their mansions and the ordinary citizen. It should always have been a warning sign that the phrase 'the real economy' was ever coined. It marks the difference between the charts, statistics and growth projections of policymakers and traders, and the everyday reality of people running businesses or going about their day jobs. In reality, there is no other kind. Finance and economics are behavioural yet real. Everything is interconnected. To many ordinary citizens, economics is a dull subject, though post-credit crisis it has become much more relevant in the discussions of all social groups.

Policymakers, IMF officials and ministers are often confined to a world of chauffeurs and five-star hotels. This encourages *groupthink*, a particular weakness when the shared narrative is already misconceived. It also cuts decision makers off from the economy – like shop owners, factory workers, exporters and others from the part of the economy dubbed 'real'. Taking time out to visit real businesses and talk to entrepreneurs about the challenges that face them might better inform policymakers as to the nature of the real economy and its prospects for growth – especially the sustainable kind of growth that is built on business development, rather than 'growth' that turns out to be a debt-fuelled consumer binge. On an excel spreadsheet in a five-star hotel, they look the same. Mistakes are often made, albeit unintentionally, when decisions are based on spreadsheets, that underestimate the complexity and interrelationships of the real economy.

Officials of the European Commission and the European Central Bank, who never have to face the voters, also live in a cloistered world. As humans, we understand the world through stories, and it tends to be the most-repeated, easily remembered stories rather than the most accurate that have the greatest impact. In a closed, powerful community, this can be dangerous. So the stories that 'the single currency will encourage economic convergence' and that 'a weakening euro is the result of unscrupulous attacks by speculators' become absorbed into the common way of thinking. The statements of the EU's leaders, as the eurozone crisis deepened in 2009–10, became so divorced from reality it was as if the two were never acquainted with one another, as I shall discuss further in the next chapter.

Typically, a taxi driver does not know why an economy hits crisis, and neither does the chairman of the central bank or the European Commissioner for Economic Affairs. But at least the taxi driver knows that he does not know.

In the 'real' productive economy, Greece's three principal export earners got lucky in the early 2000s. Towards the end of the decade, the luck ran out, and a cyclical downturn exacerbated the structural problems of Greece.

- In *tourism* the 'Al Qaeda' effect, deterring holidays in nearby Muslim countries, became diminished. However tourism remained Greece's largest industry in early 2010, accounting for around 15 per cent of the economy and almost one in five jobs, according to the World Travel and Tourism Council. Membership of the euro made Greece a relatively expensive destination for tourists, and the country had not used the boom years sufficiently to invest in luxury resorts and golf courses, as compared with rivals such as Portugal, Spain and the Middle East. The protectionist rules requiring Greek-only crews in non-EU vessels limited its benefit from the cruise industry
- In *shipping*, demand plummeted by over 90 per cent in the early part of the recession. The Baltic Dry Index fell from 11,793 on 20 May 2008 to 663 points by 5 December 2008. It has recovered somewhat since, but not to the heights of the Chinese export boom a few years earlier.
- *Agriculture* was affected by a reduction in subsidies from the European Union, following the entry of poorer Eastern European countries in the 2000s.

In Argentina, an undiversified economy had also 'gotten lucky' in a period coinciding with a currency peg. In three key areas of vulnerability, the data headed south towards the end of the decade:

- *Soya exports*: the world's leading producer of soybean oil, Argentina suffered after world soya prices spiked in 1996, reaching nearly US$ 8 per bushel but then falling to below US$ 5 per bushel (see Fig. 2.1 in chapter 2).
- *Wheat and corn*: Argentina is the world's fifth-largest exporter of wheat and the fourth largest of corn. Wheat and corn prices rose in the

mid-1990s, reaching around US$ 4 and US$ 3 per bushel respectively, but then fell to around the $2 mark.

• *Exchange rate*: the dollar was weak for much of the 1990s, helping exports, but strengthened towards the end of the decade. In 1999 Brazil, Argentina's largest trading partner, devalued the real by 30 per cent.

An underlying weakness in the Argentine economy was its overreliance on agriculture, which accounted for nearly 60 per cent of export earnings. The devaluation of the Brazilian real hit particularly hard, affecting Argentina's competitiveness both as a rival exporter and as a key market. Inward investors and Argentine companies preferred cheaper locations such as Paraguay. Inward investment to Brazil was to increase around threefold compared with Argentina since the 1990s.[16]

For Greece, the euro traded at high levels during much of the credit crisis, when it was seen as a safe haven as the USA grappled with the bank bail-outs and the collapse of Lehman Brothers in 2008. Turkey and Romania and other neighbouring countries gained a competitive edge, as their currencies devalued by over 25 per cent.

These downturns were of a cyclical nature and were not the main cause of the problems of the Greek and Argentine economies, which were plagued by structural problems. The more diverse and balanced the productive economy, the less vulnerable it is to cyclical factors. An overvalued exchange rate and stalled or (in the case of Greece) non-existent internal reforms serve to keep an economy structurally imbalanced.

Where Bail-Out is a Euphemism

Exactly as had occurred a decade earlier in Argentina, default and economic collapse became increasingly likely for Greece from the point at which the boom ended in 2008. There was no room for manoeuvre when trying to put countercyclical measures in place. The Greek economy was priced for perfection, and could not absorb a serious negative shock, owing to the extent of procyclical policies and heavy Greek indebtedness.

By end 2008 the euro was overvalued at exactly the wrong part of the business cycle. And exactly as had occurred in Argentina, policymakers delayed serious consideration of the impact of the deficit, and indeed added to it by piling more debt on to a weakened economy and calling it a 'bail-out' or rescue plan. The EU's leaders did manage one innovation compared with the failure of the Argentine government and the IMF in 2001: instead of confining the problems to one country, they made sure it was extended to others. Their comforting narrative fallacies that all would be well – fed by *overconfidence bias, consensus bias, illusion of control, confirmation bias* and *status quo bias* – combined to create a paralysing state of the *ostrich syndrome*: complete denial.

Debt has been called many things over the past couple of decades: growth, liquidity, a new paradigm, and so on. Look out for metaphors: a danger sign is when politicians and central bankers start pretending that borrowing large sums of money is 'a bail-out' or a 'defence'. Military metaphors are particularly favoured by politicians seeing their cherished currency arrangements and borrowing levels as being 'under attack'. In the Argentinian saga, the term '*blindaje*' was deployed at one point to describe a fresh loan. This means 'armour'. Since late 2009 there have been similar references by European politicians to the need to 'defend' the euro against 'speculative attacks'.

Political leaders in the EU and Greece alike appeared to sustain the belief that membership of the euro made Greece safer – when, in reality, its complacent economic management meant that location inside a hard currency area actually made it more vulnerable – just as Argentina's debt problem grew worse during the peg to the dollar.

The term 'bail-out', used repeatedly in the Argentine and Greek debt crises, has actually referred to interest-bearing loans, not subsidies or aid. In the Argentine saga, for example, the year 2001 witnessed various attempts by the IMF, and the US and Argentine governments, to counter the looming crisis. Way beyond the point at which the need for default or restructuring was obvious, the institutions insisted upon piling further debt upon the rapidly impoverishing country.

Similarly, in the case of Greece, the majority of IMF money received to date has gone to bail out foreign creditors – holders of the bulk of the Greek government debt, as described.

The Greek crisis has seen a degree of deception and self-deception similar to that in Argentina the decade before. It would be bad enough if the euphemism 'bail-out' were simply used for official press releases. Unfortunately, there are indications that it guides policy; that the decision makers believe that an interest-bearing loan, sufficient to add to the debt problems but insufficient to provide anything more than temporary liquidity relief, can work some alchemy by magically restoring confidence and economic growth. One of the most notorious examples of this was Argentina's *megacanje*, or 'megaswap', announced in April 2001. It was engineered by the Argentine finance minister Domingo Cavallo, architect of convertibility who had been brought back into government by President de la Rúa to deal with the crisis; and by David Mulford, head of the international business section of Credit Suisse First Boston. It involved bondholders agreeing to exchange old bonds for new ones. It reduced short-term payouts, but increased the amounts due on bonds maturing in the years 2006–30. For example, the 2018 bond required no interest payments until late 2006, five years after issue; but interest was payable thereafter at an annual rate of 12.25 per cent.

Few people were fooled. The swap was completed on 3 June 2001. Two days later, a report by the independent research firm CreditSights, entitled 'The Argentine Exchange: Robbing Pedro to Pay Pablo', written by Peter Petas, observed: 'The unambiguous winners from the exchange are the investment banks. The losers, ultimately, will be the Argentine people and whatever investors are unlucky enough to be holding Argentine debt when the music stops (and it will) and the country is forced into a coercive exchange or outright default.' Michael Mussa's team at the IMF calculated that the swap would save $12 billion in debt payments from 2001 to 2005, while adding $66 billion in payments from 2006 to 2030.

In Argentina a decade earlier, the failure of the *megacanje* was followed by another flawed attempt at a rescue. It was led by the US government. The Bush administration had been critical of the Treasury under the Clinton. In a classic case of the cognitive bias *not invented here*, Secretary of the Treasury Paul O'Neill contrived an intricate proposal whose main feature appeared to be that it would not have been proposed by a secretary of the treasury appointed by Bill Clinton. The deal involved an IMF loan of $8 billion, plus extra IMF assistance to help with debt restructuring. Interestingly, the free-marketeer Glenn Hubbard, head of the US Council of Economic Advisers – who generally protested against bail-outs and interventions – said that if help must be given, it should be large enough to be of real use. At the time, the amount Argentina owed its creditors was $95 billion.[17]

The 'Real' Economy Erupts

When the errors of policymakers become large, which is especially likely to happen when they hide in their bunker, bolstered by narrative fallacies fed by our familiar cognitive biases – *hubris, confirmation bias, consensus bias* and so on – the impact hits every part of the 'real' economy.

An intriguing dimension of the austerity programmes in the eurozone, begun in 2009–10, were the different reactions in different countries. While thousands of Greeks have taken to the streets in protest, both peacefully and violently, the people of Ireland have accepted similar cuts to living standards and public services in a comparatively muted fashion. 'While Athens burns, there is an equally fascinating tale on the other side of Europe which has got less attention: namely the fact that Ireland has not been convulsed by political and fiscal disarray,' wrote Gillian Tett in the *Financial Times* on 12 May 2010.

She attributed it, in part, to a stronger legal and political infrastructure, meaning, among other matters, that tax evasion by wealthy individuals is much lower than in Greece. Social cohesion seems stronger in Ireland. Though the country has had a bloody civil war, this was nearly a century ago. Moreover, it erupted over the terms of the independence agreement with the UK, not a Left-versus-Right ideological struggle as occurred in Greece and Argentina. Ireland was united in wanting independence from Britain, and in recent decades the European Union has bolstered this, making Ireland one of the EU's most loyal members to date. Of course, the caveat for economic forecasts applies equally to political ones. The fact that Irish people have been calm so far is no guarantee that they will continue to be so. Their surprising 'No' vote to the Lisbon Treaty in June 2008 was in defiance of the settled view of all the most popularly supported parties, Fine Gael, Fianna Fáil and Labour – those that typically form coalition governments. This indicates that the population does not necessarily follow the will of the architects of the European Union.

Nonetheless, the initially compliant reaction of the Irish people is in marked contrast to that of the Greeks. Probably the main explanation is that Ireland has not suffered a military dictatorship within living memory. Since independence in 1922, it has continually been a democracy, despite periods of high unemployment and poverty. The police and army are well behaved, and well regarded. By contrast, when riot police appear on the streets of Athens or Buenos Aires, nightmarish memories are evoked within the population. When a government insists upon austerity for ordinary working people in Greece or Argentina, there is a tendency to shout: 'But this cannot be! We're not a dictatorship any more!' This is not just in the subconscious. When the Argentine government defaulted in December 2001, having failed to secure further funding from the

IMF, people took to the streets. This included 'ordinary', middle-class people, not just professional demonstrators from the Trotskyist Left. Earlier that month, in a sign that matters were starting to spin out of control, the government imposed a $250 weekly limit on withdrawals from bank accounts, in a measure known as the *corralito*, prompting furious reactions from citizens unable to access their own savings.

People gathered in the Plaza de Mayo in a spontaneous protest on 20 December 2001. This is the symbolic place of protest of the mothers of the 'disappeared' – the thousands of civilians captured, tortured and murdered by the junta in the 1970s and 1980s. The 2001 demonstrators chanted: 'The Plaza belongs to the mothers, not to cowards'. They banged on pots and pans, also a repeat of a form of protest commonly used in Chile and Argentina during the dictatorships, which used to be accompanied by the cry: '*La olla esta vacia*' (the pan is empty). The humiliation for President de la Rúa , a social democrat, must have been complete. Captured on video and viewable on YouTube, one ordinary-looking young woman, seemingly not an extremist or regular protester, shouts at police on horseback using whips on protestors: 'We're not living in an era of dictatorship any more! You are idiots. Armed baboons!'[18]

Businessman Gerardo Saporosi recalls those momentous events:

At the beginning of 2002, after fleeing in a helicopter, De la Rúa resigned. That which followed was like a surrealist work of art. In three days there were five presidents. The last one called elections and Kirchner assumed power after receiving only 22 per cent of the votes. The country was paralyzed for a year, and throughout the country it was necessary to organise soup kitchens, as few people had a steady income. The powerful middle class of Argentina, which had distinguished itself from the rest of the continent by constituting some 50 per cent of the population, was reduced to around 30 per cent. That is to say, the country suffered a vertiginous process of 'Latin Americanisation' in the course of a single year.

With no capacity to pay – Argentina produced the biggest default in history in the course of a year – nor tax revenues as a result of low economic activity, new taxes with distortive effects were invented (such as the incredible tax on a cheque), and provinces began issuing their own currencies. During 2002 there were around 20 different currencies circulating in Argentina.

Greece has a similar culture of street protest to Argentina's. Even before the austerity measures that high levels of borrowing and the euro rendered inevitable, tension was high. The forces of the hydra, Greece's monstrous public sector, fuelled by the more understandable sense of injustice at tax evasion and impunity for wealthy and privileged people, were ready to be unleashed.

In an incident unrelated to the economic situation, in December 2008 a 15-year-old boy, Alexandros Grigoropoulos, was killed by the police. This prompted two weeks of riots and fights between young Greek people and police forces. On the first anniversary of this tragic event, demonstrators hurled slabs of marble and petrol bombs at police officers.

In the first few months of 2010, as bond spreads widened and austerity measures were announced, demonstrations continued, and became more explicitly about the economy and against the political elite. Yet the substance of many of the complaints were in contrast with the ferocity of the protests. There has been a refusal by trade unionists or protestors to accept that they too have been part of the problem of an unreformed economy.

On 11 March, further protests, organised by trade unions, were punctuated by violence. Youths wearing hoods and ski masks attacked groups of police on motorbikes patrolling streets near Omonia Square. Public sector workers issued defiant sentiments against the wage cuts. 'First we had a four per cent wage cut, now it's seven per cent – and we're going to lose a big chunk of the Easter bonus, too', a primary teacher told the *Financial Times*.

Yet there had been wage rises for decades for public sector workers, up to and including the previous year, as chronicled in earlier chapters. The public sector wage bill was estimated to have risen by nearly 9 per cent as recently as 2008 (see chapter 5). The reduction in 2010 was the first cut, after decades of rises, and was much more modest than the cuts in Ireland, which were absorbed largely without complaint. The Greek welfare state, the hydra, had taken over the psyche, just as all manner of falsely reassuring narrative fallacies were taking over the leaders of the European Union.

With both Argentina and Greece, the dangerous economic dynamics laid below the surface. It was not just the degree of debt; it was the nature of the debt. It was not just the extent of the spending; it was the extent of the waste. 'Dollarisation' – which was effectively the policy in Greece as well as Argentina – as much as the EU's leaders would hate to admit it, tends to encourage complacency rather than reform, especially in a clientelist political culture. Many Latin American governments have lacked strong independent central banks or checks and balances to hold policymakers to account. The same applies to Greece. Worse, by stabilising economic indicators in the short term only, and creating opportunities to borrow on the international markets, currency pegs can be fatally attractive to politicians with an eye very much on the short-term calculation of the next election. A four-year election cycle (which is short when it comes to long-term decisions regarding pensions, currency pegs etc.) clearly exacerbates this.

Walter Molano noted that rent-seeking groups 'do not willingly give up their privileged positions because of a new exchange rate regime... economists who argue in favor of dollarisation often base their prospects for change on hope'.[19]

In making a comparison with Argentina, I am not trying to claim that the countries' respective economies are the same. There are marked differences, for example in the role of the agricultural sector. There are limits to the lessons that can be learned from comparison with another context. The point is to draw attention to the lack of any apparent learning from recent experience or research on the part of the EU when it made its decision to admit Greece into the single currency. The experience of Argentina, other currency pegs and the EU's own Exchange Rate Mechanism – and the studies into dollarisation between them – should have alerted European policymakers to the risks they were taking on.

Chapter 7

THE EURO IN PRACTICE

To put it bluntly, I seem to have a whole superstructure with no foundation. But I'm working in the foundation.

—Marilyn Monroe

After Greece's entry into the euro it was not so financially attractive to northern European tourists as a holiday destination. Greece had become a hard currency area, with hard currency prices. Egypt and Turkey became more cost-effective for northern Europeans going on holiday, while for Greek shoppers Macedonia (FYROM) and Bulgaria emerged as cheaper alternatives. Towns such as Gevgalija in FYROM, just over the border, became thriving retail locations; petrol, household goods and vegetables were around half the price of Greece. Residents of northern Greek towns and cities such as Kilkis, Giannitsa or Thessaloniki would make monthly or even weekly shopping runs over the border. In June 2010, after the recession and austerity measures had begun in Greece, the *Kathimerini* newspaper was recording a weekly Saturday queue of Greek cars heading for the Bulgarian border for shopping trips.[1] Consumers across Europe have complained of a high cost of living since losing their national currencies. In Ireland, cross-border retail trips to the sterling area in the six northern counties are so institutionalised that the question: 'Have you ever crossed the border to shop?' is on the standard question-and-answer list in the 'Me and My Money' column in the *Irish Times*.

Does this uniformity of prices across the eurozone, from County Donegal to Cyprus, northern Finland to the Canaries, demonstrate an integrated economy? Superficially, it appeared so during the early to mid-2000s. One of the dangers of exchange rate stabilisation programmes, as discussed in chapters 1 and 6, is that after an initial calming effect on inflation (often accompanied by economic growth) complacency can set in. Of course, as far as the European Union leaders were concerned, the completion of the euro, including the entry of Greece, was far more than a mere 'exchange rate stabilisation' like Argentina's currency peg. It was a fully-fledged monetary union of converging European economies. So they weren't likely to be looking at the literature on 'exchange rate stabilisation' initiatives. The possibility of a parallel between the pressures building in the Greek economy and its fiscal position and those in Argentina a decade before will not have been on the agenda.

If the 12 countries of the eurozone (growing to 16 by the end of the decade), were a fully effective single monetary area, how would we know? The dilemma of whether to opt for 'convergence first', or 'convergence after' completing monetary union had been resolved by opting for the latter, despite major misgivings, including within the European Commission and European Central Bank. Given this policy choice, to what extent had true convergence been attained by 2010, a decade into monetary union?

Optimal Currency Area: How did we Measure Up?

It has often been observed that every currency union in the past has ended either in breakdown or in the creation of a nation-state. Research and practical experience broadly concur on the key elements of a successful monetary union. These include

- flexible labour markets
- flexible product and financial markets
- integration of participating economic areas
- diversity of the supply-side
- strong central government with sound fiscal policies
- similarities of inflation rates
- emphasis on growth.

After the first few, apparently smooth, years of monetary union, how were the real economies shaping up under the surface? The ECB itself contributed a working paper on the subject of optimal currency areas in 2002. The authors were too polite to point out that the monetary union just completed fell short of the requirements. There is an indication in the concluding remarks that belief in 'convergence after' could take place and was indeed beginning. It noted: 'The European experience shows that the heterogeneity of, amongst others, policy preferences, institutions and economic structures diminish only gradually.' It comments that the euro area 'is now a good currency area, by many accounts'. This is hardly a ringing endorsement, given the circumstances. The paper concludes ambiguously that 'European integration has been a catalyst for new research and has clearly highlighted the great merits, but also the limitations, of the OCA (Optimal Currency Area) theory.'[2] This shifting of the focus back from the degree to which the EU had followed the principles of an optimal currency area to the soundness of the theory itself looks suspiciously like a political statement, rather than one of economic analysis.

The ECB report notes some difficulty in assessing priority for the key features of an optimal currency area, but it would be difficult to argue that the integration of participating economic areas and fiscal coordination are optional extras. This chapter will explore the extent to which, in these two core areas, not only did the eurozone fall short of an optimal area in 1999–2001, but that complacency led to divergence, not convergence, after monetary union.

Some Benefits: Increases in Trade and Investment

Without doubt, the elimination of exchange rate risk has considerable benefits for exporters. Price transparency and the completion of the single market has helped boost trade. The effect of the single currency alone – separating out the impact of separate moves towards completing the single currency – has been estimated as adding around 5 per cent to trade. As well as reducing the hedging and transactional costs associated with a multiple currency area, there is evidence of stimulation of newly traded goods: that is, the establishment of a large single currency area encouraged firms to export a wider range of their products within the eurozone. There has also been evidence of a positive effect on foreign direct investment, especially in manufacturing. There was a particular boost to merger and acquisition activity within industry sectors.[3]

In terms of flexible labour markets, there was more limited progress. Language difficulties are an obvious barrier, particularly in the services sector, and present an obvious contrast with the USA. Legal systems, including planning and taxation regimes, are heavily nationally based, restricting the movement of professionals such as lawyers, accountants and architects. In the case of Greece, failure to open up the regulated professions, with no real impetus for change until 2010, further hampered the mobility of labour. According to OECD figures, the early years of the euro saw moves towards the deregulation of professions only in some jurisdictions, and indicated that France, Italy and Finland had actually become slightly more regulated in the key professions of accountancy, architecture, engineering and law (see Table 7.1). Many countries still continued with wage bargaining at a national, regional or sectoral level, which seriously hampers the adjustments that are necessary within monetary union. In Spain, for example, by mid-2009 reform was still no more than a proposal that had been set out by a team of economists headed by Samuel Bentolila of CEMFI, a graduate school in Madrid. The *Economist* noted: 'For most of its first decade, timid politicians were able to shelter behind the economic stability that the euro helped provide. Without a crisis it is hard to persuade voters of the need for radical change. Yet recession is the worst time to make changes that leave some groups poorer.'[4]

When reforms to make the labour market more flexible and to reform pensions were proposed by the Spanish government a year later, it prompted a general strike, with President José Zapatero accused of abandoning his socialist principles.[5]

By contrast, the three principal 'out' countries are far more liberal, with Denmark, Sweden and the UK registering 0.8, 0.9 and 1.1 respectively.

It is in the core areas of fiscal coordination and economic integration, however, that we find the heart of the test of an optimal currency

Table 7.1 Regulation of Professional Services

	1996	2003
	Figures on a scale as follows: 0 = most liberal; 6 = most restrictive	
Austria	4.2	2.0
Belgium	2.2	2.1
Finland	0.8	1.0
France	1.8	2.0
Germany	4.2	3.1
Greece	n/a	2.9
Ireland	1.2	1.3
Italy	3.3	3.6
Netherlands	1.4	1.6
Portugal	2.8	2.4
Spain	3.4	2.4

Source: OECD index. Covers accountancy, architecture, engineering and law.

area. Would the completion of monetary union spur countries toward further integration and economic reform, or had dangerous levels of complacency set in?

The Fiscal Rules: Compliance Went Down

Ironically, the one dimension where there were rules and criteria for convergence – fiscal policy – has arguably been one of the weaker features of the single currency. The Stability and Growth Pact was intended to maintain fiscal and economic discipline, and set nominally strict ceilings on public sector deficits and public debt.

When the French finance minister Christine Lagarde said in April 2010 that the Greek rescue package took time to organise because 'it's not like the USA sorting out California', this was a tacit admission that the EU had created something it could not manage. There was a single currency, but not a single political or fiscal framework.

From as early as 2003 countries fell into breach of the specified upper limits. The first culprits were not Belgium and Italy, which had caused concern in the build-up to the euro launch, but France and Germany. In the economic downturn of the early 2000s, their public sector deficits breached the 3 per cent limit.

It is well established that leaders set the tone for the conduct of everyone else. This is true in local communities and in individual organisations, and also in nation-states: Greece, like Argentina, suffered a culture of lawlessness, with members of the juntas and other politicians and rich individuals escaping crimes with impunity. But it appears also to occur at a transnational level. When France and Germany (the 'axis' that has formed the effective leadership of the EU) escaped fines or serious censure for their breach of the Stability and Growth Pact, an unhealthy precedent was set.

Italy, which was allowed to enter the euro despite not having brought its public debt to below 60 per cent of GDP, also began running deficits above 3 per cent. France and Germany escaped censure completely. In the case of Greece and Italy, sanctions were threatened but not imposed.

By the autumn of 2005 the Pact was almost inoperable. European Central Bank executive board member José Manuel González-Páramo acknowledged as much:

Portugal was the first country to breach the 3 per cent reference value in 2001. Germany and France followed in 2002, the

Netherlands and Greece in 2003, and Italy in 2004. At present, 5 of the 12 euro area countries either have or plan deficits above 3 per cent and are subject to excessive deficit procedures.

This disappointing fiscal performance in a number of countries has placed a considerable strain on the implementation of the Pact. And this became most apparent in November 2003, when the Ecofin Council decided to put on hold the excessive deficit procedures for France and Germany. This prompted a dispute between the Council and the Commission that ultimately had to be resolved by the European Court of Justice. At the time, many critics claimed that the Pact was dead. And some would probably still say that today.[6]

There was no doubting the dismay in some inner circles at the deftness of the governments of Gerhard Schroeder and Jacques Chirac to sidestep any sanctions over breaking the rules, but the implications did not seem severe at the time. ECB executive board member Otmar Issing, like Mr González-Páramo, noted: 'It was depressing to see how the German and French governments in particular flouted the Pact. First of all, Germany got its way and prevented the Commission from issuing the warning it had recommended in January 2002 (on account of a deficit expected to be 'dangerously close' to the three per cent limit). Then, in November 2003, the finance ministers yielded to German (and French) requests – or pressure – and rejected the Commission's proposed stepping-up of the procedure and had the procedure halted.'[7]

In a significant landmark, the then German chancellor Gerhard Schroeder had an article published in the *Financial Times* stating that Germany would not have its fiscal policy dictated by 'Brussels'. This was despite the fact that agreeing to the Stability and Growth Pact meant exactly that. Issing recalls that Schroeder's predecessor Helmut Kohl, just over a decade earlier, had received applause from representatives of all major parties in the Bundestag for declaring, in November 1991, that: 'It cannot be repeated often enough. Political union is the indispensable counterpart to economic and monetary union. Recent history, and not just that of Germany, teaches us that the idea of sustaining an economic and monetary union over time without political union is a fallacy.'

The message was not repeated enough. In fact, it was scarcely repeated at all, other than perhaps within the European Commission, where there was strong support for full fiscal union. The euro has not been supported by the necessary elements of a successful single currency area. It has not had a single government, nor a single fiscal policy. There is limited labour mobility.

Individual nations still issued their own sovereign bonds due to a lack of full fiscal union. It also means that the effect of trading imbalances is exacerbated. If one of the states of the US falls behind competitively with another, there are effectively fiscal transfers between the two. Moreover, the US has a single language and much greater mobility of labour. Hence the divergence in labour costs and competitiveness that were occurring in the eurozone during the 2000s meant that imbalances were becoming entrenched.

Greece's fiscal position was consistently the weakest, even after allowing for statistical window dressing. Greece's continuous current account deficit and accumulation of public debt, that helped the continuous growth of the consumer-based spending, was unsustainable. Further destabilising the situation has been the switch from a largely domestic to a largely foreign creditor profile. In 1994 some 85 per cent of Greek government debt was held by domestic financial institutions, by 2007 this ratio had been almost inverted, with 75 per cent held by foreign investors.[8]

While it is convenient to place all the blame on the Greek ministers and Goldman Sachs for disguising the level of Greek government debt,

Figure 7.1 Holders of Greek Government Debt

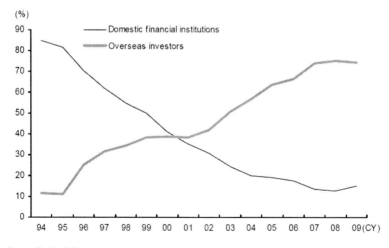

Source: Bank of Greece.

the story goes much deeper. In addition to the national dysfunctions described in earlier chapters, Europe as a whole had structural economic imbalances between north and south – aggravated under monetary union, as I shall describe. In addition, the EU's leaders were guilty of complacent stewardship: they wanted to keep the status quo, an appearance of growth and success, financed in large part by borrowing. It was not until March 2009 that the European Commission formally censured Greece for having an excessive deficit in 2007, noting that this was 'revealed by the October 2008 correction of notified data.'[9] This was backward looking; two years late – and there was no penalty.

Institutionally, it is more likely to be a case of incompetence rather than conspiracy. Parts of the EU seemed to be asleep at the wheel. There appears to be a problem also with an underestimation of scale; a failure to appreciate that they were dealing with matters of huge economic importance. There has been a tendency to use terms such as 'weakness' or 'asymmetry', when words such as 'danger' or 'incompatibility' would better illustrate the underlying risk profile. In the history of the EU, there was an ingrained tendency to deploy compromise or 'fudge' as a way round intractable disagreements between member states. This may be acceptable when dealing with workplace regulations or fisheries policy, but not with a project as ambitious as full-scale monetary union across diverse economies.

The EU Commission's statement on the Greek economy in February 2009, while calling for further structural reform and measures to tackle the deficit, added:

> Greece has experienced strong economic growth at four per cent per year over the current decade. In 2008 its GDP grew well above the euro area average and in 2009 it was still seen in positive territory in the Commission's January forecasts. However, domestic and external macroeconomic imbalances have widened considerably, which has led to very high public and foreign debt. The ongoing global economic and financial crisis is taking its toll on the economy and putting pressure on the debt burden.

Its projections for the public deficit, based on extrapolation and *overconfidence bias*, were as follows: 'The budget deficit exceeded 3 per cent in 2007 and 2008 and, according to the Greek Stability Programme, it will reach 3.7 per cent in 2009 before falling to 3.2 per cent of GDP in 2010 and 2.6 per cent by 2011.'[10]

The single currency was taken to be some sort of safety blanket, especially – but by no means uniquely – in Greece. People assumed, subconsciously or in some cases quite openly, that 'Europe would always be there to bail us out'. The entitlement culture, the sense that Europe 'owes' us Greeks, influenced the popular attitude towards the single currency and the perception of the benefits it was supposed to bring. There was an implicit feeling that this was going to be a free ride.

At the EU level, completing the fusion of the legal entities and launching the euro as a major currency was taken to represent a successful outcome in itself. There is a similarity with many complex company mergers: success is often defined as completing the financial and legal due diligence and forming the new entity, but the real task lies in full integration at ground level. The celebrations and ceremonies held for the euro in 2001 were the equivalent of a football team performing a lap of honour for the achievement of managing to stand still during the national anthem.

Many commentators stick to the problem presented by the data – but the problems of convergence were deeper than that. The extreme dysfunctions in the Greek economy and its dissimilarity with Western Europe, described in chapters 3–5, have not been factored into most analyses. Those designing the Stability and Growth Pact, being mostly Western Europeans, did not fully appreciate that they were dealing with an Eastern state that had different rules, norms, and preferences to those in the West. They did not realise the huge role of the state, the psyche of the Greeks, the bragging rights for gaming the system; nor the loose tax collection and tax-paying culture, which was ingrained in the national psyche under the Ottoman Empire.

It was not appreciated, for example, that EU-wide regulations imposed via written warnings or directives would be insufficient. There is a long list of fines that Greece has paid for breaking the EU rules. In a decision announced in July 2000, for example, the European Court of Justice for the first time imposed a penalty on a member state for failure to comply with one of its previous judgments: Greece was ordered to pay a penalty payment of €20,000 per day for failure to comply with ECJ judgements on measures to dispose of toxic and dangerous waste in the area of Chania. One tally of cases taken to the European Court of Justice between 2000 to 2004, showed the top three to be: Italy (114 cases), France (112), and Greece (93). Denmark, one of the 'opt-out' countries from the single currency, recorded just 9 cases.

An Appearance of Convergence

The sheer size of the eurozone, and the presence of leading advanced economies within it, helped it become established as a major trading currency. Greek interest rates fell sharply after replacement of its weaker former currency, the drachma: from 20 per cent in 1993 to a range of just 3–5 per cent during the period 2001–09. A similar pattern was observed in other peripheral countries. One reason for this was the perceived reduced inflation risk promised by the 'Bundesbank'-style ECB. Another was that the adoption of the euro made it easier for foreign investors to purchase peripheral country debt, without concern for currency risk.

You can see the 'bath tub'-shaped curve of either bond yields or interest rates against time for the peripherals, with high rates plummeting in the run-up to 2001, with a flat bottom for most of the decade, before rising again.

While the eurozone appeared to be converging, and its aggregate indicators were benign, internally the divergence was actually growing. The growing debt of the peripheral countries was simply the other side

Figure 7.2 Germany versus 'PIIGS', 10-year Yield Spread

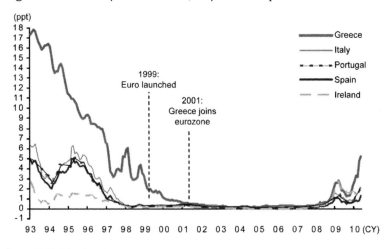

Source: ECB, Bloomberg data.

of the coin of Germany's export-led emergence out of the recession of
the early 2000s.

Trade: The Train Decouples

What about productivity and trading performance – elements of the
euro project that were simultaneously judged crucial to its success and
omitted from the plans and from the convergence criteria? Not even
the crudest measure, the current account deficit, was included in the
Stability and Growth Pact.

The planners of the euro had hoped that, by ruling out competitive
devaluations, the single currency would effectively force countries to
reform their labour markets, open up economies and usher in continual
productivity gains.

But this 'convergence after' approach was high risk. The precedents,
for example from Argentina, strongly indicated that 'convergence first'
was the more prudent path. Moreover, the dysfunctional nature of the
Greek state which was overlooked in the due diligence process for the
single currency, and by the purchasers of government bonds, meant
that the gulf between economic reality and compliance for an optimal
currency area was huge. Widespread corruption is just one example:
Germans bribing Greeks to buy their goods is not just a legal and ethical
matter, but also a huge distortion to the operation of a competitive free
market. Closed shops are another example: they are the opposite of the
principles of a flexible labour market, and were widespread in Greece.
Not until 2010, a decade after entry into the single currency, did the
Greek government begin efforts to end these practices.

At the start of the single currency, the largest trade deficit countries
were Portugal and Greece, at around 7 per cent and 3 per cent of GDP
respectively. By 2007 these had widened, and the gap between surplus
and deficit countries had become a gulf, as Table 7.2 indicates.

It is a similar story for labour costs and productivity within Greece,
with costs for the most part increasing ahead of productivity gains
while the reverse pattern was established for the EU as a whole (see
Table 7.3).

In September 2010, Barclays Capital's economics research team
published an analysis of convergence in the eurozone, and made a
direct comparison between the 11 largest eurozone states and the 11
largest states of the USA. It noted some convergence in Europe in GDP
trends since monetary union, but concluded that there was significantly

Table 7.2 Current Account Balances, Percentage of GDP

	2001	2007
Germany	0.0	+7.7
The Netherlands	+2.4	+6.5
France	+2.0	−1.2
Italy	−0.1	−2.6
Spain	−3.9	−10.1
Portugal	−9.9	−9.8
Greece	−7.3	−14.1

Source: OECD economic database.

Table 7.3 Unit Labour Costs and Productivity in Manufacturing in Greece Compared with EU Average

	2000	2001	2002	2003	2004	2005	2006
	(annual changes in %)						
Greece							
Unit labour cost	5.1	0.3	2.8	1.2	2.3	2.4	2.4
Labour productivity	1.6	1.3	1.5	1.0	1.7	2.5	3.2
EU average							
Unit labour cost	−1.1	1.9	1.9	0.4	−1.0	0.0	0.3
Labour productivity	4.3	1.3	1.5	2.7	3.7	2.5	2.6

Sources: WEO databank and IMF staff calculations. Published in Greece: Selected Issues, IMF Country Report no. 07/27, January 2007.

greater divergence, compared with the USA, particularly in the following dimensions:

- *Labour market*: compared with the US states, there was much wider divergence in unemployment rates across the eurozone states. Moreover, there was greater divergence within individual euro area countries, reflecting labour market rigidities. Europe features more employment protection legislation, generous unemployment benefits and higher marginal labour taxation. There is a high level of long-term unemployment, compared with other advanced countries.
- *Inflation rates*: these varied widely in Europe. The most marked difference was between the core and the periphery: 'If we focus on the "core 5" countries, or even the "core 5 plus Italy and Portugal",

we find that the divergence is quite similar to that of the US, or even lower in recent years.'

• *Real GDP growth*: this was sharply divergent, with some economies overheating while others remained depressed. The divergence in estimates of the output gap – the difference between actual and potential GDP – has widened between the core and the periphery. This puts strain on the 'one-size-fits-all' interest rate regime.

In conclusion, the inner 'core' economies had been converging towards an optimal currency area, but this core was diverged from the periphery, and the differences between the core and the fringe had increased since the credit crisis began.[11]

The 'catching up' period that was expected to happen automatically (because all 12 eurozone countries were on the same 'train') didn't – just as it didn't when Argentina linked its currency to a much stronger one; and just as it hadn't with the Exchange Rate Mechanism, the prototype to the euro that ended in failure in 1993.

Instead of 'catching-up', southern eurozone members fell behind. The economies being left on the station platform, in the preferred metaphor of the euro campaigners, were not the 'outs' of Denmark, Sweden and the UK, but those who had attempted to jump on board. The 'two-tier' Europe that the apostles of the single currency had thunderously warned about during the 1990s had indeed come to

Figure 7.3 House Prices in Greece, Spain, Italy and Ireland

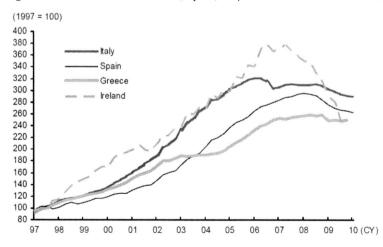

(1997 = 100)

Source: National Housing agencies.

pass: but it was two tiers *within* the eurozone, not between the 'ins' and the 'outs'.

They couldn't have been more wrong, but it shouldn't have been a surprise. When, a decade earlier, Argentina linked its economy to the dollar, the effect on trading performance deteriorated, and the country fell behind Brazil in international trade.

There was fatal *overconfidence bias* in the belief that convergence would just 'happen'. For years, however, high levels of borrowing disguised the extent to which the real economies were diverging. The wrong interest rate – too low for Ireland, Greece and Spain for much of the decade – helped create investment bubbles, especially in property. Taking a base of 100 in 1997, Greek house prices rose to 280 in Athens and 260 in all urban areas at the peak in 2008. Even higher rises were experienced in Spain, Italy, and Ireland, and the remnants of the boom can be seen in the ghost estates of Spain and Ireland.

The availability of cheap credit (see below, where the outstanding volume of Greek mortgages went up eight-fold) simply transmitted into house price increases, beyond the necessary real economy productivity gains needed to support them.

Richard Koo of Nomura provides some important details of the background to the low interest rate era of the early to mid-2000s. He points out that the dotcom boom and bust of 1998–2000 affected Germany as well as the US. The Neumarkt, the equivalent of the NASDAQ, fell 98 per cent. Individuals and companies with large investments in IT-related businesses were left holding assets that were

Figure 7.4 Greek Housing Credit Outstanding

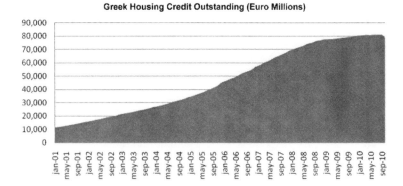

Source: Bank of Greece.

all but worthless, while their debts remained. German businesses were borrowing and investing 6.9 per cent of GDP in 2000, but by 2005 they were paying down debt at a level of 2.2 per cent of GDP – a net contraction of 9.1 per cent of GDP. It was a 'textbook balance sheet recession'. With the Maastricht Treaty formally preventing a deficit of more than 3 per cent, the eurozone's largest economy weakened. It was this development, Koo argues, that prompted the reduction in interest rates to just 2 per cent. 'This corresponds to the period when ECB president Jean-Claude Trichet boasted that the French-led ECB had succeeded in bringing interest rates to a level the German-led Bundesbank had never been able to achieve. In reality, however, interest rates were low not because the ECB had successfully reined in inflation expectations, but rather because Germany had fallen into a balance sheet recession.'

If the ECB had not lowered interest rates so far, the housing bubbles in the periphery would not have grown so much; Germany would have had to address the balance sheet recession, which was not responsive to monetary easing. The options would have been a substantial devaluation of the currency or a massive fiscal stimulus of the kind pursued by Japan and later by the US and the UK.[12]

During the boom years 2005–07 the real interest rate was just 0.8 per cent, growth averaged 2.5 per cent, which was above trend, and credit growth was continuing.

Politics Cannot Repeal Arithmetic

In the context of Greece, low borrowing rates for the private sector coincided with artificially low yields on government borrowing, leading to the debt-and-spending boom described in earlier chapters.

The core problem with the eurozone countries after monetary union was that membership actually reduced pressure on governments to undertake reforms necessary for monetary union to succeed. Italy, for example, did little to strengthen public finances or make labour markets more flexible. Productivity and competitiveness fell, while inflation remained above the eurozone average. Removal of the devaluation option meant subdued growth and a continuing debt problem. Germany also should have adjusted. While monetary union was intended to put an end to competitive devaluations, Germany effectively 'devalued' through control of wages and strong productivity growth, suppressing consumption and investment. This improved competitiveness and

Figure 7.5 Unit Labour Cost Developments 1999–2010

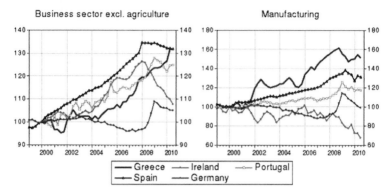

Source: Brugel calculations with OECD data.[13]

suppressed demand for imports, causing the country's trade and current account surpluses to increase. Just as Italy was unable to devalue its currency, Germany without the Deutschmark did not face any currency appreciation.

Added to this were the loans from German banks and bribes from German (and other countries for that matter) companies to boost further demand for German exports in southern Europe, as discussed in earlier chapters. Many of the major economic forces at play in the decade were forcing disequilibrium, not convergence, beneath the apparently complacent noses of policymakers and officials in Brussels and Frankfurt.

Another measure of growing divergence in the real economy comes from the deflator, an indicator of relative prices. Between 2000 and 2009, the German deflator rose just 9 per cent, as wages stayed level and the country became hypercompetitive. Spain's deflator increased 35 per cent, and Greece's 33 per cent. Just because the European countries share the euro does not mean that they cannot have different productivity levels and competitive environments. Tax regimes and product and labour laws mean countries' prices for goods and services follow different and sometimes diverging paths.

The 'competitive devaluations' so loathed by European Union leaders can be a more sensitive form of adjustment to the type that is being desperately sought within the eurozone. This is because changes to producer prices can be more 'sticky' than changes to exchange rates for a floating currency. Producers have no problem in raising prices of goods and services, but are loath to reduce them. Non-tradables in particular can be inflexible. Currency devaluations are a relatively straightforward and swift way of adjusting relative prices, while keeping nominal prices constant. The 'out' countries of the European Union may have the best of both worlds: free trade flows but more rapid and less painful adjustments to pricing when needed.

By 2007 Germany was generating the world's largest trade surplus. Eurozone nations were responsible for much of this: Germany's trade surplus with the US grew only slightly during this time, while the country actually ran deficits with key Asian nations.

In addition, as discussed earlier, German and French banks lent to successive Greek governments, and German and French arms suppliers were major benefactors of this spending spree. The pattern of German and French banks financing countries that need to finance their trade deficits is identical to the economic recycling conducted by the Japanese in the 1980s and by China now, *vis-à-vis* the USA.

Hence, Germany benefited most from eurozone membership during the decade 1999–2009. The interdependence of surplus and deficit nations was almost total. It also became unsustainable, as the exchange rates were far too high and the interest rates too low for peripheral nations with a stunted supply-side.

Despite this alarming growth in divergence throughout the decade, all the indications were that the EU's leaders believed that convergence was occurring.

Figure 7.6 German Balance of Trade

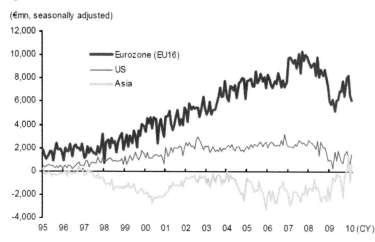

(€mn, seasonally adjusted)

Source: German Bundesbank.

Repeatedly, we have heard politicians express the hope – in defiance of all research and experience – that merging dissimilar economies together within a single currency area, or fixed exchange rate, encourages convergence. It doesn't – it merely heightens the differences and closes off the escape route, via reduced flexibility. This is one of the commonest and most dangerous examples of *overconfidence bias* that occurs in politics – that you can shortcut your way to economic development through monetary policy alone.

Even as late as 2010, long after it had become evident that catching up had not occurred, the train metaphor reappeared. Josef Joffe, editor of *Die Zeit*, commented: 'So will the euro train, made up of 16 national cars, finally derail? Possibly, but it's hard to imagine because nobody wants to decouple.' There is far too much at stake for the leaders of the eurozone to allow it to fail, he argued. He listed some of the negative consequences of breaking apart the single currency – economic instability, high interest rates and default.[14]

This is partially correct, but misses the point. Of course no one would want the euro 'train' to derail, and there would be huge repercussions if it crashed. The problem is more fundamental: the euro isn't a train, and it isn't on tracks. It's an experiment, overseen by complacent stewards. Its architects see it as a culmination, as binding and as irrevocable. It is anything but; it is an ongoing drama, with unpredictable outcomes.

Cognitive Dissonance

The hope for 'convergence after' was misplaced. Its hypothetical possibility was stymied by complacency. There are indications of cognitive dissonance and narrative fallacies among European leaders, who seem to have come to believe their own PR. Such psychological biases may appear to be a mere detail of economic and political developments, but their impact can be huge. The EU's leaders clearly believed that they had created a full monetary union, based on an optimal currency area. The reality was that, for the peripheral countries, it was just a currency peg, like Argentina's. Now there *are* differences with Argentina, but they are not reassuring:

- Five countries are involved, not just one
- Levels of borrowing are higher, in absolute and relative terms
- Exit is more difficult
- The banking system across the continent is at risk of contagion.

The Joffe quote above, and numerous others like it, reveal that the *illusion of control* fallacy is at the heart of the euro project. It gives the EU's leaders the impression that the single currency is almost entirely within their hands – unless devious Anglo-Saxons and other speculators succeed in their destabilising efforts – and that resolution and confidence will be sufficient to keep the 'train' on track. When borrowing vast sums of money on the international capital markets, however, much of that control goes to the creditors. When taking away economic policymaking from national governments and placing it with the ECB, some of the political control passes from the national government to the ordinary citizen. This is counterintuitive, because officially their views are being taken out of the equation altogether. It arises, however, because they may no longer vote for pro-EU parties in general elections. There are indications of anti-EU parties gaining more support in different European countries. Ordinary citizens are much more difficult to contain and appease than party leaders loyal to the European project. The ECB could seek to abolish national elections to make its life easier, but it may find considerable opposition to that idea.

A strong exchange rate is nothing more or less than one of the symptoms of a strong real economy; it is highly unlikely ever to be the cause. Having been able to witness the failure of Domingo Cavallo to use artificially high exchange rates to try to effect economic development in Argentina in the 1990s, as well as Europe's own failure to encourage convergence through the 1979–92 Exchange Rate Mechanism, the EU leaders really had no excuse for repeating the experiment in the 2000s. Yet they really did fall for the seductive idea once more, according to at least one candid admission. Interviewed by the BBC 'Today Programme' on 3 May 2010, German MEP Wolf Klinz said: 'For one reason or another one felt that maybe if we do have the common currency then automatically countries will move towards each other, will move closer to each other and that will foster integration.'

Nassim Nicholas Taleb suggests that a crude form of social Darwinism may have entered the Western psyche, with the narrative fallacy that organisations and economies tend to evolve towards perfection. The possibility for error and randomness are downplayed, and of course the complacency that accompanies this attitude ironically makes error more likely. He writes: 'Many [traders]…believe that companies and organisations are, thanks to competition (and the discipline of the quarterly report), irreversibly heading towards betterment. The strongest will survive, the weakest will become extinct. Things are not as simple as that.'[15]

Though the context was the investment community, he might equally as well have been describing the *overconfidence bias* within the European Union that economies within the eurozone would 'naturally' converge with one another and, given the completion of the single market and the competition this encourages, also improve their performance. The 'catching-up' process of the poorer countries that former ECB member Otmar Issing refers to was just supposed to happen, without any plan or measures being put in place to check that it was – other than the limited agenda of the Stability and Growth Pact, whose sanctions were not applied in any case.

Borrowing and PR; Hubris and Schadenfreude

There were two dimensions, however, in which the euro was a resounding success between 2002 and 2009: in addition to the ability to borrow cheaply, it benefited from excellent public relations. The euro's PR machine scored some impressive achievements, bolstered by reassuring narratives informed by the cognitive biases I have discussed. During the boom years of the Great Moderation and global expansion it was believed that 'this time it was different'; irrational exuberance was not solely confined to traders in collatoralised debt obligations (CDO), mortgage vendors in Nevada or real estate developers in Ireland. The European Union leaders enjoyed congratulating themselves over a strengthening euro, and defying the critics who had predicted a struggling currency.

Here is a selection of observations and predictions:

> My own prediction is that by the year 2002 the European Monetary Union will include its current 11 members plus Greece, Sweden, Denmark and Britain. By 2005, Slovenia, the Czech Republic, Poland, Hungary and Estonia will also be in. And by 2010, assuming all goes well and the monetary union is prosperous, no country in Europe will want to, or be able to, afford to stay out.
> — *Robert Mundell, Nobel Prize-winning economist, writing in 1999.*

> In the future the euro is going to be taking a place in the international markets in general as the money of exchange. (*It will replace the dollar*) of course – in the oil market and in any market' ...
> — *European Commissioner for Energy and Transport*
> *Loyola de Palacio, 2003.*

Of course, there were dissenting voices. I recall one economist describing the creation of the euro as 'at best, an act of uncertain merit' and another denouncing it as a 'great mistake'. A decade on, we have been able to assess the performance of EMU through a complete business cycle. And I am pleased to say that the euro has proved an economic success.

— *European Commissioner for Economic and Monetary Affairs Joaquin Almunia, address to the Peterson Institute, Washington, 11 April 2008.*

There is much irony in the fact that many of the critics of xenophobes and eurosceptics opposing the single currency can be shamelessly partisan in their anti-American sentiments. Expression of imperialist ambition emerges again and again in the statements of the architects of the euro. The single currency was to have been the global reserve currency; the centrepiece of a 'United States of Europe', which in turn was to have replaced the USA as the superpower of the West. EU zealots enjoyed predicting the end of the US dollar as the leading reserve currency. This confirms the suspicion that ambition for sheer size, rather than true convergence, lay behind the rushed decision to enlarge the single currency area to a wide number of dissimilar economies, and not to look too closely at the economic statistics.

Admissions that the ambition for the euro was imperialist, rather than helpful to economic performance, were also quite often explicit. In 2002 Romano Prodi said that 'the historic significance of the euro is to construct a bi-polar economy in the world. The two poles are the dollar and the euro'. The then Spanish president Felipe González in 1998 declared: 'The single currency is a decision of an essentially political character... We need a united Europe. We must never forget that the euro is an instrument for this project.'

To be fair, the projections of the euro overtaking the greenback were not confined to Europe. A pioneer of the optimal currency area, Canadian economist Robert Mundell, supported the single currency. In 2008 a positive and influential analysis emerged from the USA. Professor Menzie Chinn of the University of Wisconsin and Professor Jeffrey Frankel of Harvard concluded that the euro was set to replace the dollar as the world's largest reserve currency within the next 10 or 15 years, and possibly as early as 2015. It contained calculations, with the customary projections drawn out on a graph, where the share of anticipated international reserves held in euros overtakes those of dollars between 2010 and 2020.[16] This report appeared at the start of the recession and associated banking crisis, but Wolfgang Munchau, a *Financial Times* columnist, has said the crisis 'could easily accelerate the trends they have identified'.[17]

Some of these critiques are half right. The preeminence of the dollar cannot be assumed to continue indefinitely, especially as the USA has huge twin deficits itself, but its replacement or replacements will probably come from Asia.

This was not on the radar at the peak of the subprime crisis in North America, when there was a huge joy in the eurozone with the weakening US dollar. Consider the following quotes:

> Today, we know that the euro has indeed become the second most important international currency after the US dollar... In fact, with the present exchange rates the euro area GDP is higher than that of the US.
>
> — *EU commissioner Joaquin Almunia, in a speech to the Peterson Institute, April 2008.*

> The Euro at 10 is regional, stable, and a legitimate source of pride in European achievement.
>
> — *Adam Posen and Jean Pisani-Ferry (eds), 'The Euro at Ten' (Peterson Institute for International Economics, 2009).*

The intellectual grandfather of Anglo-Saxon neoliberalism, Milton Friedman, had predicted that the euro would not survive its first economic crisis. When the euro strengthened against the dollar following the collapse of Lehman Brothers and the associated banking crisis in 2008–09, the hubris and Schadenfreude went stratospheric.

In the 2009 publication *The Euro at Ten*, with contributions from numerous economists and politicians, the subtitle ran: *The Next Global Currency?* The inclusion of a question mark indicates that not all contributors were certain of its future as a reserve currency. In the minds of some, however, there was no doubt.

The editors state in their introduction:

> The euro is now in its tenth year of usage, successfully performing all the functions of a currency area for European citizens using it, and providing price stability to the euro area. The monetary union and its central bank are in process of passing the test of a major financial crisis and have held-up well so far.

Joaquin Almunia, principal cheerleader for the single currency, was the most enthusiastic. While some fellow contributors perceived problems arising in the euro area from the banking crisis and internal trading and fiscal imbalances, Almunia wrote that the euro had been 'an undisputed success'. This is not correct. Dispute was continual, and included reasoned argument from sober economists such as Wilhelm Nölling, not just flagwavers of national currencies. This statement is an example of the Stalinist tendency among the unelected EU commissioners, an inclination to think: there is no dispute if we say there is no dispute.

A further quote from his chapter follows, with my observations in italics:

> The euro...has anchored macro-economic stability [*illusion of control here, like restoring a façade and saying the house is new*] and brought historically low inflation and interest rates for much of the last decade. [*The deflationary effect of German reunification, of China's low-cost imports and the liquidity boom might have also contributed to low inflation and interest rates.*] Despite the euro area's lower-than-expected growth rate [*prediction errors and wishful thinking*] – due largely to too few structural reforms – the macro-economic stability combined with boost of trade and investment brought by the euro has helped to create 16 million more jobs, than in the United States in the same period.

Yet the lack of inevitable convergence towards global reserve currency status, and of Europe becoming a superpower, sometimes baffles the euro's supporters. For example, the authors of *The Euro at Ten* note: 'It was initially assumed that monetary integration would trigger financial integration within the euro area. In the event, Europe's financial center is London, not Frankfurt or Paris.' This observation was not accompanied by an apology to the people of the 'out' countries for having repeatedly used this argument as a scare tactic to encourage them to join the EMU experiment. On 22 June 2010, in the first budget of the new Conservative–Liberal Democrat coalition government in the UK, the chancellor George Osborne ruled out euro membership for the next five years, and announced the disbanding of the UK Treasury's Euro Preparations Unit.

Danny Alexander, chief secretary to the UK Treasury, is the former head of communications for the pressure group Britain in Europe, which campaigned for the sterling to join the euro. He said in September 2010: 'In the current economic circumstances I'm relieved that we are not in the euro... I still think there's a case for that [membership] in the long term, but that's a long way off. I think that the flexibilities that we have as an economy are helping our economy to recover.'[18]

The failure of the globalised economic world to follow the script so carefully prepared by the architects of European Monetary Union was to prove a constant source of irritation and puzzlement, which only intensified as the eurozone hit crisis in 2010.

The Swaps, the Fiddled Figures. The Saga Continues

It is not enough to say that Greece fiddled its public sector deficit statistics in the period 1999–2002 with the help of Goldman Sachs, and thus lay all of the blame on a handful of Greek government ministers and investment bank advisers from a decade ago. Their role was ignominious, but there were systemic failures. There was no desire to find hidden deficits.

By the end of the decade, however, the extent of the massaging of public sector deficits was becoming clearer. The Luxembourg-based agency Eurostat had faced an unequal battle with cynical governments in an attempt to provide a true picture. Europe's finance ministers repeatedly commented on the inadequacy of timeliness and accuracy of data compared with the USA, but seemed to have little sense of urgency in correcting the situation.

As details emerged, it transpired that more investment banks and more governments were involved in the deception. As in the North American subprime crisis, use of financial derivatives played a role in disguising the extent and riskiness of debt – in this case European sovereign debt. By 2010, The *New York Times* disclosed that: 'Instruments developed by Goldman Sachs, JP Morgan Chase and other banks enabled politicians to mask additional borrowing in Greece, Italy and possibly elsewhere.'[19]

But Brussels knew about the misleading figures. It was in the EU's short-term interest to let the pattern of borrowing and spending continue. This involved German and French banks lending to the Greek government – some German corporations bribing Greek officials – European banks lending to construction firms and mortgage lenders, and the international bond markets lending to peripheral governments. The short-term growth figures looked good, but the underlying imbalances were deteriorating. The euro became established as a global reserve currency during a period in which it was departing even further from the features of an optimal currency area.

The Implicit Guarantee: The Euro Subprime Scandal

The irony at the heart of the outburst of sectarian dislike for the USA was that the EU's own leaders were themselves guilty of the same errors as North American banks. The subprime crisis emerged from large-scale lending to low income borrowers, and was famously aggravated by securitisation. But while continental European politicians fumed at such Anglo-Saxon excesses affecting the world economy, a similar phenomenon was occurring in Europe. Governments of varying creditworthiness were bundled together and stamped with an investment grade. With the CDOs, the instruments had been rated according to the soundest of the mortgages involved, despite including debts of widely varying levels of quality. In the same way, the euro was treated as the equivalent of the Deutschmark, despite containing only one currency of such strength. And exactly as happened with the CDOs, this faked level of 'strength' was used for trading well above its true level.

The inherent risk with the bundling of CDOs and of European economies was therefore deepened by good old-fashioned *overconfidence bias*: i.e. let's assume everyone's performance levels up to the best, without any actual plans or policies to encourage this, or checking for any evidence that it was beginning to occur, and ignore the evidence that the opposite was occurring.

This led to one of the most dangerous features of the euro: the implicit guarantee that it would, and could, always bail out a weaker member; that membership of the eurozone conferred an automatic and financially infinite safety net. The EU's leaders believed it. So too did the world's bond traders. You see this in the 'bath tub' curve of peripheral government yields against those of the central governments. For years, Greek bonds traded as though they were the same as German bonds. Even then, the EU's leaders appeared to be in denial of the extent of the problem, until May 2010, when action of a sort was finally taken. If full-scale due diligence was unrealistic, a few indicators could have raised the alarm: a corruption index well below the European norm, as measured by Transparency International; or the proportion of public expenditure that goes directly on wages being around twice the level of Germany's – nearly 70 per cent of government spending in Greece compared with 38 per cent in Germany according to 2009 figures from Eurostat.

The actual mechanics of this implied safety net were never spelled out. For a decade, politicians, investors and the general public across the eurozone tacitly assumed that the euro was big enough and bold enough to cope with any problems; that it would behave in line with the strongest of its constituent members. This implicit guarantee became so strong that it undermined itself, ushering in a level of complacency that helped take debt levels and trading imbalances towards unsustainable levels.

In 2008, the graph lines of the spreads between Greek and the northern 'out' EU country government bonds and German bonds crossed over. In November 2007, the spread on Greek bonds was only +34 bps higher than Germany's. The figure for the UK, not enjoying the 'benefit' of being in the eurozone, was +65 bps. By December 2008, the Greek figure was +221 bps; that for the UK was down to +5 bps, in spite of Britain running a record public sector deficit. Projections based on extrapolation were even more useless than usual!

The distorting factor, of course, was the branding that the euro enjoyed, which then suffered a precipitous fall. The PR machine had done its work, but it could only ever have a temporary effect. The markets were starting to suspect that the sovereign debt obligations of the euro area were not quite as investment grade as they appeared. The ratings agencies followed this lead. The Greek government 'enjoyed' – if that is the term, because it encouraged more borrowing – investment grade rating for some time after some of us had been warning that the increase in government debt was reaching unsustainable levels.

By the time the short-term effects of cheap borrowing and aggressive PR had faded and yield spreads and debts were widening, it was clear that the imbalances had reached dangerous levels. Even then, EU's leaders continued in a state of denial between late 2009 and May 2010 when action of a sort was finally taken. The euro faced a choice between a first option of break-up, devaluations and defaults; and a second one of massive loans accompanied by rapid fiscal integration and internal market reform, with or without the support of local populations. Both were high-risk options, but a low-risk one was no longer available by the time the EU's leaders acknowledged the problem and stopped believing their own PR. They decided on the second of the two options: a monumental undertaking.

Selective and Short-Term Memory

The hubris and Schadenfreude seemed to induce collective amnesia. Politicians, electorates and analysts seemed to forget or ignore the divides, the pain, the arguments and the inevitable compromises that were needed to reach the signing of the Maastricht Treaty and the adoption of the euro. These divides were intracountry, between countries, intra-central banks, and so on. The euro has been in existence for just ten years, yet the history of its painful birth seems to have been forgotten.

The same pressures and problems that European countries experienced during the Exchange Rate Mechanism in the period 1979–93 reappeared in 2002–09, yet policymakers responded as though they were occurring for the first time. This was the case with the failure of monetary discipline to lessen the differences between surplus and deficit countries in trade, and the failure of governments to maintain fiscal responsibility. A 'one-size-fits-all' interest rate again caused problems, though in the rerun it was more of a case of rates that were too low, with an accompanied growth of credit and property prices; whereas in the years of the ERM high relative interest rates had hit industry, jobs and home ownership in some participating countries. There was a tendency to think 'this time it's different', and the ERM and its ignominious end was more or less written out of the European Union history.

Between 1980 and 2000 the drachma depreciated by around 85 per cent compared with the Deutschmark, reflecting the relative economic performances of Greece and Germany. On what basis was it assumed that this deterioration would be arrested simply by joining the single currency?

As the rising yields began to be noticeable it was also evident how the belief in the 'comfort blanket' effect of the euro was still causing them to be underpriced. So while the difference in yields between northern and southern Europe was growing, it was much less than that suggested by the data. By April 2009 serious mispricings emerged: Ukraine bonds were trading at a colossal spread of +6,000 bps on a debt/GDP ratio of 12 per cent, compared with Greece's +200 bps on a debt/GDP ratio of 105 per cent. The market, like the EU's political leadership, was still in denial about the scale of the underlying problem in government debt in relation to the productive capacity of the economies within the countries of the single currency.[20]

Complacency about the undefined 'protective' qualities of the euro affected the IMF. In its January 2007 Greece country report, which sounded some warnings about growing imbalances in the eurozone and the declining competitiveness of Greece, as well as noting tax evasion and Greece's underground economy, the IMF nonetheless expressed the belief that the single currency, in ways that it did not specify, reduced risks. Addressing the question of whether external imbalances should be of concern in a eurozone country, it asserted: 'Adoption of the euro has reduced the significance of the current account deficit and external indebtedness as risk factors.'[21] How? It is not spelled out. This section is couched in a euphemistic language that is popular among professional economists. There is no actual discussion of *how* the existence of the single currency reduces these risk factors. Maybe it's the Freddie Mercury school of economics: 'It's a Kind of Magic'. The cognitive biases, leading to faith in an unspecified protective quality of the single currency, appear to have affected the IMF's economists also.

Beware Buyer's Remorse

Few countries were more reluctant than Germany to give up their national currency.

Most opinion polls in the country were unsupportive of the switch to the single currency, which was quickly dubbed the 'teuro' by its citizens, a play on words as 'teuer' is German for expensive. The government did not dare run a referendum prior to entry, out of the obvious fear that the untrustworthy citizens would come up with the 'wrong' result.

Germany is now suffering an acute and potentially dangerous case of 'buyer's remorse', or decision regret. This is a well-known phenomenon in psychology, with particular relevance to decisions on investment. The psychologist David Bell has defined it as focusing on the assets you might have had if you had made the right decision. In investment, this can apply equally to the stock you sold which subsequently appreciated, and the stock you decided not to buy. Suppose you had a choice between a lottery offering $10,000 or nothing, against a guaranteed gift of $4,000. You choose the guaranteed $4,000, but later discover that the lottery would have paid out $10,000. It is difficult to avoid regret over this missed opportunity from gnawing away at you. Peter Bernstein, author of an intriguing book on the history of human understanding of risk, and our unfortunate bias towards theories based on games of chance, commented: 'Even though everyone knows it is impossible to choose only top performers, many investors suffer decision regret over those foregone assets. I believe that this kind of emotional insecurity has a lot more to do with decisions to diversify than... [the most] intellectual perorations on the subject.'[22]

Germany thought it had signed up for a Greater Deutschmark: a low inflation, no bail-out currency, backed by an independent ECB modelled explicitly on the Bundesbank, reinforced by the Stability and Growth Pact. That deal is now buried. What would have happened if we had stuck with the Deutschmark? You cannot be German, or even be living in Germany, if you are not thinking of this question at least some of the time.

'In Hindsight' – But they were Warned

When the official reports of the eurozone debt crisis come to be written, which may or may not constitute a post-mortem of the single European currency itself, they will in all likelihood contain the phrase 'in hindsight' numerous times. It recurs frequently in the text of the IMF's report on Argentina's convertibility experiment (see chapters 1 and 6).

In the context of the euro, what the phrase 'in hindsight' really means is: 'without *overconfidence bias*'. Many observers have warned of lack of convergence, inaccurate statistics on government debt, political risk, a one-size-fits-all interest rate, a lack of labour mobility, national-based fiscal systems – all well before the crisis began and, in many cases, well before the adoption of the single currency. Some German economists even launched a legal challenge to the government's decision to join the euro, explicitly on the basis of inadequate safeguards according to the criteria listed above.

And even the excuse that unexpected events took the project off course is inadequate, because the project planners themselves had taken the assumption that events could not take it off course. It's not enough for the ocean yachtsman to complain of a hurricane, if in his preparations he had discounted the possibility of hurricanes, and treated with disdain the forecasters who warned him of their possibility.

Of all the dishonest comments made by EU spokespeople in the single currency saga, the most shameful is that of EU president Herman van Rompuy on 25 May 2010. The head of a commission that for years had made false reassurances, overoptimistic projections of 'convergence' and treated its critics with disdain, he had the temerity to say – and I quote in full: 'We are clearly confronted with a tension within the system, the infamous dilemma of being a monetary union and not a fully-fledged economic and political union. This tension has been there since the single currency was created. However, the general public was not really made aware of it.'[23]

This is so directly the opposite of what occurred that it does take one's breath away. The communication was in the opposite direction, and the commission ignored it. For years the voters, and many prominent observers, had been warning again and again of the imbalances within the system and the incompleteness of measures to cope with monetary union. Two referenda held specifically on the euro, in the advanced economies of Sweden and Denmark, resulted in a 'No' vote. The warnings were legion, vocal, public, and many were reasoned and consistent. They were by no means confined to xenophobes or traditionalists. The 155 German economists who published an open letter in 1998 made clear their commitment to the *principle* of a single currency, but said that the timing was wrong and convergence incomplete.

Simon Tilford of the pro-EU Centre for European Reform published a critique of imbalances and weaknesses in the eurozone in 2006, and warned that, without reform within southern economies to enable them to adapt, in the absence of the option to devalue there was a real risk that such countries could be caught in a spiral of weakening competitiveness, higher premiums on government debt, declining political support and investors starting to question the sustainability of the single currency. Three years later he recalled how such warnings, far from being listened to by EU leaders, prompted a torrent of criticisms. 'Some critics even went so far as to accuse it [the Centre for European Reform] of euroscepticism. But it is not pro-European to ignore negative trends, especially as these trends could do a lot of damage to the whole EU if they led to some countries leaving the eurozone. The fact that we highlighted these concerns was not motivated by a desire to see the single currency fail.'[24]

He reports that his warnings were brushed aside, despite his pro-EU credentials. This shooting of the messenger is a classic sign of *herd behaviour*, the mentality of a closed order. Tilford concluded that the *overconfidence bias* scenario, of accelerated political integration within the eurozone and the move to fiscal federalism, was the least likely to occur. Writing at the peak of the euro's value as measured against the dollar, at a time when the ECB was being praised for its handling of the crisis, he acknowledged: 'this would seem to be a strange time for anyone to raise questions about the stability of the currency union. But the euro is about to face its first really serious test.'[25]

How it coped with the test as it emerged in late 2009 and during 2010 will be covered in chapter 10. Before that, however, to complete the context of the Greek and eurozone crisis, we will next consider the contribution of the international capital markets, and the beliefs that underpin their operations.

Chapter 8

LIQUIDITY BOOM

We don't see things as they are, we see them as we are.

—Anaïs Nin

How Come Greece was Allowed to Borrow $500 Billion?

At the end of the liquidity boom decade, by early 2010, most eurozone countries were burdened with dangerously high levels of sovereign debt as the world economy struggled through an uneven recovery from deep recession. To make matters worse, many of the most significant creditors were European banks, indicating systemic risk with a profile similar to the credit crisis of 2007–08. The entire continent appeared to be tottering on a financial precipice. How did this come about? How was Greece allowed to borrow so much? Why were the red flags only waved long after the risks emerged?

For all the tension between EU leaders and the investment community, for a whole decade both parties colluded in the pretence that Greece had a similar economy to Germany's. I have described how the imperialist ambition of the EU's leaders for a large euro area, rather than a converged one, distorted the process of establishing the single currency. There was shockingly weak due diligence in assessing suitability for entry into the euro, and an equally weak application of the few rules that were supposed to police its operation.

But in an age of globalised finance, why did the investment community buy the story? No one forced them to loan to successive Greek governments sums that were colossal relative to the productive scope of its economy. No one compelled them to regard the economy as being, de facto, the equivalent of Germany's or that of the Netherlands. The answers lie partly in the wall of liquidity unleashed upon global markets in the early 2000s, looking for a profitable home, and also in some of the ingrained beliefs and practices in the markets, on the buy-side and sell-side alike.

These beliefs influence the benchmarks, habits and customs of an entire industry. The jargon and acronyms convey a certain mystique to proceedings, reinforced by the self-confidence of traders. Occasionally, the beliefs that underlie their practices are highly suspect; some core beliefs are, on occasion, wrong. Sometimes they are based on an overconfidence of their understanding of what an economy constitutes and how it behaves. The habits, instincts and common practices of the investment community can actually encourage economic instability.

Howard Marks of Oaktree Capital neatly summarises in general terms the dynamics that led to the misallocation of capital, including the vast level of lending to Greece. He anticipated in 2007 that 'the credit cycle that began around 2002 will go down as one of the most extreme on record'. A selection of these are:

- *Too much capital availability makes money flow to the wrong places.* When capital is scarce, there is naturally more care and attention paid to its allocation; when there is too much capital chasing too few ideas, investments will be made that do not deserve to be made.
- *When capital goes where it shouldn't, bad things happen.* When money is everywhere, 'unqualified borrowers are offered money on a silver platter'.
- *When capital is in oversupply, investors compete for deals by accepting low returns and a slender margin for error.* There is auctioning; bidding is effectively saying you will take less for your money.
- *Widespread disregard for risk creates great risk.* Symptoms of this phenomenon are statements such as: 'Someone will always pay me more for it'; 'If I don't move quickly, someone else will buy it', and 'Nothing can go wrong.'
- *Inadequate due diligence leads to investment losses.* The best defence against loss is deep analysis, but in hot markets people worry about missing out.
- *Psychological and technical factors can swamp fundamentals.* In the long term, markets are driven by fundamentals; but in the short term considerable distortions are caused by investor psychology and technical factors that affect supply and demand for assets.[1]

A Liquidity Boom: The Early 2000s

The Greek, and eurozone, debt crisis was the result of a perfect storm. In previous chapters, I've discussed how the monstrous, wasteful Greek public sector created a demand for ever-increasing expenditure, with little return for the public good, and how the designers of the eurozone had 'fudged' criteria for entry into an optimal currency zone. But the crisis would not have taken on the scale that it did without huge volumes of investment funds being ploughed into eurozone government bonds. A succession of factors contributed to this.

In the first few years of the century we experienced the risk factors listed above. Additionally there were interest rates that were too low, designed to stimulate the economy, and an excessive faith in ratings agencies – a particular problem that I shall address later in this chapter.

All these factors combined with particular acuteness in the period 2000–07. The dotcom boom and bust, and the heavy borrowing and overbuilding of optical fibre capacity, led to severe corporate strain and a market downturn, coinciding with accountancy scandals at Enron and others. There were the terrorist attacks on the USA on 11 September 2001. The Federal Reserve took interest rates to as low as 1 per cent. Interest rates were low also in Germany and Japan. In the case of Germany, the policy response to the collapse of the Neumarkt was a significant factor in creating a loose monetary regime and prompting lending to peripheral eurozone countries.

With equity returns collapsing – between 2000 and 2003 the Neumarkt fell by 98 per cent and the NASDAQ by almost 80 per cent, while the Dow Jones fell by nearly 40 per cent and the FTSE100 more than halved – investors looked for returns from less conventional avenues, such as emerging market securities, leverage and financial innovations like securitised assets. The risk profile increased.

Benchmarking, Convergence and Carry

One of the most notorious quotes from the height of the subprime boom came from the former CEO of Citigroup Chuck Prince. 'When the music stops, in terms of liquidity, things will get complicated [but]… as long as the music is playing, you've got to get up and dance.'

This single quote gets us to the heart of the problem very quickly. *Herd behaviour*. The procyclical attitude. Lazy benchmarking. Copying your peers for short-term purposes. Warren Buffet's fourth part of the 'Institutional Imperative' indicates that the behaviour of 'peer companies, whether they are expanding, acquiring, setting executive compensation or whatever, will be mindlessly imitated. Institutional dynamics, not venality or stupidity, set businesses on these courses, which are too often misguided'. That is, companies and investors will copy each other on the latest fad, or hottest item, because of the well-known axiom that, in the words of Keynes, 'it is better to fail conventionally than succeed unconventionally'. Hence, we often see investors piling into the same asset class or industrial sector, pushing up valuations and leading to overvaluation and future poor performance. This can be described as the *bandwagon effect*.

On the buy-side, fixed income institutional investors are always searching for enhanced returns. The jargon is called 'yield pick-up'. There are three ways this can be done: one is to extend the duration of the investment; another is to decrease the credit quality; and a third is to increase the illiquidity of the investment. All of these should provide increased yield *vis-à-vis* the shorter duration, higher quality and greater liquidity investments. Towards the end of an investment cycle, investors get pushed into the first route in their desperate hunt for yield, taking the maximum amount of risk for lower returns.

At the start of the 2000s and the birth of the euro, Alan Greenspan, then chairman of the Federal Reserve, kept interest rates close to zero per cent in the years following the dotcom boom and bust and the terrorist attacks on the USA in September 2001. As noted in the last chapter, there were similar policies in Europe, with rates falling to 2 per cent.

This created the liquidity and carry trade bonanza. 'Carry trades' are where investors create small daily gains, based on interest rate differentials. However, as we know, every five or ten years, a crisis happens and all the previous gains can be lost from carry trades in a very short period of time. Our familiar *problem of induction* and tendency to extrapolate are key factors here. A vivid image is created by the following phrase, which characterises the carry trade as: 'picking up nickels in front of the steamroller'.[2]

So why are investors obsessed with carry trades? It is well established in prospect theory that given a choice between risky outcomes we are about two times as averse to losses as we are to gains. So investors love to make small positive gains; they experience twice the pain when making losses; so they often choose to invest in *seemingly* safer assets that generate small daily gains. Small daily losses, by contrast, are too painful. There is no automatic discipline to analyse the risks being taken on in the upward slope of the bubble curve. Customers want a narrative of upwardly mobile earnings, not a sober analysis of hidden risks.

The time horizon is also a factor: investors will accept more risk over a longer time-frame. With herd-like behaviour, many stick to the small daily gains that appear to be safer when the time horizons are smaller. And as we shall discuss, time horizons have been getting shorter and shorter.[3]

ADHD in the Markets

The search for yield becomes difficult, often desperate. Investors are in a competitive environment, and are judged on performance, usually within a short-term framework – weekly, monthly, quarterly. They suffer from a form of ADHD or attention deficit hyperactivity disorder; a desire to demonstrate constant action. James Montier notes that the average holding period for stock is now six months – compared with several years in the 1950s and 1960s. Yet he observes: 'At a one-year time horizon, the vast majority of your total return comes from changes in valuation – which are effectively random fluctuations in price. However, at a five-year time horizon, 80 per cent of your total return is generated by the price you pay for the investment plus the growth in the underlying cash flow. These are the aspects of investment that fundamental investors should understand, and they clearly only matter in the long term.'[4]

This obsession with the short term is part of the problem. The completion of the euro coincided with the policy of near-zero interest rates globally. Investors obsessed with carry and benchmarking – with support from the faulty logic that the European Union provided a blanket of support, making credit analysis and differentiation obsolete – were 'forced' to try to squeeze the last basis points out of the so-called 'European Convergence Trade'. This was based on tacit faith in the unspecified protective qualities of the single currency, which was even referred to in an official IMF report (see chapter 7), and in the supposedly inevitable process in which the peripheral European countries would see their inflation and interest rates converge with Germany's; first the 'in' countries, then the 'outs'. Few anticipated that the process might operate in the opposite direction.

The launch of the euro created a new, seemingly liquid pool in government bonds. Convergence appeared to be a safe bet. The early price gains of bonds in the PIIGS countries (Portugal, Italy, Ireland, Greece and Spain) in the convergence trade fuelled a false sense of security. This is a classic example of how the perceived reality of a benign credit environment led to an increased and self-fulfilling buying mechanism. We see the 'bath-tub' shaped curve, with peripheral government bond yields falling to near par with Germany's in the early 2000s, but then climbing again from 2009 onwards.

Robert Shiller has described these confidence multipliers as 'price-to-price feedback'. While prices rally, people begin to believe that the prices are giving them information that the PIIGS were performing and converging, justifying further purchases and price increases, creating a virtuous cycle – or rather, the illusion of a virtuous cycle that was just the upward slope of an investment bubble. The concept of convergence is consistent with a worldview that treats economic trends as continuous, with forecasts based on extrapolation.

This affects politicians too: a positive feedback loop occurs in which rising prices and lower yields in bonds can convince finance ministers in emerging markets that the fundamentals have improved, as Desmond Lachman observes. This was certainly the case with Greece – it was also the case with Argentina in the 1990s. Lachman adds that short-termism encourages this trend: 'The short-term horizon of today's emerging market money managers is to be explained in large measure by the footloose nature of mutual fund money, which means today's money managers are expected to show good performance on a month-by-month basis.'[5]

In the real world, however, such trends cannot go on indefinitely. At some point, boring concepts such as relative value and credit analysis with capacity and character to pay come back into the picture. For a decade however, the story was 'party on', allowing Greece to borrow a whopping €180 billion more from 2000 to 2010. On no reasonable analysis of the relatively small and semi-developed nature of the Greek tax base and productive economy could such sums be considered reasonable – as previous chapters illustrate. Yet credit default swaps were trading at +10 bps at one point in time in 2007. From 2004 to 2007, Greek bonds were essentially trading almost like German bunds. This compression of bond yields effectively mispriced the inherent risks, as investors, in their insatiable hunt for yield, believed they were getting a nice little pick-up in yield for free. It took a global credit crunch for investors to begin to focus their minds again.

One of the damaging beliefs behind this type of behaviour in the carry trade is the *ceteris paribus* fallacy – a shorthand, borrowed from the physical sciences, that simply means 'all other things remaining the same'. This helped bolster faith in the apparent stability of the eurozone. Unfortunately, in the real economic world, *ceteris paribus* does not exist. It can only exist in the situation where all human beings are dead. All other economic elements are *never* equal nor can *ever* be held constant.

All finance is behavioural. When you are sat in front of the screen, you feel fear and greed. My experience indicates that bad decisions tend to be made when emotions are running high. Another thing is that when people give you a story, different influences on decision making – analytical and emotional issues – appeal to your emotional side, and the prospect of making a lot of money contributes to greed.

You can argue that investors shouldn't follow each other into high-yield activity without full regard to the risk. The problem is that if all your competitors are doing this and realising short-term gains, you are not doing well in your customers' eyes; i.e. if I don't follow, I'm going to be underperforming *vis-à-vis* my competitors. Everyone has to follow the market – but doing so means taking on more and more risk.

Collusive Denial

It is important here to look at the behaviour and beliefs behind the damaging investment mistakes of the past ten years. The liquidity boom resulted in part from the policy of low interest rates; however, this policy in itself did not cause the extreme distortions of bubble economics. Cheap money does not force people to misjudge risk and ignore warnings. There are deeper, damaging beliefs at work. A prime example of how investment bubbles are encouraged in periods of high liquidity can be illustrated in the following comment from a respectable private bank:

> Dear Investors,
> Please find attached a list of investment grade bonds that might be of interest to you. With deposit rates nearly zero, and no sign that rates will hike in the short term, these bonds offer a good alternative to cash deposits. Also bid/ask spreads in the corporate fixed income space have tightened, meaning that trading out of the bond when cash is needed does not represent an opportunity cost anymore.

The list of bonds attached by this venerable private bank ranged from single A- to BBB-rated paper, with maturities from one year to ten years, some of them trading at +110 per cent of par. How these could be considered 'cash equivalent' is beyond me. Investors here were set up for future volatility and hence serious disappointments (the volatility of cash is zero). At the end of a cycle liquidity premiums, credit analysis and relative value are underestimated. There was the assumption that the liquidity bid was here to stay forever, thus propping up assets, and valuations had gotten ahead of themselves. Please note some of these 'cash equivalents' mentioned in the above list lost over 50 per cent of their value, and bid-offer spreads widened to over 10 percentage points. It seems like a lot of work to be able to make potentially 2 per cent to 4 per cent annually.

In bubble economies, smart money is in a very precarious position. It could either sit on the sidelines and focus on the continued deterioration of macroeconomic conditions, or it could join its peers and reluctantly buy. The conundrum arising from the investors who remained uninvested is that they may have suffered client withdrawals as they underperformed their peers on a short- and medium-term basis. This procyclical bias is why investors were accumulating risky assets, regardless of the macroeconomic fundamentals, and why, as Chuck Prince said, they 'continued to dance'.

Issuers took advantage of the situation by tapping into this liquidity and issuing endless amounts of new bonds. This created the illusion that the fundamentals were sound and that they capital markets were strong, and so the procyclical Ponzi scheme grew bigger and bigger during the mid-2000s.

These dynamics also fuel *herd behaviour* as investment patterns become fads, which then become bubbles, leading to more money following the wrong strategy, whether it be tulip bulbs, Louisiana land, dotcom shares, collatorised debt obligations – or eurozone bonds. Momentum investing leads to people 'following the ant in front of you'. Keynes witheringly described the fads of the financial markets as being like newspaper competitions in which the competitors have to pick the 6 prettiest faces from 100 photographs – the winners being those whose choice most nearly corresponds to the average of all selections. He added: 'when the capital development of a country becomes a by-product of the activities of a casino, the job is likely to be ill-done'.

The lure of 'high yield' – which is how 'high-risk' prospects are branded when it comes to selling the product – is a large part of the Greek and euro debt crisis story, just as it was with the subprime crisis and the Latin America debt crisis of the 1980s. Debt crises are caused as much by lenders as by borrowers. Investors get bored with low-risk, low-return products and modest bonuses, and the sell-side are aware of this, as much as any salesmen. There's a blatant contradiction between faith in rational human agents that forms the supposed ideological belief of investment bankers, and the appeal to irrationality in their marketing campaigns. Seductive marketing labels, such as 'subprime', 'Alt-A', 'high-yield' and 'emerging' markets are used to appeal to emotional centres, not analytical ones. So while investors may argue that they did not know the full extent of Greece's debt position until late 2009, this argument is lame. Concern over reliability of the data goes back to at least 2003 and there is no excuse for failing to exercise due diligence on the state of the productive economy, the extent of corruption and waste, or the deteriorating trading position *vis-à-vis* Germany.

Richard Koo of Nomura is correct to point out: 'These issues [structural problems in the Greek economy] have existed for decades. No wonder the Greek people are asking "Why now?" The overseas lenders, after all, were well aware of these problems when they lent the money... I think a major cause of the current crisis is that lenders neglected to perform due diligence.'[6]

He coins the phrase 'collusive denial' to describe the psychological twist that borrowers and lenders got themselves into. He adds: 'In recent US congressional hearings, Goldman Sachs was criticised for selling financial instruments containing home mortgages for which the lender had not verified the borrower's income. If Greece's structural problems were as bad as they have been made out to be, the Western European financial institutions that ignored these problems in a search for higher yields should surely bear a similar responsibility.

'In that sense, I think a kind of *collusive denial* existed between the borrower and the lenders. Lenders thought that Greece would continue to muddle through despite its many problems, and Greece assumed there would always be buyers for its debt even if it continued to run substantial fiscal deficits.'

Relativity, and Ketchup Pricing

Benchmarking is a symptom of a human psychological tendency to judge things in terms of relativity. We saw in chapters 1 and 5 how investors felt compelled by the orthodoxy of benchmarking – and the institutionalised buying patterns around the EMBI-Plus Index – to continue buying Argentine government debt well after the point at which a credit analysis would raise question marks over the ability of the Buenos Aires government to be able to pay back in full. The music was playing, and everyone was dancing.

Relativity can be seen as a Darwinian issue: that, as people we are still wired to judge ourselves in relation to our peers. We would rather earn $33,000 per year when our peers are earning $30,000, than earn $40,000 when our peers are earning $43,000. Clearly, this phenomenon goes some way to explaining the huge rise in investment bank bonuses in the 'go-go' years.

Economists and investors are easily tempted to look at relative values, and decline to ask searching questions about the fundamentals – a phenomenon clearly at play in the peripheral eurozone government bond market. For example, there is a tendency to look at bond prices relative to other bond prices, rather than capacity to repay; or to look at the price of a house compared to one around the corner, rather than the average take-home pay of the region. Larry Summers, who has held senior economics positions in the Clinton and Obama administrations, has referred to 'ketchup economists' as those who would note that a two-quart bottle of ketchup sold for twice the price of a one-quart bottle as evidence of a perfectly efficient market.

The Politicians' Short-Termism, and Disrespect for the Business Cycle

We have seen how Peronism and its counterparts in other countries, especially Greece, sees economics as a means of seizing cash and distributing favours. There are milder, sometimes almost subconscious, versions in all jurisdictions. When the music is playing an infectious beat, our elected representatives also start to tap their feet.

As well as deploying resources out of short-termist calculation, many politicians used favourable short-term indicators not only to shower favours, but to overstate their own influence. They sought to wish away economic instability through rhetoric. Most notoriously, the UK prime minister Gordon Brown declared 'no more boom and bust', as this hubristic leader from the land of King Canute decided he could outlaw the business cycle. In a similar manner, eurozone politicians lauded the single currency for its near magical powers in creating 'stability' and credited themselves with having caused low inflation, ignoring the contributory factors such as growing supplies of cheap Chinese goods.

Politicians during this period had a fear of recessions, and seemed to believe that all manner of lax monetary policies and deficit-created stimuli were justified. The irony, of course, is that this was just another type of boom that was running the risk of an even bigger bust. The low rates set in 2000–05 sowed the seeds for this crisis. The praise heaped upon the 'masters of the universe' in the investment banking world by many political leaders added to the collective complacency. Low rates and attempts to moderate volatility simply led to investors taking on more risk and more carry. It gave a false sense of security, given the official euphemism the 'Great Moderation'.

Bubbles get farthest out of line with reality when actively encouraged by policymakers. Alan Greenspan helped fuel the US housing boom in the mid-2000s. In late 2004 the Federal Reserve chairman had complacently observed that: 'While local economies may experience significant speculative price imbalances, a national severe price distortion seems most unlikely.'

A business or economic cycle is an inevitability, like the tides of the sea. Economic activity surges, and then falls back. The proper policy response, for investors and politicians, is to take out sensible countercyclical measures as a defence. The mistake is either to ignore or wish away the cycle (politicians), or to behave in a procyclical way (very common among investors) exacerbated by a short-term focus.

One reason, however, why myths such as the 'Great Moderation' and 'this time is different' and 'the end of boom and bust' become popularised is that the cycle can head further in one direction – and for longer – than a reasonable observer would expect.

Being able to understand business cycles, and also how they overshoot, especially when money is cheap, is not new. James Montier points out that John Stuart Mill's definition from 1867 has stood the test of time: 'Displacement → Credit creation → Euphoria → Critical stage/Financial distress → Revulsion.'

Montier provides a readable description on how even intelligent investors and companies hold on to their positions and deny the reality of an oncoming recession, even as the evidence builds up around them. 'Analysts lag reality. They only change their mind when there is irrefutable proof they were wrong, and then they only change their minds very slowly – a process known as "anchoring" and "slow adjustment."'[7] These anchoring effects were one of the main reasons why it took all the participants so long to come to terms with the Greek crisis.

Efficient Market Hypothesis, Hyperactivity, and Obsession with the Short Term

The beliefs of the past few decades have been that free markets set accurate prices and allocate capital efficiently. The irony has been that those most fervent in such beliefs have been responsible for misallocation of capital on a colossal scale: the dotcom boom, the accountancy scandals, the subprime mortgages and the subprime sovereign debt.

Belief in abstract forces that tend towards benign outcomes, such as 'convergence' or 'equilibrium', have replaced proper inquiry into the dynamics of real markets. In the real world, prices do not 'automatically' seek equilibrium. What we have in real markets is free human will, guided by individual intelligence in some cases, alarming stupidity in others, and also by complex individual and group psychological dynamics. Information is incomplete, and can never include the future.

The institutional focus on short-term indicators is closely linked to the intense pressure for a continual upwardly mobile story to relate, as measured by financial indicators. As well as a belief in a supposed natural tendency for markets to correct themselves and move towards convergence or equilibrium, there is also a desire for constant activity and constant upward motion. Market players are not allowed to analyse risk in depth, nor sit back and say 'times are tough, let's wait it out'. They need to feel they are doing something all the time. The resultant hyperactivity itself causes problems.

Warren Buffett has written of *herd behaviour* and *hyperactivity* as common causes of misallocation of capital and of executive time. His term 'institutional imperative' refers to the tendency to imitate the behaviour of others, to overestimate one's own influence and ability and to prefer action to calm, considered analysis.

Hyperactivity fits with the intensely short-term focus of the markets. Chief executives will relate in private that they have knowingly damaged a company's longer-term growth prospects through measures that make the next quarterly report look good. In a similar way, investors will take indicators showing strong recent growth as sufficient evidence in itself for capacity for future growth, as though the performance of a company or an economy can become an exercise in perpetual motion, with never any need for pause, nor investment in human capital and future capacity, nor adaptation to acknowledge physical barriers such as a saturated market or depleting natural resources.

Linked to hyperactivity is *overconfidence*; there is belief in convergence and equilibrium, and also that organisations and economies are auto-correcting and tending towards optimisation and peak performance. If there are risks ahead of a market downturn, often there is a tendency to assume: 'Just write positive monthly or quarterly profits and when the market turns we will be able to time our exit.'

Efficient market hypothesis as a concept grew in popularity during the 1970s and 1980s, even as events such as the oil price shock and the 1987 stock market crash strongly indicated non-linearity and unpredictability. These were not sufficient to dent faith in what Paul Krugman refers to as the 'beautiful idea' of perfectly priced markets based on complete information, which are automatically adjusting.[8] This was used to shape the model know as the Capital Asset Pricing Model, or CAPM, which assumes that investors rationally balance risk against reward, including financial derivatives.

Ridiculing the Whistleblowers

Every time that a cabal of economists and the people who listen to them create a 'new paradigm' in which 'this time is different', there is group pressure to ridicule the dissenting voices. This is *herd behaviour*. In 2005, at a conference held to honour the then chairman of the Federal Reserve, Alan Greenspan, Raghuram Rajan of the University of Chicago presented a paper warning that, under Greenspan's tenure, levels of debt and loose monetary policy were creating a dangerous level of risk. He was mocked 'by almost all present', according to Paul Krugman.[9]

In a similar vein, Nouriel Roubini, who has consistently made correct calls on the eurozone crisis, has been dubbed 'Doctor Doom'. Indeed, all the critics of eurozone imbalances and sovereign debt crisis were dismissed, as I shall discuss in further detail in the next chapter. Rounding on the dissenting voice is a classic symptom of *herd behaviour*. James Montier summarises the key features of *groupthink*:

- An illusion of invulnerability
- Collective rationalisation: discounting the warnings and not reevaluating assumptions
- Belief in inherent morality
- Stereotyped views of out-groups
- Direct pressure on dissenters: members under pressure not to voice any critical viewpoints
- Self-censorship
- Illusion of unanimity
- Appointment of 'mind guards': members protect the group from information that is contradictory to shared beliefs.[10]

Of course, this has affected the EU's leaders every bit as much as the investment community, as I shall discuss further in the next chapter.

Wrong Signals

Investors look for the continuous happy story on headline growth – whether it is of GDP or profits, often without exploring its dynamics or sustainability. As discussed in previous chapters, a good GDP growth story can be borrowed on the international capital markets.

As the Buttonwood blog in the *Economist* noted in June 2010: [The] speculators' guilt lies more in the bubbles than their bursting.' The cycle has been repeated numerous times. The blog added:

> In the early 1990s belief in the Asian growth story caused capital to flow into the region. Money was diverted into speculative investments, particularly property. Without the boom, there would have been no need for a bust. Similarly, the same speculators whom European politicians are now excoriating are the ones who played the 'convergence trade' in the 1990s. They bought the bonds of peripheral European governments in the hope that their yields would converge with those of Germany. The trade worked. Speculators made money, governments benefited from lower borrowing costs and nobody complained.[11]

The codependence of short-termist investors and short-termist governments is a seriously destabilising relationship. When we see them erupt with rage at each other, we see something akin to self-loathing.

Stability: Elusive, Illusive

While the investment community searches for convergence, continual profits and growth, central bankers look for order of a different kind: stability. Both share a tendency towards *overconfidence bias* – to believe in the good story, and towards *illusion of control* – assuming that *they* have attained this harmonious state of affairs, and not inquiring too deeply into underlying risks; their belief being that 'it will be so if we say it is so'.

Otmar Issing, founder member of the European Central Bank, states: 'Not knowing whether prices will remain stable in the future causes uncertainty.'[12] This, a typical central banker statement, is intended as an illustration of cause and effect, but it is in fact a tautology.

The policy of 'stable prices' beloved of central bankers stems from the belief that the economy is a simple system with known parameters. In reality, it is a complex system determined by human behaviour, with frequent irruptions from 'unknown unknowns'. If you fix prices or exchange rates, then the very act of doing so is likely to cause relationships to become seriously unfixed in another part of the system. Affecting one part affects it all. Fixing exchange rates and interest rates may work in economic areas where the patterns of production, distribution, purchasing and income levels are similar (states of the USA; the Benelux nations plus the German-speaking countries of Europe), but it is highly unlikely to work when fixing exchange rates across highly dissimilar economic regions (pegging Argentina to the USA; Mediterranean countries to countries in northern Europe).

Endogenous, Exogenous

When economists using the English language want to sound serious and academic, they use Latin or Greek terms. The custom, borrowed from law (which prefers Latin) and the physical sciences (where the preference is for Greek), is often to give an air of seriousness even when, or perhaps especially when, the underlying thinking is flaky. *Ceteris paribus* is Latin for 'all things the same', which you can have in a laboratory, but not in society, so its use is not applicable to economics. Another pair of phrases, Greek in origin, are 'endogenous' and 'exogenous'. These have been extremely popular in recent decades. They may be no more valid than the theoretical and quite useless concept of *ceteris paribus*.

'Endogenous' refers to matters that are 'internal' – factors that relate directly to the economic unit being governed. So, endogenous factors to the Greek economy might include wage levels, public spending and so on within the country. Exogenous factors include oil prices or the foreign policy of Turkey.

The problem with giving the two terms equal billing is that it disguises the fact that 'exogenous' factors can be of a scale several thousand times bigger than endogenous ones, and several thousand times bigger than anything experienced before. Creating this artificial separation also disguises the fact that everything is interconnected. It is a similar way of thinking to basing theories of probability on games of chance. In games, there are no 'unknown unknowns'. In economics, a previously unknown unknown can suddenly come to dominate the environment. In a game, while there may be improbable outcomes, no one will come along unexpectedly and completely change the rules and the context. Unfortunately, we seem to be wired as a species to favour the inside over the outside view; because we are more familiar with what we know, we underestimate the likely impact of what we don't know. Giving equal or greater attention to 'endogenous' elements leads to *illusion of control* and the phenomenon of 'tunnelling' – focusing disproportionately on what you know, and not being prepared sufficiently for unexpected events.[13]

The Washington Consensus

In the 1990s, Argentina was held up as a model of free-market reform, in line with the principles of the Washington Consensus, which has held intellectual sway over the IMF, World Bank and most investment banks for the past couple of decades. Its key elements are:

- *Deregulation*: it is held that regulations that impede market entry or restrict competition should be minimised, with exceptions only on grounds of safety, environmental and consumer protection, and for the overview of financial institutions.
- *Liberalisation* of the capital account of the balance of payments is another key tenet. This ensures people can invest funds overseas, and allows funds from overseas to be invested in the home country.
- *Free Trade*: lifting of tariffs, quotas and so on for imports and exports encourages competition and long-term growth.
- *Fiscal responsibility*: governments should not run large deficits that have to be paid back by future generations. Deficits tend to cause higher inflation and lower productivity. Deficits should only be used for occasional stabilisation purposes.[14]

While some concerns were raised about Argentina's public sector deficit towards the end of the decade, it was held to have made impressive strides towards this orthodoxy. The Consensus indicated that Argentina ought to have been one of the more successful emerging economies. As chronicled in chapters 1 and 5, it hit crisis, both on the supply-side and in terms of public finances.

Does this mean that the Consensus, and even the concepts of free trade and free movement of capital are mistaken? It is probably more the case that they are inadequate – helpful in the right context, dangerous in others. Belief in *ceteris paribus* leads many thinkers to overlook context.

In Greece, all the wrong things were deregulated, and all the wrong things regulated. We had a kleptocratic state and a culture of lawlessness that meant that billions of euros of easily borrowed capital were squandered. We also had a sclerotic supply-side, held back by closed shops, overregulation and the cronyism and corruption of an oligarchical business structure. In this context, exposure to international capital markets was a disaster. But this doesn't make the free market a bad idea! It just means that it is a powerful tool that must be handled with care. In the case of Greece, it was like handing over an aircraft carrier to a person without naval or airforce training. Free trade and access to global markets can only be safely introduced by a state that upholds the law, clamps down on corruption, invests in human capital and supports the development of specialist business clusters, while maintaining fiscal prudence.

The other factor common to Argentina and Greece was an overvalued exchange rate. As chronicled in chapters 1 and 5, this had a negative effect on the supply-side, to the extent that companies from Brazil, which devalued the real, and Turkey, which has a floating currency, are in the process of overtaking their rivals.

Even the commonsense principles on fiscal responsibility become a burden for an overvalued currency once a downward spiral has set in. The IMF/European Union efforts to try to get Greece (and earlier, Argentina) to reduce its budget are creating a debt spiral and increasing the percentage of tax extracted from a smaller and smaller economy. There is no easy way out of that spiral.

Policymakers need to make qualitative judgements to replace their overreliance on quantitative data and checklists. They should look at patterns of trade, investment in human capital, probity, honouring of contracts and so on. Does the supply-side resemble Sweden, or Greece? What is the level of corruption? In Greece extreme misallocations of precious (borrowed) public funds resulted from favours being returned to businesses, such as Siemens and their Greek introducers.

There is increasing evidence that highly advanced business clusters have multiple beneficial effects on the local economy. If there is a Google or a BMW in the province, not only does this create jobs directly by producing goods that the world wants to buy, but the high level of skills generated mean that former apprentices and alumni tend to set up profitable start-ups; also, suppliers have to meet exacting standards, creating world-class businesses that can supply other commercial clients, and so on. There is not only the impact of the Google or BMW business, but also that of the wider Google and BMW diaspora.

This type of analysis needs to be incorporated into macroeconomic planning, which has a tendency to focus on fiscal and monetary policy more than trade and business, as though the tiller were more important than the engine.

Just as the Greek public sector became an uncontrolled, all-consuming hydra, so did the global financial system. In the words of Simon Johnson of the Peterson Institute for International Economics, speaking January 2009:

> A supersised financial system – the obesity of banks and shadow banks – helped create the vulnerabilities that made the September [2008] crisis possible. This financial system captured its regulators and took on far more risk than it could manage (or even understand). And this is a statement not just about US banks, but also about most parts of the global financial system. The answer lies with the political economy of the US financial system, including the power politics of large financial firms. These grew large relative to the institutions that support and constrain them. In effect, we created an emerging-market type of structure.[15]

It is likely that a problem stemming from a simplistic syllogism arose in the years following the collapse of the Berlin Wall. Throughout much of the twentieth century the West was fighting an ideological war against Communism and other proponents of the planned economy. The 'free market' – in reality, a mixed economy – was clearly vastly superior to the socialist economies, but this became hardened into a simplistic mantra that all economies resembling the free market must become equally strong; also that there was a simple, linear relationship between the degree of liberalisation and the degree of wealth creation. The reality is far more complex.

Worse, in the early 2000s finance became a monstrous hydra in its own right, fomenting myriad Ponzi schemes and other bubbles as herd-like investors chased short-term or illusory returns. Finance became large relative to GDP, and credit grew rapidly in the boom. Small states such as Greece overborrowed; others such as Iceland and Ireland were exposed to similar liabilities through the activities of their banks. By 2010, the head of Ireland's central bank, Patrick Honohan, declared: 'From 2003 to 2007, the Irish banking system imported funds equivalent to over 50 per cent of GDP to fund a runaway property and construction bubble.'[16] The authorities have begun to take action against the most high-profile culprit, Sean Fitzpatrick, the former chairman of Anglo Irish Bank, who took out large, personal, secret loans from the bank and is now bankrupt. In September 2010, testifying before the finance committee of the Dáil

(Irish Parliament) the finance minister Brian Lenihan refused to rule out a haircut for holders of Anglo Irish Bank's €2.4 billion subordinated debt. At the same time, an Irish official told a British newspaper that the government was beginning to 'explore the appropriate burden-sharing arrangements'. Anglo Irish may ultimately cost Irish taxpayers as much as €25 billion[17] – a vast sum for a relatively small economy. As with other jurisdictions, there were very close relationships between Sean Fitzpatrick, other senior bankers and the political elite.

The irony here is that, by the 2000s, the 'free market' system has become so highly dysfunctional that it is more like an emerging market. The largest institutions operate like rent-seeking oligarchs, buying up the influence of governments, relying on the tacit promise of bail-outs and prolonging their rent-seeking opportunities. Profits at the banks are fed by a large and increasing volume of transactions founded on a relatively small base of physical assets – an inherently unstable dynamic.

Economist Simon Johnson is experienced in dealing with the tightly bound elites of politicians and oligarchs in emerging markets, and now recognises that pattern in the West, including the USA, noting 'just as we have the world's most advanced economy, military and technology, we also have its most advanced oligarchy'. Banking bail-outs have become progressively more favourable to the banks themselves as the 'rescue' has continued, while political lobbying has seen the following legislative changes:

• Insistence on free movement of capital across borders
• Repeal of Depression-era regulations separating commercial and investment banking
• Congressional ban on the regulation of credit default swaps
• Major increases in leverage allowed by investment banks
• A light hand at the Securities and Exchange Commission in regulatory enforcement.
• Intentional failure to update regulations to keep pace with financial innovation.[18]

Accompanying this lobbying activity and the globalisation of finance, the Washington Consensus, originally intended as no more than a minimum policy framework for the Americas established by the US government, World Bank and IMF in 1989, seems to have assumed the status of a comprehensive ideology that is both necessary and sufficient for economic success. It does little more than emphasise fiscal responsibility, privatisation, trade liberalisation, property rights and tax reform, and its more honest proponents stress its limitations.[19]

This understanding is long established, but not widely disseminated. Joseph Stiglitz in 1998 warned that the emphasis in the Washington Consensus on trade liberalisation, deregulation and privatisation did not ensure competition, which additionally requires regulation, auditing and transparency. The warning was prophetic: the banks could not police themselves, and should not have been allowed to. For too many policymakers, the Washington Consensus became almost the sole guide to policy, backed by reliance on a handful of numeric indicators, such as money supply, inflation, budget and trade deficits. In some cases 'economists would fly into a country, look at and attempt to verify these data, and make macro-economic recommendations for policy reforms all in the space of a couple of weeks.' He pointed to some fairly obvious omissions concerning the supply-side, such as education and technology development, and that the reforms did not always support one another, making trade-offs necessary.[20]

An overview of the Washington Consensus by Nancy Birdsall of the Center for Global Development, with Augusto de la Torre and Felipe Valencia Caicedo of the World Bank, has also highlighted the danger of premature financial liberalisation prior to effective regulation. It identifies three areas of weakness in applying the principles of the Consensus: failure to implement all the reforms fully; errors in the manner of implementation, such as sequencing problems; and, as Stiglitz noted, an absence of crucial elements for economic development, such as research and education.[21]

Capital inflow 'bonanzas' can be more of a curse than a blessing, especially for emerging economies according to Carmen and Vincent Reinhart following their study of such phenomena in both advanced and emerging countries, which covered 181 nations over the period 1980–2007 plus a subset of 66 countries in the period 1960–2007. Such inflows are associated with a higher likelihood of debt default and banking, inflation and currency crashes. In particular, they note how, when a heavy inflow persists, this can lull policymakers into believing that a temporary phenomenon has become permanent. Developing nations are particularly prone to procyclical fiscal policies during this period, accentuating the destabilising effects of the inflows, which tend to be punctuated by a sudden stop.[22] One could add that, in the case of Greece (and other periphery countries), the problem was exacerbated because EU officials refused to acknowledge that the country had developing-market features. Paul Volcker has warned that, where global capital flows are unimpeded and large in scale, there is a perverse disincentive for emerging economies to pursue good policies, because they will attract dangerous amounts of inflow! The capital they attract is seen as an endorsement of the fact that the policies are good, so the country attracts yet more capital, creating an investment bubble.[23] Recent policies of quantitative easing, and protests from some emerging economies, indicate that this lesson has not been thoroughly learned. Capital inflows are increasingly viewed as a destabilising influence in developing economies.[24]

Some investment banks have cleverly used the language of the Washington Consensus while undermining some of its principles to secure political favours, up to and including state bail-outs. It has naively been assumed that unrestricted global flows of capital automatically lead to competitive markets and sound use of capital. This has not been the experience in practice. The volume of capital deployed has been huge, relative to the productive capacity and taxpayer bases, and debt levels have risen sufficiently to overwhelm some smaller economies, especially Iceland, Ireland and Greece. The volume of capital was simply too much for small economies to absorb. This has led to the current dangerous situation, especially as the era of infinite and cheap capital has ended, meaning that financing deficits will become more expensive, and the temptations for financial protectionism greater.[25]

Chapter 9

THE ENTERTAINERS

There are two kinds of forecasters: those who don't know, and those who don't know that they don't know.

—J. K. Galbraith

Around 2008 the satirical Alex cartoon in the business section of the British paper the *Daily Telegraph* ran with the following dialogue:

'People keep asking me how long the recession is going to last. What shall I say?'
'Tell them 18 months.'
'Why 18 months?'
'It's not so far off that they will despair, but it's long enough for them to forget that you made the prediction.'

To a large extent, economic forecasts are made for emotional reasons, rather than technocratic ones. Predictions are typically made without much knowledge of the complexity of the *existing* web of economic interrelationships, never mind future patterns.

Given the fondness of professional economists for predictions, one would imagine that there is a wealth of evidence showing the merit of predictions; perhaps a league table showing which economists are more reliable than others at anticipating future prices or other events. Such studies as exist are not supportive. Economists are no better, it would seem, than journalists at anticipating future events, but neither are very accurate – both are less precise than weather forecasters. Those with PhDs and/or seven-figure salaries are no better than students.[1]

The common quip is that the economist is the type of expert who can explain tomorrow why the thing he predicted yesterday did not happen today. The get-out clause when asked for an explanation is that unexpected events changed the rules of the game. But there is a blatant contradiction here, and intellectual sloppiness: models and predictions are taken to be valid on the tacit assumption that there will be no black swans. Yet the excuse when they go wrong is that there was a black swan!

Credit Rating Agencies: Backward or Forward Looking?

Credit ratings are an area where concepts of past and future become horribly mixed up. They can only be based on historic data, because time travel remains beyond the scope of human beings. Yet they exist to provide a yardstick on the likelihood of a debtor making good their repayments in the future, based on information available today. The credit ratings agencies, like all other forecasters, have no way of knowing what the future holds. Ratings agencies have risen in significance, and investors have dumbed down, basing a lot of their decisions on relative ratings.

Rating agencies receive a lot of bad press. They are in a *nasty* business or, if you like, the 'short put' business similar to private banking and security firms. If they do their job correctly they receive no special pats on the back, because they are just doing their job. Any 'surprise' will be by definition negative for them and they will be drawn into an endless round of criticism.

The errors attract more headlines, of course. In my career, the ones I remember fondly are the Parmalat debacle, Enron, subprime, Lehman Brothers and Greece – all of which were a complete miss.

According to the US Financial Crisis Inquiry Commission, just one of the big three, Moody's, rated some $4,700 billion of residential mortgage-backed securities between 2000 and 2007, and $736 billion of CDOs. Phil Angelides, chairman of the FCIC, told hearings in June 2010 that Moody's was a 'triple A factory'. He added: 'Investors who relied on Moody's ratings did not fare so well.' Following the subprime crisis, the Securities and Exchange Commission has issued new rules requiring much greater transparency on the ratings process, via rule 17g-5. The European Commission issued similar rules.[2]

In July 2010, China-based Dagong Global Credit Rating stripped the USA, UK and France of their AAA rating, giving higher ratings to China, Germany, the Netherlands and Canada. It gave stronger weighting to wealth-creating capacity, rather than any historical record of stability of law and government institutions.

This indicates, as agencies admit, that ratings are more of an art than a science. In the short term, in Europe, the ratings were correct, in that Greece did not default. But you can be right for the wrong reason.

In defence of the ratings agencies, Parmalat and Enron were cases of fraud, but this begs the question: should the information that investors, agencies and others rely upon be exclusively financial? In earlier chapters, I have described how the crude data required for compliance with the Maastricht criteria for inclusion in the single currency hid a realm of serious risk issues that lay below the surface. Like Enron's financial accounts, data can be seriously misleading.

So there are two problems: a tendency to forget that ratings agencies cannot see into the *future*; and a disinclination to dig for the real story behind the figures that are published *today*. There is a need both for a more three-dimensional picture, and for more modesty, or caution. In an outspoken attack in May 2010, Bill Gross, managing director of Pimco, the bond house, accused ratings agencies of 'blind faith' in sovereign solvency: 'Their quantitative models appeared to have a Mensa-like IQ of at least 160, but their commonsense rating was close to 60, resembling an idiot savant with a full command of the mathematics, but no idea of how to apply them.'[3]

They used historical assumptions that were based on a very different regime. They fell for the seduction of *past extrapolation, problem of induction, overconfidence* and *no margin of error*, or *no ranges* – the amount of subsequent downgrades was just astonishing. Unfortunately for them nobody remembers the thousands of correct and accurate ratings they produced (over the short term) – such is the nature of their 'thankless' job.

In the subprime crisis, the agencies were one of the main culprits of the debacle, in that they gave ratings to bonds they could not accurately rate. The degree of collatoralisation made the products so opaque that the actual risk in the underlying assets was invisible.

When this unravelled, and Greece was no longer able to borrow from the markets in May 2010, a successor entity emerged: the European Financial Stability Facility (EFSF), set up to provide €440 billion of liquidity to help indebted EU countries through the crisis; the so-called 'bail-out', which in reality is simply more borrowing. The EFSF possesses many of the same features as previous eurozone entities and collatoralised mortgages. It is a special purpose vehicle, backed by individual guarantees provided by participating countries, which are the single currency users – the 'out' countries negotiated to remain outside of the arrangement at the weekend conference on 9 May 2010 where arrangements were finalised. The countries will be expected to contribute to the fund, and to create a 20 per cent 'cushion' on top. But the essential problems remain: will the markets lend to this entity at low yields? Will the ratings agencies give it an investment grading? In September 2010, the ECB duly received its desired AAA rating for the EFSF, which it was reversely-engineered to achieve, and hence investors will be encouraged to pile in. Despite this, it will be expensive for individual nations to borrow from; the main purpose of the EFSF is political, rather than economic: it has been created to buy time.

A common criticism of ratings agencies is that they are subject to potential conflicts of interest. They get paid by the issuers they rate, similar to auditors who get remunerated by the firms they audit. There is at least the suspicion of a subconscious desire to avoid issuing a rating that would harm the business prospects of a major customer. Also, ratings agencies themselves belong to corporations that have the goal of maximising shareholder value. There is a generalised potential conflict here: give too many low ratings and there won't be enough business. Also, they constantly look for growth opportunities, such as 'unsponsored' ratings, where companies who do not pay or request for the rating nonetheless receive one, with some sort of unspoken threat involved.

The ratings issued by the lead agencies – Moody's, Fitch, Standard & Poor's – are institutionalised. They are accepted as the regulatory standard, and numerous laws, banking regulations, capital requirements and pensions fund guidelines are formed around them. In the US the SEC calls them 'Nationally Recognized Statistical Rating Organizations'. In effect this stamp of approval is international, hence they play an institutionally ingrained role. The ECB and the European Commission have published proposals for reform.[4]

The agencies believe they are adding value – and indeed in most cases they are correct. A double-AA bond defaults less often than a single B. However, when they are wrong, the hidden sharp binary drop of the bond prices creates a huge amount of distress. If a bond that is rated BBB trading in the 90s drops to sub-investment grade (euphemistically called 'high yield' by dealers when they trying to sell it, or if you have already established a short position called 'junk') this results in forced sellers, because of the institutionalised way in which ratings are written into guidelines, as described above. These sellers are legally *not allowed* to hold sub-investment grade bonds, hence the rapid and sudden drop in bond prices. What happens when a bond is suddenly downgraded ten notches? Numerous collateral pools, repos and other levered instruments built on the previous 'solid' rating are affected, creating a downward spiral. Due to the 'short put' characteristics of debt and credit, multiple, overnight downgrades are numerous, while upgrades are slower, usually a couple of notches at a time. I cannot actually remember any bond that has been upgraded as aggressively as many downgrades (although this is most definitely my *recency bias* at play). Hence, fairly or unfairly, they get a lot of bad press. The way in which the ratings are 'wired in' to the system exacerbates instability.

Triple-A should indicate not just low probability for a default, but low probability of downgrading as well.

Other issues arise. They do sometimes promote a form of laziness, and they allow for distortions as many regulators and investors effectively just hand over the investment decision-making process to them. This outsourcing behaviour can create huge problems, especially when coupled with rating agencies' 'I can predict the future' attitude, in combination with other market malaises such as benchmarking and league tables.

Look at the example of the marketing material below. You can see higher returns, for similar maturity, on the same ratings. This is an example of selling on the basis of relative prices rather than fundamentals, and outsourcing the risk assessment to the ratings agencies, based on the headline rating. Simply put, if a LUKOIL bond rated BBB- is trading at 5.29 per cent yield and a TNK–BP bond with the same maturity and same rating is bought at 6.5 per cent, it must be cheap. The questions that immediately arise are: is the market correct in its assessment of LUKOIL yield for the inherent risks? Are the rating agencies assessing both companies correctly? Do the investment banks sell deals with 'relatively cheap' arguments? The answer to the final question is scarily, 'yes'.

Another issue with rating agencies is that they are not supposed to time market volatility. Yet they are criticised dramatically for falling

Table 9.1 BP TNK – Eurobond New Issue Terms

Issuer	TNK–BP Finance S.A.
Guarantor	TNK–BP International Limited
Proceeds	to fund a loan to TNK–BP Russia
Ratings	Baa2 / BBB− / BBB−
Size	Up to US$ 1 billion
Maturities	5-year and/or 10-year
Tranches	5-year
	10-year
Yield guidance	6.50% area
	7.50% area

Table 9.2 Benchmark Comparable Bonds (Offer Yields)

			(%)
LUKoil	Baa2/BBB−/BBB−	11/2014	5.29
LUKoil	Baa2/BBB−/BBB−	11/2019	6.92
Gazprom	Baa1/BBB+/BBB+	7/2014	5.81
Gazprom	Baa1/BBB+/BBB+	4/2018	6.86

behind the curve or, in case of sovereigns, unjustifiably downgrading them. They rate over the course of the cycle, and hence are slower moving than market prices. This is how they are designed to be, yet they get a lot of criticism for this.

There was a huge and constant debate about what would happen if Greece got downgraded and fell out of the ECB's collateral eligibility requirement. As the ECB stated: 'At least one credit assessment from an accepted external credit assessment institution for the issue (or, in its absence, for the issuer) must comply with the Eurosystem's credit quality threshold.'

Questions were asked when S&P downgraded Greece and Portugal together in April 2010. The euro politicians went wild with conspiracy theories. On 29 April, one day after the S&P downgrade, Wolfgang Schäuble, German finance minister, said: 'No market participant is prevented from not taking rating agencies too seriously.' Guido Westerwelle, Germany's foreign minister, called for an 'independent' European rating agency, which could avoid the conflicts of interest that he claimed US-based agencies faced. These calls would have had more conviction if prominent European leaders had questioned the investment-grade ratings given to Mediterranean countries in earlier years, which had facilitated the decade-long borrowing boom. The behaviour of EU politicians and credit agencies alike was irresponsible and procyclical.

While there are many examples where, with the weapon of hindsight, we can show how ratings agencies got it wrong, we shall only include one, which I find humorous. The following quote is from the Moody's paper 'Spain Portugal Greece Contagion or Confusion', published on 10 February 2010:

It is worth remembering that there is, as yet, no hard evidence that any euro area government faces an imminent risk of losing market access. The five-year bond issued by Greece in late January was substantially over-subscribed, and the country's debt agency ended up issuing €8 billion instead of the planned €3–€5 billion, albeit at the cost of a large widening of yield spreads relative to other European sovereign issuers. Therefore, speculation that Greece, or any other government, might not be able to roll over existing debt falling due in the spring has so far been based on perception rather than fact.

Even so, in the event that a critical mass of investors starts *believing* (their emphasis) that a government's liquidity is impaired, this could become a self-fulfilling prophesy. Moreover, if enough investors believed that a government's debt is on an unsustainable path, it is unlikely that they would be willing to purchase bonds except at a very high price (which could itself put the debt on an unsustainable path). In such a situation, a credible alternative source of liquidity would allow a country to fend off financing and ultimately potential payment difficulties, until it regains the trust of commercial markets.

No, it wasn't 'imminent'. It took a whole 76 days – from 10 February to 27 April, when Greece's government bonds were downgraded to junk, rendering borrowing on the open markets effectively impossible.

Noting that the bond issue was oversubscribed shows the authors did not understand the way in which the bond market functions: for example the actions of 'flippers' – those who purchase with the intention of selling again quickly; or the overinflating of orders to achieve better allocations. This is a bias of looking simply at one number, and not the underlying fundamentals of the quality of the order book and the 'hotness' of the issue.

Howard Marks of Oaktree Capital Management refers to the reliance on ratings, noting: 'Some require ratings before taking actions they're considering. But ratings must be taken with a big grain of salt… They routinely rate securities too high when things are going well and then overcorrect… My advice: expect CEOs, regulators, ratings agencies and other market participants to make mistakes.'[5]

Investors frequently believe that any investment is better than cash. Because it's the lowest risk, it's assumed to have the lowest prospective return. This overconfidence and bias towards activity has been a significant force in the eurozone crisis.

So much has been written about the recent record of ratings agencies and their role in the subprime debacle that I cannot add more to the historical record. What I can add is that an astonishing degree of complacency has reasserted itself just a couple of years down the line, and that the markets have returned to understating similar levels of risk.

Investment Banks

Investment banks are often demonised for their role in the dotcom stocks hypes and the subprime crisis, dodgy derivative deals, credit default swap (CDS) trading and so on. Allegations of conflicts of interests abound. They provide services for both sides of the capital flow, for investors and issuers. On the one hand they offer research and market-making services for investors, and on the other advice, deal structuring and capital-raising services for issuers. They also trade on their own account, obviously impartially guarding the interests of their clients at all times.

In 2010 Greece had to issue a significant amount of debt. Let us see which investment banks were the international lead managers for these deals:

- 26 January: €8 billion, 5-year bond: Credit Suisse, Deutsche Bank, Goldman Sachs, Morgan Stanley.
- 4 March: €5 billion, 10-year bond: HSBC and Barclays Capital.
- 29 March: €5 billion, 7-year bond: Société Générale, ING Bank, Bank of America Merrill Lynch.

EU politicians were not the only ones to display excessive confidence in their declarations of the indestructibility of the euro (see chapters 6 and 8). The IMF declared in 2007 that: 'Greece has no spillover potential' as it chronicled the success of the eurozone.

Let's see how investment banks, and the professional entertainers that they employ, fared in their predictions and spotting the Greek crisis.

HSBC

Greece is No Iceland or Dubai, 27 November 2009

Extend at the front-end of the Greek curve Greek government yields already implied the loss of investment grade status, effectively trading three notches below the current rating level

(A1/A-), an outcome that could be avoided if the necessary measures are taken now.

Investors may be skeptical that anything will change but the new government must act to head off the risk of sanctions being imposed in 2010. As another reference for the attractive valuation of Greek debt, the 5-year CDS is very close to the same level as Turkey which does not reflect the ratings differential or Greece's EMU status.

Why should Greece trade tighter to Turkey – just because rating agencies said so? Or because Greece is in the EMU? Faulty and narrow logic is being applied. Here we see evidence of overreliance on ratings and the concept of relative prices and so-called 'ketchup economics'. There is also bias in the tacit belief in a security effect of membership of the EMU – something that has never been defined or explained. It's interesting to observe, again and again, investment banks ignoring credit fundamentals, and using one argument – euro membership – for supporting their credit thesis.

It continues:

> It is not in the eurozone's interest to make an example out of Greece, by applying sanctions and ultimately imposing fines on the Republic for failing to comply. This could result in difficult placement of future bond issues and then ultimately, although HSBC believes this is extremely unlikely to happen, the humiliation of going to the IMF… The big difference between Greece and Iceland or Dubai is its membership of the single currency.

That was published just six months before IMF help was called for. Interestingly, HSBC was one of the two lead managers for Greece's €5 billion, ten-year bond in January 2010. I wonder if they were worried about placing the bonds?

Greece Equities 2010 Strategy Report, 18 January 2010

The global macroeconomic crisis has focused attention on Greece's macro fault lines, notably a triple deficit: fiscal (unsustainable budgetary calculus), external (competitiveness erosion) and credibility (poor fiscal track record and statistics quality). We argue, though, that not all is dark: Greece's economic imbalances are

not unprecedented. However, although providing a shield against
headwinds, EMU membership also eliminates easy ways out:
budgetary discipline and structural reforms are urgently needed. We
adopt a 'constructive' near-term base case, implying some progress
in fiscal adjustment but at the expense of a weak growth recovery.

Not sure exactly what all the above was about or how it can be construed
as 'constructive', but nevertheless, let's delve in deeper.

Maybe year-end de-risking and negative press has placed
additional pressure on GGBs [Greek government bonds].
Tellingly, according to HSBC calculations, 10Y bond spreads
have widened by much more than warranted by their current
average (of the three agencies) rating. Greek CDS trade higher
than those of countries that do not benefit from the protection
against external payment crises afforded by Greece's membership
in the eurozone (Hungary, Turkey).

Love of rating agencies, and blind belief in the protection of EU, are
apparent here again.

The Greek economy is crucially shielded by economic/funding
headwinds through eurozone membership.

Why? How can we confidently jump to the conclusion that once we
are in the EMU economic and funding headwinds disappear? What
exactly is the EU 'shield', and how does it protect? This narrative fallacy
that was prevalent in Greek public opinion seems to have permeated
through the investment spectrum.

Moody's considers the risk that the sovereign debt of a member
state becomes ineligible for ECB repo operations to be very
remote. Notably, Greece has the best debt profile of any EMU
member, with the highest average maturity (7.8 years) and the need
to rollover just ten per cent of its total debt in 2010 (compared to
c. 25 per cent for Ireland and Spain).

Narrow logic and *numeracy bias* are evident here: there is a highly selective
use of data with key information – i.e. the sheer quantum of external
debt for a small economy – missing from the analysis.

In any case we all know you cannot take equity analysts seriously. What about the fixed-income analysts? Surely they were closer to the mark? We will see below.

Société Générale

Fixed-Income Special: Outlook for Greece in 2010, 8 December 2009

On the first page they kindly offered us a summary of the key points, conveniently with bigger fonts.

Key points:

*** This current bout of nervousness around GGBs will not go far, unless the credit world were ever to join the sell-off. It does make sense to make space for fresh GGB issuance in early 2010. However in the overall context of stable and low rates, markets will still remain in risk-loving mode.

Unlucky folks, nervousness indeed did increase, and the market did go into extreme risk-aversion mode. Sorry, the *ceteris paribus* argument did not hold and the tail wagged the dog here. It got worse:

*** Much silly talk on Greece. Of course anything is possible. Pigs can fly and Armageddon could be for tomorrow. Just silly talk.

There is overconfidence here, as well as skillful use of *ad absurdem* – where a philosopher uses exaggeration to set the context for an explanation that is inadequate or oversimplified. The oversimplification seeks to rule out any lateral thinking or scenario planning.

*** In line with our guarded support for carry trades in early 2010, **we see potential for tightening of spreads between GGBs and some other sovereigns in H1 2010**.

As we know, spreads had widened by over +1,000 bps by May 2010, from approximately +200 bps when this was written.

*** Our 2010 *Outlook* does foresee extremely serious challenges facing the weaker sovereigns. But this is prefixed on a lame recovery over the next year. It is a story for beyond 2010, when sovereigns could be in an even weaker position to resist what shocks may come their way by then.

There is a good point here regarding the sovereigns, but sorry to say some overconfidence in the prediction. By the way, in all of the above the bold is Société Générale's emphasis.

By 21 December 2009 Greek bonds had widened slightly more, and Socgen, with the *status quo bias* of their 8 December report in full play, produced another strongly opinionated piece:

Multi-Asset Snapshot: Greece Heavily Oversold. Start Positioning for a Sharp Rally, 21 December 2009

Greek spreads too high. Short-dated Greek bonds are pricing in forward spreads over Bunds way in excess of even BBB.

Two interesting points on this: (1) They assume rating agencies are accurate, and (2) they seem to know with such certainty what an 'excess' is. It continues: 'We are afraid for the stability of the eurozone sovereigns, but for 2013 and beyond...' – a clever trick features here, with *cognitive dissonance* in evidence: by acknowledging a real and identified risk but then pushing it out into the future, you can effectively ignore it. This is similar to saying: 'I know smoking is bad for me, but only in the future and by then I will have time to change my habits and deal with the problems.'

No funding problems. The debt of the Hellenic Republic has the highest maturity of any eurozone member. So Greece should have no problem funding itself over the coming year and probably at much lower yields than today.

This is an example of *numeracy bias* with respect to the highest maturity. There is also extreme narrowness to the judgment – taking into account only one factor. Robert Cialdini called this the 'Single-piece-of-good-evidence' approach.[6] Using the analytical brain is time consuming and uses huge amounts of effort. In today's rapidly changing, multitasking and information overload era, the brain often opts for using automatic shortcut decision-making techniques in choosing one single piece of information to make a decision. Analysts and investors, by stating one piece of information – Greece is in the EMU, or Greece is trading wider to what the ratings suggest – are examples of the investment community succumbing to this bias.

Towards the end of the report the authors make the following argument based on the *recency effect* and *narrow range* biases – in which we let recent headlines dominate our consideration – and are biased to the 'single piece of good evidence' or similar:

> More generally, we share the misgivings of the rating agencies on the lack of political commitment to be public deficit down (in Greece and elsewhere). We see ever deeper troubles for sovereigns extending well beyond 2010 (on anaemic growth prospects). [Please note the authors' need for a story to justify].
>
> However 2010 will be more like 2009. We view the sell-off of late as just another hiccup, and a buying opportunity. It is still too early to envisage crunch time for sovereigns in 2010. As S&P itself notes in its latest appraisal, Greece has the highest duration of any eurozone sovereign. And EMU membership gives it very good protection against occasional difficulties in 2010. How ironic.

There is a disinclination to specify the precise nature of the protection that EMU membership affords. We see an ability to spot patterns everywhere, and clear *ostrich effect* bias with the 'just another hiccup' comment. Indeed, how ironic.

Nomura

Greek Mythology: Down But Not Out, Nomura Rates Insights Report, 8 December 2009

In this document, we come across the following assertion:

> The volatility in peripheral spreads, and in particular Greek spreads, to core markets seems to have reached panic proportions. Valid credit concerns exist but we think much of the recent widening is a function of year-end liquidity constraints.

Greek 5-year CDS spreads were at +208 bps on 8 December 2009. They peaked at over +1000 bps on 6 May 2010. If +200 bps was 'panic proportions', let's call +1000 bps 'end-of-civilisation' proportions. Interestingly a cute narrative fallacy is being used to simplify and promote the idea of 'All will be ok', namely 'year-end liquidity constraints'.

It continues:

> As such we are trying to differentiate here between what is a worrying but by no means catastrophic fiscal situation and market pricing. In our view, the degree of support from the EU, given the political risks involved, will likely surprise the markets, as should the degree to which balance sheet constraints and liquidity conditions are exacerbating the move. *A normalised progression of the 10-year Bund/Greek spread from September to January period this year is evolving along almost <u>exactly</u> the same path as it did last year. The key message then is that the post year-end return of liquidity tends to see a strong outperformance from peripherals.*

By producing a graph from September 2008 to January 2009, and superimposing September 2009 to December 2009, the analysts were able to detect a pattern, and they extrapolated forward. This is pattern detection is an innate human ability. With the 'History repeats itself' argument they were able to 'predict the future'. Do you see the pattern? Sorry for the pun. Please note the Bund/Greek spread during the periods depicted was between +80 bps and +160 bps.

Bank of America Merrill Lynch

20 Questions for 2010, 7 January 2010

Bank of America Merrill Lynch posed some very interesting questions in this January 2010 report: In the cover page the bank asked:

> Could Greece, Spain, Ireland derail the eurozone?

The emphatic answer was: 'No, they are too small'. There seems to be a huge element of certainty and oversimplification here for a complex multifaceted, interlinked and rapidly evolving situation. With just five words they managed to solve the problem. This is a classic example of the *oversimplification* bias.

Also, the question they pose is conveniently very narrow. This is a classic case of 'framing'. Framing according to Wikipedia is 'using an approach or description of the situation or issue that is too narrow' – that is, it arbitrarily crops certain elements out of the picture, like someone framing a photograph. What about Portugal or Italy? Isn't the Portuguese economy closely linked to the Spanish, and the Italian economy to the Greek and Spanish ones? By asking a narrow question, they could answer it easily, based on an answer they had probably preselected.

In the report they expand and emphasise:

> These places are just too small. Together they account for a *mere* [my emphasis] 16 per cent of the eurozone. Ireland (1.8%) and Greece (2.7%) are minnows. With 11.6 per cent of euro GDP, Spain is not that big either.

Excuse me. Since when is 16 per cent 'mere'? Or 11.6 per cent not too big? In addition to the behavioural biases, this in my view is just faulty logic, with a heavy dose of wishful thinking. It continues:

> The crisis trio will be likely to lag the overall eurozone recovery. But they are small open economies. They look set to benefit from the upturn in their major trading partners in Europe and beyond.

So the dog is wagging the tail here, and no likelihood of the vice versa. Further on the authors pose another valid question:

> How serious is the risk of a Greek sovereign default? Could the eurozone even fall apart?

They open with the comment that 'The dust is settling in Greece'. Be reminded that this is 7 January, with the Greek Ministry of Finance looking forward to the pleasant task of the forthcoming €50 billion of refinancing and with a CDS spread at the time of only +270 bps. In full stride the authors continue:

> The outlook for Greece's sovereign rating remains negative. [That's bad isn't it?] But the country is unlikely to face short-term liquidity problems.

I feel relieved now. We may be falling off a skyscraper, but rest assured that as we pass by the fiftieth floor we still haven't hit anything.

Helpfully, they offer a cunning suggestion to Greece's multifaceted problem:

> We believe that Greece will manage to issue debt albeit at an inflated coupon. It will therefore make do without EU and IMF help.

Pardon me? So 'inflate' the coupon a bit and problem solved? Noted, the EU and IMF are not needed here.

Greece: What If?, 27 January 2010

Within a *mere* 20 days by 27 January in the report 'Greece: What if?' their tune had slightly changed. On the cover page they wrote:

Could Greece trigger a new wave of market turbulence?
In the recent financial turmoil, credit markets have often sent the first clear warning of trouble ahead. Although Greece itself is small, the recent blow-out in Greek credit default spreads to a peak of 365 bps has caught investor attention: could Greece trigger a new wave of turbulence in global asset markets?

Contagion risk makes default even less likely
Greece faces grave problems. Its public deficit is high, its fiscal statistics are unreliable and the ratings agencies have downgraded its debt. However, Greece has finally started to adjust. We remain confident that the Greek government will be able to fund itself on its own. In the unlikely event that Greece lost its access to funding markets, we believe that it would get help from its European partners to avoid a default: precisely because of the potential contagion risk, we think other EU countries would not want to live through what might happen otherwise.

Good points, but weren't Greece, Ireland and Spain *between them* too small just 20 days ago? Witness the massive U-turn.

Economic backdrop: Greece matters
As we have argued before, we are confident that Greece will not default on its public debt. In normal times, small countries such as Greece – with an economy the size of Massachusetts

or Michigan – would not have a significant impact on global markets. But times are still not normal.

Notice the U-turn with the psychological shortcut identified by the psychologist and author Philip Tetlock: 'I would have been right if things had not changed', ex-post justification. One would think that use of such a technique would invalidate the customary *overconfidence bias* that emanates from such papers, but no matter.

Later on they, begrudgingly, do offer some more wide scenarios, whilst always clinging tightly to their prior beliefs in true *status quo* or *attachment to prior beliefs* fashion. This is also known as the 'Semmelweis reflex', or 'the tendency to reject new evidence that contradicts an established paradigm', and is closely related to other cognitive biases, especially those associated with *groupthink* (see definition earlier in chapter 8, under the heading 'Ridiculing the Whistleblowers').

But what if help was needed?
We remain confident that Greece will not need to be bailed out. But – for the sake of argument – could the EU actually help Greece if it really had to? Most likely 'yes'.

Replace 'confident' with 'overconfident'. It continues:

As economists, we are not legal experts.

Change economists for entertainers and we are on the right track, boys and girls.

In the highly unlikely event that assistance might be needed, such theoretical help could take various forms, in our view.

They just can't seem to break free of those *status quo* beliefs.

Any theoretical help would almost certainly be tied to harsh IMF-style fiscal conditions. However, the IMF itself would probably play only a limited advisory and not a leading role. IMF chief Dominique Strauss-Kahn indicated on 14 January that, since Greece is a eurozone country it would be 'totally normal that the eurozone and the European Central Bank try and work out its problems alone'.

Please notice the *certainty effect* throughout these reports: that the EU would come to the rescue no matter what – and would have the capacity to rescue the situation. It is the 100 per cent belief that what is anticipated (and usually wished for) will take place, and is also known as the *sure thing effect*. There is a considerable amount of research on the human preference for confidence over expertise.[7]

Later, in February, the entertainers did seem to wake up to the fact that predicting the future is fraught with difficulties.

BNP Paribas

BNP Paribas did produce interesting research on the Greek situation, setting out four scenarios. Scenarios! How refreshing not to have the arrogance to predict with certainty what will happen, or on what is right or wrong. This is precisely what the investors and others need on a regular basis. While avoiding some of the commoner errors of excessive certainty, sadly the tendency does creep back in if you read the small print.

Greece: Bridging the Fiscal Gap: Four Scenarios, 8 February 2010

Let us look at their scenarios:

- *Scenario I*: adjustment (35 per cent probability on a 2-year horizon)
- *Scenario II*: financial support/bail-out (48 per cent probability on a 2-year horizon)
- *Scenario III*: debt restructuring/soft default (15 per cent probability on a 2-year horizon)
- *Scenario IV*: disorderly default (2 per cent probability on a 2-year horizon)

48 per cent, 2 per cent, 15 per cent, 35 per cent. That's pretty precise. Also nice and round. Unfortunately, while they were doing so well, they fall for the *precision bias* or *range aversion* bias. Such precise figures are no more meaningful than a footballer saying he is '110 per cent committed' to his current club (which is usually a sign he's seeking a transfer).

In the strange world of economics, you can 'predict the future' if you give an exact number and you appear pleasingly precise and scientific, and of course you cannot be accused of misleading people provided each number is less than 100! If the fourth scenario occurs, that you rated at 2 per cent probability, you have the alibi that you never actually ruled it out.

Heaven behold anyone should give us a range! These biases refer to how decision makers prefer to give a precise forecast number, usually a round number and one that does not differ too much from past circumstances. Financial analysts tend to fall for this cognitive trap when looking at GDP growth, company sales and so on.

The effect of this is that a single estimate goes against looking at a broad range of possibilities and the potential risks.

This tends to make policymakers blind to other possibilities, which are the further biases of

- tunnel vision
- mental myopia.

This can lead to the *illusion of certainty*, 'anchoring', and so on. Where do these biases originate from? On the emotional side it probably stems from 'uncertainty aversion' – a primal need to avoid the unease of mental doubts and conflicts. This leads to a preference for a 'magical certainty'. On the cognitive side, it saves time not having to think of infinite amounts of permutations. This is linked closely to the phenomena of 'anchoring', 'framing' and *numeracy bias* based on past data, as discussed.

Also, did they identify *all* the possible scenarios? Surely not. Why couldn't they include a new category called 'other'? Well, for one the head of the research team would not have allowed it; if the analyst had insisted it would have been in vain. I can imagine the conversation:

'But what could "Other" entail?' asked the head of the research team.

'It's not important,' should have been the answer, 'only that they exist and they deserve a non-zero probability, if only out of respect.'

'But give me an example,' retorted the head of research.

Caving in, the analyst could have retorted all or none of the below:

- All the 10 million Greeks living abroad gave the Greek Ministry of Finance €10,000 each.
- Vast proven oil reserves were found in the Aegean or Ionian seas.

- China and Greece agree on a compulsory tourist exchange of 10 per cent of each population to visit the other country yearly.*
- Germany to volunteer to Greece war reparations, adjusted for inflation.**

Disinterested Banks Saw it Differently

Other investment banks were playing a different tune. Out of the so-called bulge bracket firms, conspicuously absent from Greek government bond issues, was a former darling of the Greek Ministry of Finance and frequent winner of Greek deals: UBS. JP Morgan was also absent, as it was black marked following the structured bond Acropolis transactions scandals mentioned earlier.

At about the same time UBS was making different types of statements. A report by Simon Penn from 16 December 2009 asked the unthinkable with the following title: 'Would EMU Exit Aid Greece?' He asks open and thoughtful questions: 'What if this were the least worst option? What if staying inside the EMU could wreak more damage?'

He makes the very good analysis and then concludes: 'Here's a likely sequence of events: EU Assistance for Greece, with governments lending money to aid it with bond redemptions and coupon payments, coupled with an ECB pledge to purchase its debt, in other words, fudge in the short-term'. Throw in the IMF and actual purchase of bonds and this is significantly different from the projections of the other banks listed above, and close to the actual turn of events.

JP Morgan released a research report named 'How to avoid a Greek tragedy?' on 16 December 2009. This was at least in the right ballpark, talking about actions and potential catastrophes.

Let's recap. The following investment banks handled tranches of Greek government bond issues during 2010: Credit Suisse, Deutsche Bank, Goldman Sachs, Morgan Stanley, HSBC, Barclays Capital, Société Générale, ING Bank and Bank of America Merrill Lynch. And those responsible for some of the most markedly optimistic assessments of Greek government solvency, summarised above, were: HSBC, Société

---

*   Credit to Deputy Prime Minister Theodoros Pangalos for this one, though I added the compulsory bit.

** Actually, this one is also Theodoros's. Well done old chap for all this out-of-the-box thinking.

Générale, Bank of America Merrill Lynch, Nomura and BNP Paribas. There is some overlap between the two lists.

Those giving more downbeat assessments: UBS and JP Morgan. The number of issues between them? Ah, that's right – none.

What About the Buy-Side?

As is evident from the above, the sell-side did not do a great job in anticipating the Greek debt crisis. What about the buy-side? Of course, in the world of the entertainers, there's a pleasing alternative to the term high risk, and that's to call it 'high yield'. On 5 May 2009, Bloomberg reported how some judged that others saw the rise in spreads as a temporary spike and a buying opportunity:

> ING, Pictet & Cie, Baring Investment Services and F&C Asset Management Plc said bonds of the so-called peripheral euro nations are cheap after the global recession led to debt-rating downgrades. 'We've been adding countries like Greece, Portugal and to a lesser extent, Ireland. The breakup of the euro or defaults aren't likely', said Baring's Alan Wilde, head of fixed income and currencies.
>
> Mickael Benhaim, who helps manage about US$103 billion as head of global bonds at Pictet in Geneva, was quoted as saying: 'The current levels reflect excessive pessimism ... The wide spreads are offering a good profit-making opportunity. I'm not in the camp that believes the eurozone won't survive.'

Faith in convergence was strong, the report noted:

> Since the euro debuted in 1999, German 10-year bunds paid an average 60 bps less in interest than Greek debt and 27 bps lower than Portuguese notes. The difference in yield, or spread, on Greek notes will fall to within 1.75 percentage points of German debt of the same maturity by year-end, from 3 percentage points on March 12, the most since January 1999, according to ING. Investors would get a 10 per cent return should the prediction prove accurate.

Because the buy-side had amassed such huge amounts of Greek government bonds, there was clear evidence of a lack of proper fundamental analysis.

Figure 9.1 Greece, Portugal, Spain and Germany 5-year Sovereign CDS Spreads

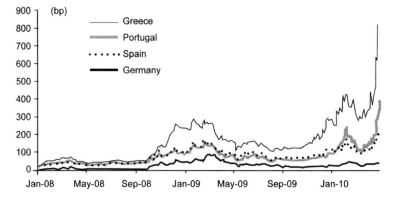

Source: Datastream.

This 'collusive denial' might not be that irrational or flawed from the investors' personal perspective. The investors took comfort from headline assumptions and *current* truths during a small period of time, namely that (a) there was no exchange risk, and (b) that strong credit ratings based on 'current fundamentals' would hold. Over several years they were right. If investors had looked at the euro experiment through a longer spectrum of time, maybe over 50 years rather than 10, they might have been able to see that it was too short a period to judge. However, this might have been irrelevant for them. As people with families to feed, in a competitive dog-eat-dog industry, they needed to manage career risk (i.e. avoid underperforming their peers in overly short periods of time quarter-on-quarter for example), and so the above longer-term view was probably somewhat of a theoretical luxury.

Assimilation: The Unpredictable Becomes the Inevitable

In all of the comment above, note the rapidity with which 'extreme' or 'hypothetical' possibilities are first of all disregarded, then acknowledged as being possible, then actually come to pass, and then finally are quickly accepted as having been almost inevitable. The entertainers assimilate stories quickly into their collective narrative in the hope that we soon forget that they had projected a very different world. This is a common phenomenon by all humans in which we fool ourselves that the world is much more benign and understandable than it is. We forget that history has happened in real time and not in the write-up afterwards.

We forget how taken by surprise we were by events.

In the eurozone crisis, reports written with thunderous certainty about the safety of the euro, the remoteness of the possibility of a Greek default or the impossibility of serious contagion were written in early 2010, just a few weeks before financing became impossible on the open market and default was prevented only by promises of massive loans by the EU. In the next chapter we will chronicle these events and some of the startlingly false (but confidently uttered) predictions.

As noted above, one of the more marked U-turns occurred within a period of just 20 days. Where were the *mea culpas*, the inquiries by the entertainers into why their predictions were wrong, not just by a few percentage points but by a quantum leap?

What seems to occur is that the new context quickly becomes the new normalcy; the entertainers draw upon their considerable supplies of amnesia and overconfidence and move on. This ease with which groups of human beings assimilate a new pattern and assume it to have been inevitable is just one of the many examples of narrative fallacy and psychological short-circuiting that we seem to be capable of, and which have played a leading role in this drama.

This process is a factor behind our tendency to underestimate the likelihood of the low-probability, high-impact event. The probability of *each* one may be low; but the probability of *any* of them occurring is actually high. And the scale of the impact keeps increasing with the globalisation of finance. As a fellow fund manager commented to me, 'this financial crisis represents a once-in-a-lifetime buying opportunity that has occurred already twice in my career' (the prior opportunity was the Russian crisis in 1998).

Danish academic Bent Flyvbjerg reminds us that concepts in economics are socially defined and inherently subjective: 'The kind of economic theory which can reliably predict changes in exchange rates and stock market trends has yet to appear. Moreover, as stated, economic theories exist by virtue of the practices by which people define the concepts of money, property, economic behaviour, etc., and these can change at any time and thereby undermine the theories' ability to predict. We do not have, and probably never will have, a theory which can predict the changes in these practices.'[8]

There is a bias towards measurement and numbers, and against descriptive narrative. Data, no matter how selective or unreliable, is seen as 'hard', and description, no matter how authentic and thorough, as 'soft'. As we saw in the last chapter, the Maastricht convergence criteria consisted entirely of data. As well as 'money, property' etc., one could add 'public sector deficit as a proportion of GDP' to Flyvbjerg's list of socially-defined entities. In 2001 the Greek public sector deficit was taken to be a number. It turned out that it was a multifaceted issue.

Since around the eighteenth century the 'science' of risk has been dominated by theories based on the study of games of chance. This brings with it the tacit assumption that the real economic world has knowable parameters and calculable probabilities. Recognition of this error is not new. Frank Knight, a contemporary of John Maynard Keynes, emphasised the difference between risk and uncertainty. In 1921, he wrote: 'Uncertainty must be taken in a sense radically distinct from the familiar notion of Risk, from which it has never been properly separated... It will appear that a *measurable* uncertainty, or "risk" proper... is so far different from an *unmeasurable* one that it is not in effect an uncertainty at all.'[9]

Unfortunately, Knight's active period coincided with the peak of classical economics and Marxism, and the attritional war fought between them. When, in 1989, Marxism lost, it looked as though classical economics was the winner. Big mistake. They were both wrong. For years, faith in the wisdom or otherwise of 'the markets' has been seen in Western political culture as a 'Left-Right' issue; hence Knight's work was undervalued. This is a profound misunderstanding. People who believe in the importance of the markets have to understand them better – and that means accepting uncertainty and miscalculation. Consider the following statement:

> Neither market prices nor the underlying reality is fully determined. Both suffer from an element of uncertainty that cannot be quantified. I call the interaction between the two functions reflexivity. Frank Knight recognised and explicated this element of unquantifiable uncertainty in a book published in 1921. But the Efficient Market Hypothesis and Rational Expectations Theory have deliberately ignored it. And that's what made them so misleading.

This comment was made not by a social democrat, but by uber-capitalist George Soros.[10]

Quantitative, 'black-box'-based or trend-following funds base their investment strategy on mathematical models that look for past patterns and extrapolate into the future, looking for 'buying signals' and 'breakout levels'. These strategies are designed by statisticians and are operated by computers, and are not run on trying to determine investment fundamentals. The issue which arises is that mathematical models and historical trends can't tell you when past market behaviour has been irrational and flawed.

The IMF

In an extraordinarily contrite publication following the banking crisis and recession, the IMF admitted that it had been too much 'in awe' of the institutions in the largest economies, and that it had suffered from 'intellectual capture'. It had mistakenly assumed that the apparent sophistication of financial markets meant lower risk. The IMF also acknowledged it was wrong to omit advanced economies from the 'Vulnerability Exercise' that had followed the Asian crisis of the late 1990s, 'despite internal discussions and calls to this effect from Board members and others'.

It also identified the influence of cognitive biases in leading policymakers and IMF assessors astray. In particular it refers to *groupthink* and *confirmation bias*, which led to faith in the 'Great Moderation', and insufficient questioning of optimistic assumptions around the self-regulation of markets, risk in financial innovation and the capability of banks to manage risk. It explains in confessional detail both the way in which the biases took hold and the limitations of the beliefs that took collective hold as a result. Faith in market efficiency was one such belief. The prevailing view among IMF macroeconomists 'was that market discipline and self-regulation would be sufficient to stave off serious problems in financial institutions'. There was also excessive faith in quantitative models, with the report acknowledging an 'over-reliance by many economists on models as the only valid tool to analyse economic circumstances that are too complex for modeling'. This admission, though typically understated, is actually an historic change given the dominance of mathematical modeling in recent decades. These observations demonstrate *groupthink*, with individuals tending to think the same, and *confirmation bias*, filtering out indicators that would challenge their beliefs.

The 'capture' by institutions in the most powerful countries – the Fund's major shareholders – is also the subject of remorse at the IMF, with the report acknowledging an attitude in which 'you cannot speak the truth to authorities', since 'you're owned by these governments'. There is also hubris, a tendency not to acknowledge the limitations of policymakers' knowledge, evident for example in the faith that the 'sophistication' of financial markets meant lower risk, when it is now clear that no one knew the full extent of the risk in the securitisation of subprime mortgages.

This report is welcome. If such a sceptical, inquiring attitude forms the basis for IMF approaches in the future it will become much better placed to advise and assist governments on systemic financial risk.[11]

It would be heartening indeed if national governments and the European Union Commission were to learn from the modesty and intelligence of this document and follow suit. The European Union, with its tendency to blame speculators and Anglo-Saxons for its policy errors, has considerable distance to travel in this regard.

The Entertainers Entertain

The narrow logic that we saw repeatedly in the excerpts from sell-side advisers earlier in the chapter feature the fatal tendency to confuse the map for the territory, systemically underestimating the possibility of unknown unknowns and other out-of-the-box thinking. The close cousins of these characteristics are *overconfidence*, overfamiliar narratives, predictions based on extrapolation and the mathematical models based on a *ceteris paribus* that cannot exist. Fat tail outliers happen more often than you expect. You can live with this, as long as you accept it and learn to spot the danger signs of a cognitive bias in a new and unfamiliar context.

My belief is that free markets are usually the best mechanism for the allocation of capital, sensible pricing and a realistic valuation of risk. However, behavioural biases and human actions occasionally (or frequently depending on your time horizon) do create situations where prices move away from fundamentals for extended periods. We need to move towards an understanding of the non-linear, unpredictable nature of real markets.

The investment community, on the buy-side and the sell-side alike, were contributors to the Greek and eurozone crisis. Those who, in the words of Chuck Prince, kept on dancing as the music was playing helped create an unaffordable boom and then bust in the eurozone government bond market. In early 2010, the music stopped.

Chapter 10

A TEMPORARY BAIL-OUT?
A CRISIS MADE WORSE BY
SATISFICING

*The Constables, and the Bow Street men from London ... ran their heads very
hard against wrong ideas, and persisted in trying to fit the circumstances to the
ideas, instead of trying to extract ideas from the circumstances.*
—Charles Dickens, *Great Expectations*

Sovereign debts mounted following the banking crisis, taking them
well above the 'ceiling' set in the Maastricht Treaty in many eurozone
countries. There was no mechanism within the eurozone for expelling
a member with excessive deficits. Neither was there a mechanism short
of expulsion for dealing with an overly indebted nation. There had
been a mechanism for *preventing* excessive deficits, but it wasn't used. So
when Greece's official public sector deficit suddenly doubled to over
12 per cent in late 2009, the EU Commission, the Ecofin Council and
the European Central Bank had no procedure to put in place. They
had to adapt as they went along. Before even an improvised rescue plan
could be executed, however, they had to acknowledge the nature of the
problem. An obstacle to this process was the fact that they appeared to
have believed their own PR: that the euro was a stable currency that
had guaranteed 'price stability', that it had helped protect European
economies from the banking crisis, and that any attempts to talk it down
came from malicious speculators or xenophobes. This state of prolonged
denial resulted in a fatal delay of several months while officials tried to
restore confidence, leaving the underlying crisis to deteriorate.

A Rescue is Needed! Get the Euphemisms Ready!

As part of their confidence-building exercise they did, however, change
their preferred metaphor. In early 2010, the single currency ceased to

be a train; it became a shield. This was remarkably similar imagery to the '*blindaje*' that the Argentine currency apparently needed in the 1990s. The global crisis – all the fault of those nasty Yanks with their subprime lending – meant that evil speculators were 'attacking' the proud single currency, the great achievement of European vision and the binding force for securing peace, abolishing poverty and so on. Fortunately, while the trusty shield of currency union protected eurozone economies from a worse fate than it might otherwise have faced, it needed strengthening from renewed onslaught. Desperate times called for desperate measures.

'The euro is a protection shield against the crisis,' said European Commission president José Manuel Barroso on 5 February 2010. Switching the metaphor slightly, but with a similar message, former MEP Richard Corbett said in 2009: 'The euro has been a rock of stability, as illustrated by the contrasting fortunes of Iceland and Ireland.'

It was not the first appearance of this imagery, less dynamic than the 'train', but reassuring in its promise of protection. In the run-up to the launch of the single currency, the then Commissioner for Economic and Monetary Affairs Yves Thibault de Silguy said: 'The euro is like a breastplate that will become more and more resistant. The stability of the currencies within its area is without question.'

Unfortunately, without any true economic convergence or fiscal discipline, and with limited coordination between governments and high and growing levels of sovereign debt, there was no actual shield to put in place, in a financial sense, in early 2010. So the two shining successes of the euro's ten-year existence were pressed into service: borrowing and PR.

Again and again, we heard that the problem was one of 'confidence' or of 'credibility' in the euro – as though the contradictions and errors of its architecture could be ushered away with more of this magical quality, and that 'confidence' could be created by the neatest turn of phrase at a press conference, or via the most authoritative demeanour.

For months, indeed years, the fiscal position of Greece had caused concern. It had been clearly visible on the radar screen, but few realised its significance. Especially at EU level there was a tendency to downplay the growing crisis and to shoot the messenger. A comprehensive assessment of elevated risk by Simon Tilford of the pro-euro Centre for European Reform in 2006 was dismissed – a case of the pressure on dissenters that *groupthink* or *herd behaviour* often induces. While he had some supporters within the economics department of the EU Commission, elsewhere there was criticism that was 'dismissive', he says. So when the phrase 'in hindsight' appears in the post-mortems, take care to recall that these individuals were warned.

The response to the mounting crisis of sovereign debt and widening spreads, misleadingly referred to as a 'bail-out', can be neatly divided into three phases:

- **Phase I** – October 2009 – 25 March 2010: denial and PR.
- **Phase II** – 25 March 2010 – 9 May 2010: tentative U-turn; denial, PR and an announcement of an intention to borrow in the range €25–45 billion – but no actual money put on the table.
- **Phase III** – 9 May 2010 onwards: U-turn completed; actual and intended borrowing of nearly one trillion euro in total; the ECB steps in as lender of last resort; hope of buying enough time to enforce fiscal convergence through a tougher Stability and Growth Pact, and of trading convergence as the periphery learns to compete with the core.

The Cost of Debt Rises; Warnings Mount

Dangers were emerging in the use of enhanced liquidity measures to mask solvency problems within the eurozone and acute stress within Greece and the banking system. The engine of global recovery seemed to be liquidity. But what were its effects? Well, a good example could be the €442 billion one-year money the ECB auctioned at 1 per cent to European banks in June 2009. Since the banks seemed in no hurry to lend, and creditworthy borrowers not in a rush to borrow, this money got recycled mostly in bond buy-backs and other securities transactions (this was effectively disguised money printing by the ECB). Banks at the time had good quarterly results, beating expectations despite a worrying increase in non-performing loans (NPLs). However, note that the main source of these profits was from 'securities transactions' and not the traditional NII or fee income. These securities transactions were basically ECB lending banks cash at 1 per cent to buy Greek government bonds, with minimal haircut requirements. Wasn't this just a colossal Ponzi scheme? Answers on a postcard please.

Before chronicling the institutional denial in phase I, it is worth listing the warnings of the high risks that were building up in the eurozone, and the experience of those seasoned observers issuing the red alerts.

Desmond Lachman. As noted earlier, Lachman was one of the first to warn of likely default in Argentina while at Smith Barney. In January 2010 he wrote an article in the *Financial Times*, observing that: 'I have seen more than my share of supposedly immutable fixed exchange rate arrangements come unstuck. I have also observed at close quarters the rather well-defined and predictable stages through which countries go as their currency regimes unravel. This experience informs me that, much like Argentina a decade ago, Greece is approaching the final stages of its currency arrangement. There is every prospect that within two to three years, after much official money is thrown its way, Greece's euro membership will end with a bang.'[1]

Nouriel Roubini. The Professor of Economics at New York University consistently warned of the danger that the Greek situation posed, and was critical of the perceived inadequacy of the 'bail-outs'. In February 2010 he warned: 'Greece has long been an accident waiting to happen due to heavy public debt and lack of competitiveness. But its problems are not unique. On their resolution rides the fate of its neighbours, the eurozone and perhaps the European Union itself.'[2]

Wilhelm Nölling. The German economist, a consistent critic of the way in which the single currency had been set up, declared along with his colleagues in March 2010 that: 'Greece faces the threat of state bankruptcy. No longer is there any illusion that membership of Europe's economic and monetary union provides protection from harsh realities. Since it entered the euro area in 2001, Greece has sacrificed competitiveness and amassed enormous trade deficits. Theoretically, to make up the economic ground lost in less than a decade, the Greeks would need to devalue by 40 per cent. But in a monetary union, that is impossible... There is, sadly, only one way to escape this vicious circle. The Greeks will have to leave the euro, recreate the drachma and re-enter the still-existing exchange rate mechanism of the European Monetary System, the so-called ERM-II, from which they departed in 2001.'[3]

George Soros. The hedge fund manager, who became famous for making €1.2 billion while anticipating the collapse of the Exchange Rate Mechanism in 1992–93, said at an event hosted by the *Economist* in April 2010 that Greece was facing a 'death spiral' owing to the cost of borrowing in the rescue package announced on 11 April. 'While it's better than what the market is currently willing to offer, it's still rather high. It is a question of solvency. If you start charging very high rates as the market does in anticipation of solvency then that pushes you into insolvency.'[4]

Simon Tilford. The chief economist at the Centre for European Reform noted that the stresses within the eurozone had been growing during the decade, not diminishing. Unlike Nölling and his colleagues, Tilford is not a eurosceptic. That did not spare him criticism for talking the currency down.

We were entering a psychologically dangerous situation, in which the ideological and vanity-induced commitment to saving the single currency was on a collision course with fiscal and economic reality. Taking heed of the warnings would have meant admission of error on a scale that was politically and psychologically difficult. In a situation where there is at least a hypothetical possibility of success with the course of action that is preferred for emotional reasons, there is a tendency to rule out all the others on the grounds of an 'if only' argument. An alternative route with a better chance of success may be available, but if this is taken, participants would be vulnerable to the charge that: 'You didn't give plan A enough of a chance – if only you had tried it for longer/with more enthusiasm.' Hence, it is likely that many heads of government proceeded with the announcements in March, April and May 2010 knowing that the initiatives were almost certainly doomed.

In such a situation, a group often exhibits what is known as 'satisficing' – clinging to the first course of action that gains approval, rather than an optimum solution. In tightly bound ideological groups exhibiting *herd behaviour*, certain options are automatically regarded as taboo, so the discussion is arbitrarily narrowed.

Phase I – Denial and PR (October 2009 – 25 March 2010)

With every month that passed after restating the deficit to nearly 13 per cent of GDP in late 2009, Greece found borrowing more difficult and more expensive. Early in 2010, Greece started displaying classic symptoms of credit stress. An inverted credit default swap (CDS) curve emerged in January – with yields on short-term debt exceeding those on long-term obligations. There was a +338 bps on five-year CDS, compared with +300 bps on ten-year CDS, meaning the market was pricing in a higher probability of default in the short term than the long term. At the time the only other Western European country with this feature was Iceland.

The canaries in the coal mine were starting to perish.

In the months leading up to the onset of full-scale eurozone crisis, the Greek government was aware of growing problems with public spending. Indeed, it had declared that the revised public deficit figure was an alarming 12.7 per cent, and it almost certainly underestimated the implications of this announcement. The newly elected prime minister and finance minister, George Papandreou and George Papaconstantinou, stayed true to the spirit of Hellenic Peronism. They wanted to keep the borrowing and spending going, although they were beginning to see the need for some cuts. In autumn 2009 they committed to an ultimately humiliating attempt to borrow from the Chinese.

In November, an individual close to the negotiations told Dow Jones Newswires: 'They [Greek government representatives] are looking for a deal where the banks will bid to buy at least €25 billion in Greek bond issuance next year. It's still at a very early stage.' The individual added that the Greeks were also looking for a commitment from the Chinese to buy some bonds in the secondary market. The Greek financial website Axiaplus.gr said in the same month that Prime Minister George Papandreou had been personally involved in secret talks with the Bank of China and two other unnamed Chinese lenders. The investment banks Goldman Sachs and JP Morgan were also party to the talks.[5]

In mid-January, Greece has successfully issued €8 billion of five-year bonds at 6.1 per cent. But just a few days later, more details emerged of the thwarted China deal, in a manner that unsettled investors. The *Financial Times* picked up on the rumoured €25 billion deal. With characteristic clumsiness, Greek ministers issued a denial. Then Yu Yongding, a former adviser to the Chinese central bank, was reported by Bloomberg as saying that China shouldn't buy a 'large chunk' of Greek government debt to help rescue the nation because the securities were more risky than US Treasuries.

In an emailed response to questions, Yu added: 'It is unreasonable for an economist to support a diversification away from an unsafe asset class to a much more unsafe asset class. Let European governments and the ECB rescue Greece.'

It got worse. Yu's statement continued: 'Even if pricing is attractive, one key problem for Greek government bonds is the lack of credibility. We trust US statistics on debt and deficits. The numbers are not pretty but we have a pretty good idea, so we would know what we are buying. In contrast, Greece's statistics have been sharply criticised by the European Commission.'[6]

That laborious work on accurate data, signalled as a priority by the Ecofin Council some years earlier but not acted upon with sufficient rigour or urgency during the years of apparent success for the single currency, was another problem kicked into the long grass by the EU that would come back to bite it. This was not unlike the self-declared 'Ninja' (no income, no job) loans, where due diligence on subprime borrowers was reduced to nothing in the mortgage frenzy of the early 2000s.

Spreads subsequently widened considerably, aggravating the sense of crisis. More damaging than Yu's use of the words 'much more unsafe' and 'rescue' were the fact that the comments came from a source with plenty of skin in the game, and without an ulterior motive for 'attacking' the euro, in the militaristic metaphor used by EU spokespeople. He was not a eurosceptic politician, nor an Anglo-Saxon economist with an ideological agenda; he was simply an investor worried about losing money. The Chinese government had absolutely no interest in talking down the currency. Both in terms of its holdings in euros, and its trading interest in the eurozone, it had every motive for the success of the single currency.

The China initiative was not the last attempt by Greece to secure funds from outside the eurozone. A US roadshow was to feature during phase II of the 'rescue'.

Although the markets were waking up to the scale of the risk in Greece's growing sovereign debt, the customary drip-feed of denial emanated from EU spokespeople. This was despite the fact that even the most basic maths indicated that a continent-wide crisis was looming. Talk of 'bail-outs' began to appear in the business and economics pages from the more bearish commentators in late 2009 and early 2010, and they were met with angry denials.

For example: 'The "no bailout" principle is anchored in the EU Treaty and has to be taken absolutely seriously... An exit or something similar from the eurozone would be totally unrealistic for Greece, and also not do-able,' said Ewald Nowotny, ECB executive board member and Austrian central bank chairman in December 2009.

German economy minister Rainer Bruderle announced in early March that: 'Papandreou has said that he didn't want one cent. The German government will not give one cent anyway.'

In March 2010, Greece raised €5 billion ($7.4 billion) from its third syndicated bond offering of the year in a seven-year offering. The bond attracted bids of around €7 billion, said Petros Christodoulou, head of Greece's Public Debt Management Authority, or PDMA. 'Given the peculiarity of a seven-year offering which targets only specific investors, the placement was very successful,' he commented.

The next day the Public Debt Management Agency attempted to auction €1 billion by tapping the outstanding 2022 bonds at a yield of 6 per cent, some +40 bps lower than the benchmark ten-year yield. In the end they raised less than half the target figure – just €390 million. This trading-style tap, to try opportunistically to iron out the yield curve anomalies and settlement issues occurring, would be the last deal the bond markets would accept.

Hostages to Fortune, by Europe's Comical Alis

'Greece', declared Jean-Claude Trichet, president of the ECB in December 2009, 'is not Argentina'. Indeed, it isn't. But its economy is more like Argentina's than it is like Germany's or Belgium's, and eurozone policy has been based upon the tacit assumption that the reverse is true.

This quote is an obvious case of *overconfidence bias*. Some optimism in political and economic leaders is called for. The narrative of a politician or other leader can have a positive impact on confidence among consumers and the markets. But there has to be a positive trend to nurture. Just as monetary union cannot create a strong economy, positive rhetoric cannot fabricate a recovery; it can only encourage whatever positive developments there might be. Thunderous, positive declarations that are in denial of the reality on the ground serve only to weaken the credibility of the spokespeople involved, and distract attention from the necessary remedial action. In the past couple of years, Europe's leaders have dealt with the ugly consequences of an orgy of sovereign debt through a combination of positive rhetoric and arranging even more debt. They are in danger of becoming no more credible than Comical Ali, Saddam Hussain's press spokesman during the 2003 war, who proudly boasted to TV reporters of defeating the invaders even as US tanks entered Baghdad.

Four months after Trichet's hostage to fortune, he was quoted in Belgian newspaper *Le Soir* as saying: 'A Greek default is out of the question, according to the information at my disposal.' This was said just a month before the downgrading of Greek debt to junk status, meaning that default was only spared by the commitment of other eurozone countries to take on more debt and lend to Greece. In the same article, *Le Soir* commentator Pierre-Henri Thomas reprised Trichet's earlier quote, but pointed out that the differences between Greece and Argentina simply served to raise the stakes – for the whole of Europe, not just the Hellenic Republic:

> Greece is not Argentina. It is part of a monetary union, in a zone that is one of the richest in the world. In the current, deleterious climate, the countries have to cut their cloth according to their means, agree to lend at reasonable levels… if not, the market that speculates on an absence of European spirit will win. And for Europe, all is lost.[7]

Trichet had made the astonishing comment during the banking crisis that 'the euro area does not suffer from any imbalances' – a claim that was erroneous, complacent and overconfident given the huge and increasing divergence between northern and southern Europe. Even as late as March 2010 he claimed that there was a 'special' virtue in the European single currency, a vague and arrogant assertion. Such comments do not help shore up confidence.

He was not the only culprit. As evidence mounted of serious crisis within the eurozone, the PR machine went on. A selection of hostages to fortune are as follows:

> Today, the EMU is limiting the impact of the crisis in Europe and in the rest of the world as well.
> —*Joaquin Almunia, from 'The Euro at Ten', June 2009.*

> The credibility of the euro is not defined by individual economies, especially when they are small. Therefore there is no possibility of exchange orchestrated attack against Greece, as was done in Argentina in 2001 and earlier with Malaysia, Thailand or the UK before.
> —*N. Christodoulakis, writing on 17 January 2010.*

Although somewhat fashionable in the United States or the United Kingdom, talk of a euro area break-up is mistaken, based at best

on shallow comprehension of the functioning of the Economic and Monetary Union...
> —*Jean Pisani-Ferry and Adam Posen (eds), from the introduction to 'The Euro at Ten', June 2009.*

A bail-out is not necessary and will not exist...
> —*Joaquin Almunia, then EU commissioner for economic and monetary affairs, 29 January 2010.*

There is a zero probability for euro area to break up. Bond spreads today exaggerate credit risks.
> —*Commissioner Joaquin Almunia, 11 Feb 2009.*

If a crisis emerges in one euro area country, there is a solution... Before visiting the IMF, you can be sure there is a solution and you can be sure that it is not clever to talk in public about this solution... But this solution exists. Don't fear for this moment – we are equipped intellectually, politically and economically to face this crisis scenario, but by definition these kinds of things should not be explained in public.
> —*Commissioner Almunia, 3 March 2009.*

No EMU member will leave the euro and no country is facing funding difficulties.
> —*Luxembourg finance minister Jean-Claude Juncker, 31 March 2009.*

We certainly won't see a state bankruptcy in Greece.
> —*Ewald Nowotny, ECB executive board member and Austrian central bank chairman, 27 November 2009.*

The European Commission stands ready to assist the Greek government in setting out the comprehensive consolidation and reform program, in the framework of the treaty provisions for euro-area member states.
> —*Commissioner Almunia, 9 December 2009.*

What happens in one member state affects all others, especially as we have a common currency, which means we have a common responsibility.
> —*German chancellor Angela Merkel, 10 December 2009.*

The euro area is a monetary zone of complete solidarity.
—*French finance minister Christine Lagarde, 11 December 2009.*

The IMF is not needed in Greece. We have to solve the problems
with our own fortitude.
—*German finance minister Wolfgang Schäuble, 14 January 2010.*

The European Commission is capable of providing financial aid to
Greece if it were needed.
—*Dominique Strauss-Khan, managing director of the IMF, 14
January 2010.*

According to many critics, the delay in responding to the mounting
crisis in late 2009 and early 2010 was the fault of the German
government. Chancellor Angela Merkel's reluctance to step in was
in line with the 'no bail-out' clauses of the Maastricht Treaty and
Germany's own constitutional law. She faced a regional election on
9 May in North Rhine Westphalia, and an increasingly eurosceptic
press. The cost of the 'bail-out' was simply increased by her delayed
action, the critics alleged.

A dysfunction such as this was inevitable, however. The bigger picture
in early 2010 was that a situation in which a single currency designed by
individuals who believed in fiscal union, but run by governments which
didn't, was no longer sustainable. The fiscal and trading convergence
hoped for had not occurred; instead, the periphery and the core were
further apart at the end of the decade than at the beginning. Anyone
who had witnessed the Argentine currency peg would have expected
this pattern to be the most likely. Moreover, the reasons for Chancellor
Angela Merkel's delay had a familiar ring: a possible legal challenge
to any assistance to Greece, given that the German courts had ruled
subsidies unlawful; and a lack of popular enthusiasm for saving the
single currency at all costs. The decision by the designers of the euro
in the late 1990s to ignore the legal objections raised by the German
economists, along with the disapproval of much of the German general
public and the formal warning letter signed by 155 other economists
was to return to haunt them. If Merkel had moved earlier, she might
not have been in power long enough to complete the deal. Even as it
was, she lost the 9 May North Rhine Westphalia election, the same
day as the final and most substantial deal. The approval of the two
'bail-outs' was by wafer-thin majorities in the Bundestag.

The criticism of Merkel over this delay is another example of EU bureaucrats not fully understanding democracy, and the need to bring people with you. It's another example of *illusion of control*. It also absolved them of their culpability in the delay, in which hubris, and a stubborn refusal to acknowledge the impact of past mistakes, was a more significant factor in the delayed response than Merkel's negotiations with her electorate, media and legal system. Moreover, the German complaints about moral hazard were not trivial. A pattern of 'bail-outs' for countries that had not managed their finances would undermine any single currency, although this argument was weakened by Germany's own breaches of the Stability and Growth Pact earlier in the decade.

The refusal by EU institutions to acknowledge the implications of German euroscepticism in the late 1990s and again in 2010 by the architects of the single currency was the bigger error. What happened, of course, was that euroscepticism only increased in the continent's biggest economy. Where before the EU faced only one hostile press in a major economy – Britain's – now it faced two. The newspaper *Bild* in particular became staunchly eurosceptic and virulently outspoken on the Greek question. The retirement and pension provisions were particularly explosive. Even pro-European Germans questioned why they should work until 67 to subsidise retirement for Greek public sector workers in their 50s or even, in some circumstances, in their 40s. The later U-turn on the ECB's independence, where it ceased to resemble the Bundesbank, was treated with withering scorn in Germany's media. There is also a cultural factor, something not considered worthy of inclusion in the convergence criteria: in German culture, a law is a law, and you obey it. In some of the Mediterranean countries, a law is no more than a negotiating position, and sometimes not even that. So for Germans, tearing up the independence of the ECB, which had been formally based on Bundesbank principles, which in turn were founded on the objective of never again risking the hyperinflation of the 1920s, was bound to be considered as the worst sort of betrayal. Not a pragmatic way through a crisis.

By March, the pressure had built to the point where 'something had to be done'. Unfortunately, the exclusive reliance on PR and borrowing remained, along with the view that the threat to the euro lay in external forces seeking to 'attack' it for unscrupulous reasons. On 18 March, Prime Minister George Papandreou said: 'I'm not seeking funds but I want to see an instrument on the table…a loan that would be enough to ensure that spreads and speculators both retreat.'

Quite how adding to the debt burden and interest payments would alleviate pressure was not made clear. The belief that more debt and better PR constituted a 'shield' was obviously by now deeply ingrained.

Also in mid-March, the *Financial Times* reported that Greek officials had been holding informal discussions with the IMF on a structural adjustment facility. It would 'probably amount to €8 billion – €10 billion over three years, with disbursement depending on progress on structural reforms'.[8] Please note the overconfidence and the magnitude of error in the forecasting.

Blaming the Speculators

There is a case to be made for a positive strand to rhetoric during any crisis, and there is danger with procyclical rhetoric in a recession just as much as in a boom. Prophesies of doom can become self-fulfilling; Jeremiahs get their own talk shows. The problem with Europe's leaders is not that they are being too positive or too negative, but that they are fighting the wrong battles, identifying the wrong culprits and failing to learn the lessons.

Like central bankers, politicians are confusing the symptoms for the disease. This is seen clearly in the rage against speculators, and the inaccurate military metaphors that accompany the bids to save the euro.

Blaming the speculators for declining bond prices is like blaming the bailiffs for your foreclosure. The better course of action is to maintain mortgage repayments and to live within your means. When Germany banned the naked short selling of CDS in May 2010, this was reasonable: traders have no skin in the game with this practice, and it is not essential to the functioning of the markets. The ban however does not solve the problems of the euro, which are driven by an incomplete infrastructure and excessive borrowing, as chronicled in chapters 2 and 6. The ban is just a gesture – like insisting that the bailiffs wear suits and behave in a polite fashion as they repossess your house.

Phase II: Denial, PR and the Promise of More Borrowing (25 March 2010 – 9 May 2010)

In the first week of April, the climate changed sharply. Greek–German government debt spread jumped to +456 bps. Greece's one-year credit default swaps breached +650 bps, widening by +175 bps in just a couple of days.

Just a month later, on 27 April 2010, borrowing on the markets became effectively impossible as Greek government bonds were downgraded. Standard & Poor's cut its rating to BB+/B, outlook negative – effectively junk. With €9 billion of repayments due just three weeks later on 19 May, urgent decisions were needed by the Greek government and the EU's political leadership.

The day after the 'junk' downgrade, economist Nouriel Roubini renewed his warning: 'Continuing on the path of least resistance – a "plan A" of official financing banking on a mix of deep fiscal cuts, inadequate structural reforms and hopes that markets will stay open, with growth doing much of the heavy lifting – is a risky bet that is very likely to fail.'[9]

He urged the EU's leaders to learn the lessons from recent restructurings of sovereign debts in emerging markets – Pakistan and Ukraine in 1999, Uruguay in 2002 and the Dominican Republic in 2005 – warning that 'much time has been lost in denial'. Of course, the underlying problem was that Europe's leaders were a long way from admitting that a eurozone member displayed characteristics of an emerging market. Policymakers can only contemplate a course of action if they think it applies to them.

Despite the lack of a precedent for success, and with the Argentinian precedent of likely failure, the EU's leaders stuck with plan A. They announced a massive European Union liquidity programme, agreed on 10 May, amounting to a potential €750 billion. The agreement tore up the rules on 'no bail-outs' and on the ECB's independence. Article 125 of the Lisbon Treaty states that the Union, or any member state, 'shall not be liable for or assume the commitments of central government, regional, local or public authorities…of any [other] member state.' Article 123 expressly forbids by the ECB to operate credit facilities for the benefit of a member state. The only fig leaf of legal protection for the moves was Article 122, which permits assistance in the event of 'natural disasters or exceptional occurrences beyond its [the member state's] control'.

In the early months of 2010, the widening spreads clearly indicated that the charade was over. April and May deadlines for refinancing meant that the issue was pressing. Even in their lumbering state of denial, the EU's institutions recognised that something must be done. However, the EU's decision-making process, in which proposals by the Commission must be approved by full meetings of the relevant council of ministers, is slow. In this particular negotiation, there were potentially irreconcilable differences between Germany and other key states. In particular, the German government's view was that Greece qualified as an overindebted country in crisis, and therefore qualified for assistance from the IMF. This would have the additional benefit, from the German point of view, of limiting direct exposure of the crisis to German taxpayers. This was anathema to those in the Commission and other governments who believed that the euro was a mature, independent currency that should be able to sort out its own affairs. Accepting IMF help would be an admission of defeat in an initiative that was historic, not just technical.

A week after Papandreou requested a loan 'that would ensure speculators retreat', and six months after the restatement of Greece's deficit, the EU Council of Ministers finally made an announcement. The statement was a compromise. Although Germany had accepted the idea of contributing to a loan arrangement, it had won the power of veto and the involvement of the IMF. On the one hand, Germany won on the question of ruling out concessional or subsidised interest rates for loan repayments. On the other hand, the ECB's decision to maintain the minimum credit threshold under its collateral system at BBB– was a concession to Greece, as the lowering of the threshold had been expected to be phased out by 2011.

The statement insisted that, at the point of declaration, no assistance had been given or sought. This was technically correct, but irrelevant. Everyone in the markets knew that the test would in the following months, when two huge tranches of refinancing by Greece became due – an estimated €5 billion in April, and a further €10–15 billion in May.

The key part of the statement ran:

> This mechanism, complementing International Monetary Fund financing, has to be considered *ultima ratio*, meaning in particular that market financing is insufficient. Any disbursement on the bilateral loans would be decided by the euro area member states by unanimity subject to strong conditionality and based on an assessment by the European Commission and the European Central Bank. We expect euro member states to participate on the basis of their respective ECB capital key.

The optimism that this was nothing more than a temporary measure, designed to offer a bridge and bolster confidence, is evident in the

25 March statement: 'The objective of this mechanism will not be to provide financing at average euro area interest rates, but to set incentives to return to market financing as soon as possible by risk adequate pricing. Interest rates will be non-concessional, i.e. will not contain any subsidy element. Decisions under this mechanism will be taken in full consistency with the treaty framework and national laws.'

Reading between the lines, it is easy to see the inherent instability of this 'solution'; a measure designed to reduce the impact of sovereign debt and ward off contagion, it itself added to debt. The sentence on participation in line with the ECB capital key meant that, for example, Spain, itself becoming vulnerable to contagion, had to stump up around €2 billion, which led to difficult questions for President José Luis Zapatero.

The day after the EU announcement, Zapatero replied that: 'Spain will offer support commensurate to its weighting according to GDP and population.' Spanish government sources 'indicated that the sum would be around €2 billion, with a percentage (of the total support package) that could reach 12.2 per cent, though the agreed text indicated a quota in line with capital in the ECB, which for Spain would be a little over 8 per cent'. Responding to critics, which included opposition leader Mariano Rajoy, who doubted that Spain could take on this burden given its own deficit of 11.4 per cent of GDP, Zapatero said: 'It doesn't involve giving money to Greece; rather offering loans, which they repay with interest.' Total public debt for Spain, set to reach 66 per cent of GDP in 2010, was around 20 points lower than the EU average, he added.[10]

EU president Herman van Rompuy made a characteristically vague, rhetorical declaration, based on *optimism bias* and *illusion of control*: 'We hope that it will reassure all the holders of Greek bonds that the eurozone will never let Greece fail. If there were any danger, the other members of the eurozone would intervene.'

By the time of this statement, you could argue that Greece had already failed. Even on a charitable interpretation of the data available, the state was insolvent. As for the rest of the eurozone automatically intervening, this was increasingly being opposed by German citizens and many of her politicians, economists and central bankers. The public statement was an obvious compromise. And undermining van Rompuy's comments was the public position of Jean-Claude Trichet, president of the ECB, who had declared that a formal role for the IMF would be 'very bad'. He told French television: 'We hope that eurozone members will exercise fully and totally their responsibilities to the Treaty, in spirit and to the letter.'

In a move consistent with the perceived need for fiscal union, but almost calculated to enrage eurosceptics, the EU's formal statement noted: 'We consider that the European Council should become the economic government of the European Union and we propose to increase its role in economic surveillance and the definition of the European Union growth strategy.' Years after Germany, France, Italy and others had breached the Stability and Growth Pact with impunity, stricter adherence was being ushered in, together with austerity measures for the most indebted states. But the horse had crossed the state line and taken up residency far away before this particular stable door was bolted.

The statement itself, though nominally released on behalf of all eurozone members, effectively resulted from a meeting between German chancellor Angela Merkel and French president Nicolas Sarkozy just before the EU summit on 25 March. It left unclear the extent to which the IMF would be involved in monitoring the arrangement, given that its funds were being called upon. The statement emphasised that no assistance had been called for, nor given, but failed to specify the detailed conditions under which it would be provided.

With every contradiction and U-turn by the EU in the first half of 2010 the credibility of its spokespeople weakened. It was a collective performance more similar to that of a football club falling into the relegation zone and issuing denials over the sale of players or the sacking of its manager than a mature political institution preparing for the next phase of economic development.

The hope that the 25 March declaration might generate some elusive confidence ignored certain facts of the markets. Some traders had been stopped by their bosses from purchasing Greek bonds; others had made losses and in any case the actual creditworthiness of Greek bonds had been exposed. The call for solidarity and contributions by Trichet was at odds with the evident reluctance of the German government and people to engage in what felt like a 'bail-out'. The very involvement of the IMF for one of the eurozone countries meant that the euro was not a fully-fledged currency. Wolfgang Munchau, a *Financial Times* columnist generally supportive of the euro, was dismissive: 'The politics of smoke and mirrors cannot fool all the people all of the time. This will not end well.'

On 29 March, the Monday after the announcement, demand was just €6 billion for the €5 billion to be raised by Greece, even at swaps +310 bps.

The spreads narrowed briefly after 25 March, but soon after began widening, and by the beginning of April Greece was trading at more than +400 bps above Germany, higher than before the announcement. There were echoes of the demise of the Exchange Rate Mechanism, when interest rate rises designed to shore up a currency's value were so obviously an act of desperation that they had the opposite effect. The downward spiral was now entrenched, in which increasing yields, rather than attracting investors, simply served to weaken confidence and encourage sales.

In a similar vein to the bid to attract Chinese money, Greek ministers tried a 'US roadshow' in early April, but the decision to brand itself as an emerging market was at odds with the claim to be part of a 'hard currency' area. The idea met a cool reception. 'Given where the spreads are, something has to happen between now and the roadshow,' Scott Mather, head of global portfolio management at Pimco, told the *Financial Times*. 'The higher the yield, the more unsustainable the situation is. It is not a situation where just a higher yield will bring in longer-term investors. It is the opposite of what they want to see.'[11]

Something had been done, but it hadn't worked. Something else had to be tried. On 11 April, a further announcement emerged. An extraordinary teleconference was held on that day, a Sunday, between representatives of the Ecofin Council, the European Commission, the IMF and the ECB, and a pledge of up to €30 billion in bilateral loans from the eurozone for Greece was drafted, supported by a further €15 billion from the IMF. The terms for the EU part of the loan guarantee were for 'non-concessional' rates, but at between 5 and 5.5 per cent, it would be less than the then marketrate. Germany and France would between them provide around half the funding.

Even at this stage, the Greek government insisted it would seek to stick to market financing, and that the loan guarantee was a reserve measure that would hopefully bolster confidence. This optimism did not reflect the gravity of the situation. Far from increasing confidence, further delay simply saw it erode. Moreover, delay was an institutional inevitability because of the EU's decision-making procedures. In the USA a major economic decision by the president, treasury secretary and chairman of the Federal Reserve can be made swiftly and clearly. In the EU, each government had to approve the measure, and in some cases, this required parliamentary approval. Slowness of decision making and legal wranglings over the legality of 'bail-outs', in an age of the internet and globalised finance, was a chronic weakness.

The result was drift. 'The house is burning down, and the eurozone is sitting around debating the constitutionality of calling the fire brigade or filling a bucket of water,' Alan Beattie acidly commented in April in the *Financial Times*.

The painfully obvious need to address different constituencies with conflicting reassurances weakened sentiment further. It was simultaneously necessary to try to convince the markets that this was a bail-out, and the German taxpayers that it wasn't. In a repeat of the pattern following the 25 March announcement, spreads narrowed for a short period, but then widened again as the implications sank in.

The German newspaper *Handelsblatt* claimed that the total financial support for Greece could reach as much as €90 billion. It quoted a member of the German government, who said that the €30 billion (for the first year) was 'just a first step' and that the financial support for Greece would be 'at least double the size'. Predictably, economics professors J. Starbatty and W. Hankel were reported by *Rheinische Post* to be filing a lawsuit with Germany's Constitutional Court with the intention of blocking any European Union loans to Greece. This was on the basis that the loans would violate the EU's Maastricht Treaty on monetary union and would therefore constitute an illegal subsidy. The report quoted Mr Starbatty as saying that Greece should voluntarily leave the 16-nation euro region.

Towards the end of the month, the *Bild* newspaper commented: 'Supposedly we have no money for tax cuts, no money for school upgrades, no money to maintain parks, no money to fix our streets... but suddenly our politicians have billions of euros for the Greeks who have deceived Europe.'

While EU officials were denying the possibility of restructuring Greek debt, economists within the major banks were beginning to regard it as inevitable, and to draw up scenario analyses on that basis. The front loading of the debt, with 50 per cent becoming due in the next five years, was of particular concern.

Prime Minister George Papandreou, speaking on Friday 23 April from the Aegean island of Kastelorizo, said he had asked the finance minister to 'take all the necessary steps' to draw down the €30 billion of European loans available following the 11 April announcement. This was just a month after the EU defensively pointed out that no assistance had been requested or provided, and only ten days after the Greek government said it intended to press ahead with market financing. The final straw had been a further revision of the Greek debt figures, with Eurostat stating that the public sector deficit was a massive 13.6 per cent, increased from 12.7 per cent of GDP.

On 7 May, the Bundestag approved the German contribution to the €30 billion agreed in the 11 April statement. Within one hour, there was a legal complaint lodged against the alleged unconstitutionality of this move. In any case, it was evident by this stage that the measure was not working. Phase II had failed. There was to be another Sunday meeting – and an even bigger announcement.

In early May, a few days after the 'junk' rating, events took a particularly sinister turn. This also marked the point at which Greece's problems became Europe's. A summary of events follows.

An Infernal Week, 2–9 May 2010

Tuesday 4 May: start of 48-hour strike by public sector workers in Greece. Large demonstrations. It is one week since the Greek government's credit rating was downgraded to 'junk' status.

Wednesday 5 May: continuation of strike; demonstrations turn violent, culminating in the torching of a branch of the Marfin Bank in central Greece, killing three members of staff. Papandreou condemns the murders. Chancellor Angela Merkel urges the reluctant German Parliament to back the rescue plan for Greece, saying 'Europe's future is at stake.'

Thursday 6 May: banks stay closed for the day as a mark of respect. The Greek Parliament approves austerity measures, in line with the EU conditions for the €140 billion bail-out. New Democracy opposes. Large protest outside Parliament, but largely peaceful. New York stock exchange experiences largest single-day fall, in percentage terms, since October 1987. Bill Gross, head of bond house Pimco, condemns ratings agencies for 'blind faith' in sovereign solvency.

Friday 7 May: Athens' streets return to normal; shoppers and foreign visitors replace protesters in the central squares. German Parliament approves the loans. The Bundestag, the lower house, voted 390–72 with 139 abstentions in favour of the loan package. In Spain, the spread on government debt becomes front page news: Spanish short-term debt has a yield six times higher than Germany's. *El País* describes it as an 'infernal week'.

Sunday 9 May: European Union finance ministers, with the support of the IMF, agree a huge package, called 'shock and awe': €720 billion of government-backed loan guarantees and a commitment to buy European sovereign bonds. Exit polls project that Angela Merkel's party has lost a regional election in North Rhine Westphalia, depriving her of a majority in the upper house.

Talks... The Euro's Demise

The week after that 'infernal' week, serious discussion ensued over the possibility of the euro's possible demise. It was already a bumpy week for the single currency. Although there was a bounce in the euro's value on Monday 10 May, declines followed later that week as the markets absorbed the arithmetic of the new debt burdens. Spain's president José Luis Zapatero announced swingeing cuts in public sector wages and entitlements. He was to secure his austerity package at the end of May – but only by one vote. In June he unveiled his plans for labour market reform.

More damagingly for the euro, however, was a report in the Madrid paper *El Pais* that startled Europe's capitals by claiming that President Sarkozy of France had threatened to pull out of the euro at the summit the week before – and that it was this threat that prompted Angela Merkel, the German chancellor to sign up to the rescue deal. The report quoted unnamed regional leaders of Zapatero's Spanish socialist party, the PSOE, after the Spanish president had briefed them on the summit.

Naturally, the French and German governments issued immediate, vehement denials. The next day, Saturday 15 May, *El Pais* duly published these denials. Significantly, however, it did not issue a retraction. The key parts of the original article, on Friday 14 May 2010 are:

José Luis Zapatero has engaged in many internal and public meetings this week to convince people of the monumental issues that Europe has been facing. This is what happened this Wednesday at the meeting that he held with regional leaders of the PSOE in Ferraz. They held discussions for more than two hours, and he [Zapatero] re-used, to support his case, phrases attributed to the French President Nicolas Sarkozy during the key summit meeting last week in Brussels. He emphasised that Sarkozy had threatened to take France out of the euro.

The President spent an unhappy weekend between Brussels and Madrid ... the tensions among Europe's leaders were such that a moment was reached when they divided into two blocs: on the one side, France, Spain and Italy. On the other, Germany. Zapatero commented that Sarkozy called for 'commitment by all, to help Greece, each in their own way, or France will reconsider its place in the euro.

Another of the regional leaders present reported that Zapatero told them: 'Sarkozy slammed his fist on the table and threatened to pull out of the euro, which obliged Angela Merkel to come to an agreement.

The source also said that Sarkozy had suggested that France, Spain and Italy form a common bloc against Germany, breaking the traditional France–Germany axis, which for so long has directed Europe.[12]

As Paris and Berlin issued their denials in early May, it was later reported by the *Wall Street Journal* that French finance minister Christine Lagarde had stated during this same period that 'the eurozone was on the verge of breaking apart'. This same report, published in September 2010, revealed the existence of an ultra-secret taskforce that had been set up in 2008 to discuss contingency plans in the event of a eurozone government requiring bail-out. It had been meeting during the whole period that thunderous declarations of the 'success' of the single currency were publicly being voiced. The *Wall Street Journal* investigation, 'based on dozens of interviews with officials from around the EU', found that:

> The secret taskforce, coordinated by the committee chairman, had been meeting surreptitiously since November 2008 to craft a plan should a Hungary-style crisis strike a euro nation. Membership was limited to senior policymakers – usually just below ministerial level – from France, Germany, the European Commission, Europe's central bank and the office of Jean-Claude Juncker, the Luxembourg premier who heads an assembly of euro finance ministers.
>
> The task force met in the shadows of the EU's many councils and summits in Brussels, Luxembourg and other capitals, often gathering at 6 a.m. or huddling over sandwiches late at night. Participants kept colleagues in their own governments in the dark, for fear leaks would trigger rampant speculation in financial markets.[13]

The report also confirms the widely reported story that President Sarkozy had strongly opposed the involvement of the IMF, but that Chancellor

Merkel had insisted on its participation, partly as it had the experience, but also that its austerity measures should serve as a deterrent to other overindebted nations.

I don't doubt the existence of this task force, but given the panicky reactions of EU decision makers in early 2010, it didn't seem to have done its job very well.

On the Thursday evening, 14 May, former chairman of the US Federal Reserve Paul Volcker asked if the euro was doomed. In a speech in London he said: 'You have the great problem of a potential disintegration of the euro. The essential element of discipline in economic policy and in fiscal policy that was hoped for has so far not been rewarded in some countries.'

Phase III: Actual and Potential Borrowing of €750 Billion

When the key financial indicators headed in the wrong direction, they did so rapidly. Pick your stat: two-year yields rising +150 bps intraday on 6 April – and a further +50 bps the next day; *Financial Times* 'Lex' able to describe 'limited' financial contagion on 7 April, just a month before Spain's yield is six times Germany's, and so on. A graph showing Greek 10-year spread to the bund against time, between November 2009 and April 2010, looks like a profile of the Balkan mountains, with the peaks becoming higher and higher.

In a world of vast quantities of global finance, leverage and imperfect access to information, sudden reversals and overshoots are common. By early May 2010, the 'bail-out' that wasn't – a promise of extra borrowing but no actual money – was obviously not working.

EU heads of government were increasingly angry with 'speculators' for talking the currency down and taking short positions, but they could not ignore the stark reality of the market, which meant that, at the yields they were expecting for Greek bonds, and with a 19 May deadline for €8.5 million of debt that was maturing, it was increasingly likely that market refinancing was going to be unaffordable. Indeed, George Papandreou had already called upon the rescue measures in his 23 April statement.

To prevent a repeat of the Buenos Aires drama of December 2001, the EU had to act fast. An emergency meeting was convened on Sunday 9 May.

The press release that emerged was rushed into print in advance of the Asian markets opening on Monday 10 May. Its title was: 'European stabilisation mechanism to preserve financial stability'. This is beyond euphemism, and beyond satire. In terse paragraphs not even filling two pages, the communiqué announced the end of the 'no bail-out' principle of the Maastricht Treaty. It cited Article 122.2 of the Treaty, permitting financial support for member states 'in difficulties caused by exceptional circumstances beyond member states' control'. This was a highly contentious interpretation, given that the systemic shock came at least as much from excessive government spending and lack of convergence as it had from the international credit crisis. Most had understood Article 122.2 as applying to an event such as a major natural disaster or hostile military action against the EU.

The agreement was for support of €60 billion, in the context of a joint EU/IMF operation, with activation 'subject to strong conditionality', and confirmed that the first disbursement to Greece would be before 19 May. In addition, ministers agreed to a special purpose vehicle up to a volume of €440 billion. 'The IMF will participate in financing arrangements and is expected to provide at least half as much as the EU contribution through its usual facilities.'

The potential scale of the package was therefore approaching three quarters of a trillion euros, and was quickly dubbed 'shock and awe'. Commentators were impressed by the scale of the package, but not the nature of the technical details. It had bought the EU time – estimates were typically 18 months to two years – but the task of securing sufficient convergence in such time made such a window look inadequate. The EU was trying to complete in two years what it had failed to achieve in the previous three decades: create an optimal currency area across the continent.

The cold arithmetic of the Greek fiscal position and economy was the weakest part of the plan. Evidence of a vicious downward spiral in the Greek economy, with contraction and austerity accompanied by a deepening recession and increasing debt and therefore interest rate repayments, indicated that the country could be even less able to begin to repay its debt two years down the line than it was in early 2010. Looking at the figures, rather than the press release headline, it looked as though things were going to get worse before they got worse.

Some northern European countries, Germany, Austria, Finland and the Netherlands, had reportedly wanted a requirement for national parliaments to vote before the special purpose vehicle makes any loan, but lost the argument. The bigger picture was that the fiscal burden was being shifted from the periphery to the core; but such was the scale of the economic imbalances within the eurozone that the periphery was going to be squeezed also.

Some commentary was astonishing. The IMF, in apparent keenness to bolster support for the package, even made the observation just after the huge 'bail-out' was announced that restructuring debt would not help Greece's capacity to grow. This is not true – it could help considerably. Most of the adjustment in Greece is needed to eliminate its large primary deficit – the deficit net of interest payments. This is the main issue for Greece, not the level of the debt. The package added a cool €14 billion to interest payments, on top of the debt Greece was already exposed to. How could rescheduling not alleviate that?

The off-balance-sheet nature of the special purpose vehicle, which was to be an entity to borrow funds as needed and then lend it out to a country in need, caused concern, especially in conjunction with the news of the direct measures that the ECB intended to make. Jean-Claude Trichet, the ECB president, was reportedly 570 km away in Switzerland when finance ministers meeting in Brussels coolly tore up the bank's founding principles, just days after denying that it was considering the matter. Under enormous pressure, the ECB board agreed to buy eurozone government and private bonds to ensure depth and liquidity in markets. The ECB decided to eliminate the minimum ratings requirements for purchasing government bonds in its collateral system.

On 10 May, Trichet admitted that there was not unanimous support for the measure on the ECB board. 'On bond purchases we had an overwhelming majority [of the 22 members],' he said. ECB executive board member Juergen Stark, Bundesbank president Axel Weber and Luxembourg central banker Yves Mersch were among those rumoured to have opposed bond purchases. *Der Spiegel* named Weber, Stark and the Netherlands central bank governor Nout Wellink as dissenters.

Weber went public with his concerns. In an interview with Germany's *Boersen-Zeitung* immediately after the announcement, he said: 'The purchase of government bonds poses significant stability risks and that's why I'm critical toward this part of the ECB council's decision.' The Bundesbank confirmed the comments.

The ECB announced its intention to 'sterilise' the purchases – that is, ensure that they did not add to money supply. There was some scepticism about this promise, however.

The radical departure was unsettling to the markets, and to German public opinion.

As the first €16.5 billion of purchases was confirmed by the ECB on 17 May, some comment was devastating. David Bloom, head of foreign exchange strategy at HSBC, said: 'Prior to the current crisis the euro was deemed to be the Deutschmark in disguise. But the rise in sovereign risk has changed this perspective. It now seems that people think it is a drachma in disguise.'[14]

Former Bundesbank president Karl Otto Pohl said on 18 May: 'The foundation of the euro has fundamentally changed as a result of the decision by eurozone governments to transform themselves into a transfer union. This is a violation of every rule. In the treaties governing the functioning of the European Union, it's explicitly stated that no country is liable for the debts of any other. But what we are doing right now is exactly that.'

The phase of central banks bailing out banks had moved to the phenomenon of central banks bailing out central banks, uncertain as to whether printing money would or would not help the process. Either the eurozone was entering a forced consolidation in which it would become an optimal currency union, or it was simply a monster devouring its own children. By the beginning of July, the ECB admitted that it had already purchased €59 billion of government bonds, and had been buying at a rate of about €5 billion a week. Philippe Mills, chief executive of the French debt management agency, confirmed that the ECB 'is buying mainly Greek debt, a little bit of Portugal, a little bit of Ireland. That's it'. The central bank would not disclose its specific holdings, but estimates were that Greek debt accounted for around €50 billion.

The immediate crisis had passed, however. Greece duly received a €14.5 billion loan from the European Union on 18 May, a day before the deadline, and was able to repay its immediate debt.

Despite all the U-turns and turmoil during May, what was noticeable was that the value of the euro, though softer, did not collapse. On 14 May it was trading at a respectable US$1.238. By early July it had edged up a little to $1.258. After the 10 June decision to leave interest rates on hold, ECB president Jean-Claude Trichet said: 'The euro is a very credible currency, a currency that has a track record of keeping its value [and] is a major asset for investors.' It was a defensive statement, but one that helped maintain an element of confidence.

For the plan to work, however, public opinion had to withstand the extreme adjustment being planned, and the European banking system had to remain solvent through a potentially dangerous downward spiral. The 9 May announcement had not ended the pressure, just moved it to different parts of the eurozone economy. If the single currency was going to be bludgeoned into survival, there were going to have to be some casualties. Big casualties.

Risk Spreads Back to the Banks

Throughout all this drama, the banking system was still showing symptoms of strain. The EU was not ignoring this; indeed it planned a series of 'stress tests' for banks in the weeks after the 'bail-out'. In early July, it emerged that smaller institutions would be included in the tests. This followed the need for the Bank of Spain to rescue some of the regional *cajas* at a time when the country itself was starting to come under severe fiscal strain. Concern grew that both the *cajas* in Spain and the *Landesbanken* in Germany were undercapitalised. In the case of the Iberian peninsular, much of the problem stemmed from the property bubble, in turn exacerbated by the low interest rates that resulted from being in the single currency. German and French banks, in particular, were exposed to Greek private and public debt (see chapters 1 and 4). This was an extra motive for the EU leadership to seek to do the utmost to prevent any default or rescheduling of Greek debt.

In May, the Bank of Spain intervened for a second time with a rescue, taking over effective control of Cajasur and encouraging a merger with another bank, following similar action in March 2009 to rescue the Caja Castilla la Mancha, which had registered a loss of €740 million. Cajasur lost €596 million in 2009. In each case, significant sums of cash had been withdrawn by depositors. There were similarities with the state bail-outs in the UK and Ireland of Northern Rock and Anglo Irish Bank respectively. All countries had been seriously affected by bad loans associated with the property boom.

The Spanish government set up the Ordered Bank Restructuring Fund (FROB). Socialist president José Luis Zapatero secured the support of Leader of the Opposition Mariano Rajoy for this measure. On the day of the Cajasur rescue, Finance Minister Elena Salgado referred to it as 'this small problem', noting that its assets represented just 0.6 per cent of the Spanish banking sector, and confirmed a policy of merging the smaller regional banks. The Spanish financial system was 'absolutely solvent', she said. As with all such statements, the fact that it had to be made can be deemed more telling than its content. Spain had already begun to feel the effects of contagion, and spreads on its debt were widening. The Ibex index fell more than the rest of Europe on the day of the announcement.[15] The Bank of Spain adopted a policy of reducing the number of regional banks from 45 to 20.

In this context an EU-wide stress test was widely welcomed. *Optimism bias*, however, appeared to affect the process. Wolfgang Munchau in the *Financial Times* on 4 July pointed to the stress tests including a uniform haircut of just 3 per cent – a figure he described as 'a joke'. A stress test is supposed to be an exercise in tough scenario planning, not rosy forecasting.

> It is official EU policy to deny the reality that Greece might default or restructure. A genuine stress test might expose the EU's position as indefensible. Those opposed to any inclusion of sovereign risk into the stress tests argue that the mere assumption of a haircut might turn into a self-fulfilling prophecy.

The exercise seemed to be designed to ensure that the banks would pass the test. If this happened, he added: 'It would signal to the outside world that the EU is treating its debt crisis, which is a banking crisis at heart, as a public relations exercise.'[16]

IMF Gets Tough

The IMF, perhaps mindful of the fierce criticism it received over its handling of the Argentine crisis, offered a full and detailed risk assessment after the first two 'bail-out' announcements and before the third. Published on 5 May 2010, and approved by Poul Thomsen and Martin Muhleisen, it acknowledged that the risk was systemic, extending to public and private sectors, prospects for economic growth, and to the banking system. It announced the establishment of a Financial Stability Fund, backed by the international financing package, to 'ensure adequate capitalisation of the banking system'. It promised close collaboration with the European Commission and the ECB.

The report was unusually forthright:

> Risks to the program are high. The adjustment needs are unprecedented and will take time, so fatigue could set in. Any unforeseen shock could weigh on the economy and the banking system even if the fiscal program is on track. Greece needs to persevere to ensure continued international support.[17]

A complicating factor with involvement of the IMF is that it cannot by law write down its own exposure. This would mean that, in the event of a haircut, other creditors would have to take a bigger hit.

Public Opinion has its Revenge

The real strain of the euro rescue, however, was going to be faced by the people asked to accept the austerity measures as an accelerated economic convergence programme attempted to undo a decade of complacency and divergence.

Between 2007 and 2010, with the banking collapses followed by Europe's sovereign debt crisis, private debt became public debt. This added to the severe imbalances that, far from being reduced by the supposed 'catching up' in the single currency, had become much more extreme. Germany and the Netherlands had moved further into trading surplus, Greece and Portugal much further into deficit, while similar imbalances were evident on public sector debt.

The combination of pressures meant that economic risk had now become political risk. With the ECB and the European Commission now taking over the economic policy of the peripheral countries through a tougher Stability and Growth Pact, there was no obvious outlet for political frustration. Austerity measure followed austerity measure.

In the run-up to monetary union the ECB and the European Commission took little heed of public opinion, and made little effort to win over the public – which was sceptical in many of the 11 founder countries, especially Germany and Finland – to give enthusiastic support for monetary union.

For the past decade during the boom years, the debt-and-spending cycle, irrational exuberance and popular opinion could be temporarily ignored. Now, as we enter the most dangerous phase of the euro project, it determines everything. The ECB, which has now taken the place of national governments as the determinant of economic policy, is insisting upon austerity measures; not only in the deficit countries, but even in the surplus countries – Germany itself is seeking to cut around €80 billion. Public opinion will either accept it, or not. Plain old public opinion, for decades ignored and derided by the EU's leaders, is now all they have to rely upon for survival.

Of course, the ECB does not have to face the voters. It has its 'independence'. But governments do. If governments no longer control economic policy or public spending what, exactly, are they asking the voters to support when they go to the polls? Both Spain and Greece have active left-wing parties, and a history of right-wing dictatorships. They also have centre-left governments that are imposing the type of austerity measures and labour market reforms they were elected to resist. Both have nationalist movements from the right wing.

The political risk is that mainstream parties in Spain and Greece, that in recent years have formed governments, but which are no longer able to set their own economic policy, are going to be in competition with parties calling for withdrawal from the European single currency and the reestablishment of national sovereignty.

During the boom years, voters returned parties to government that supported the European project. But voters at general elections vote on a variety of subjects, and on the character of a party and its leader. Voting preferences often diverge sharply between European Union issues and national elections.

Pro-European unity campaigners, with their *overconfidence bias* and 'train' metaphor, have often expressed the prediction that public opinion differences between the 'in' countries and the 'outs' would naturally converge, and that opposition in the 'out' countries of Denmark, Sweden and the UK would begin to fall. But what if the opposite happens – that sceptic countries become more sceptical and the attitude spreads to the 'in' countries?

Opinion-poll support for joining the euro has fallen in Sweden, Denmark and the UK; in the case of Sweden and Britain, opposition has been the norm. Within the eurozone, what if mainstream social democrat and Christian democrat parties see their votes collapse, and anti-EU parties of the Left and Right pick up support?

The Netherlands, arguably the eurozone's economically most successful country, witnessed a significant surge of eurosceptic support in the general election in June 2010. The big gainer was the eurosceptic, anti-Islam Freedom Party of Geert Wilders, which won 24 seats, 3 more than the Christian Democrats, the party of outgoing prime minister Jan Peter Balkenende.

Later in the same month in Belgium, the New Flemish Alliance (N-VA) of Bart De Wever made huge advances, moving from five seats in the lower house of the Belgian Parliament in the last elections to 27 seats, making it the largest party in the country. Again, the euro is not the issue for Mr De Wever, but the rise of nationalism in Benelux is an unexpected development with an unpredictable outcome for Europe. The resentment within Belgium is a microcosm for the eurozone as a whole: a solvent, export-orientated north wanting separation from a welfare-orientated south.

In Slovakia, the government enraged the European Commission by refusing to stump up its share of the bail-out. This was on the grounds that the small country had already experienced austerity measures to deal with its own fiscal difficulties, and did not see that it was right or affordable to 'bail out' Greece. In Ireland, the pro-EU establishment party Fianna Fáil is seeing its support collapse, and one of the beneficiaries is the anti-EU party Sinn Féin.

Even at the start of the 'bail-out' package and austerity programmes, support was thin. On 21 May just 319 out of the 622 members of the Bundestag voted for Germany's €148 billion contribution to the 9 May deal. Another 195 abstained and 73 voted against. When Spanish president José Luis Zapatero asked Parliament to approve his austerity package, it scraped home on 27 May by just one vote, and speculation over his continued leadership of the Spanish Socialist Workers' Party (PSOE) followed. Failure of the opposition parties – the Social Democratic Party (SPD) in Germany and the People's Party (PP) in Spain – to support such programmes may have been opportunistic, but a lack of enthusiasm for bail-out and reform, even before the nasty

Figure 10.1 European Bonds Spreads 2010

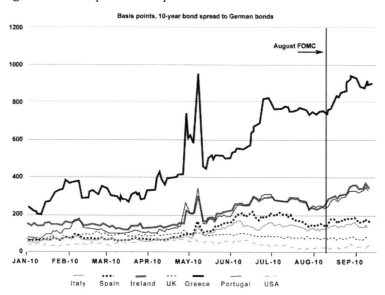

Source: Bloomberg.

medicine was taken, was ominous. Opposition parties could not have been opportunistic if public opinion had been solidly behind defending the euro at all costs.

By the end of the summer, spreads had returned to the level they had been before the colossal 'bail-out' in May, with stress particularly acute in Ireland and Greece, as Figure 10.1 shows.

All the institutional efforts since the visible start of the crisis in the winter of 2009–10 have been designed to shore up confidence in the eurozone. Many commentators and EU officials have been taken aback by how suddenly confidence collapsed. This is the wrong focus, however. The big puzzle is not why it collapsed, but why it held up for so long. Any analysis of the sums involved in lending to the governments of such small economies on the eurozone periphery, in some ways still underdeveloped, would show that it was unsustainable. People only started doing the solvency mathematics towards the end of the decade. They concluded that the debt refinancing burden would become unaffordable by around 2013, and so began pulling out immediately. The big economic lessons are to be learnt not so much from the collapse, which was inevitable, but rather from the extraordinary sustainability of an illusion earlier in the decade: the collusive denial that sustained the carry trades in the euro; and the belief in the 'train' or the 'shield', which was built on nothing more substantial than political persuasion and PR and yet was held in good faith by the major economic institutions of the world.

Chapter 11

THE MAN IN THE ARENA

It is not the critic who counts: not the man who points out how the strong man stumbles or where the doer of deeds could have done better. The credit belongs to the man who is actually in the arena, whose face is marred by dust and sweat and blood, who strives valiantly, who errs and comes up short again and again, because there is no effort without error or shortcoming, but who knows the great enthusiasms, the great devotions, who spends himself for a worthy cause; who, at the best, knows, in the end, the triumph of high achievement, and who, at the worst, if he fails, at least fails while daring greatly, so that his place shall never be with those cold and timid souls who knew neither victory nor defeat.

—Theodore Roosevelt, 'Citizenship in a Republic',
speech at the Sorbonne, Paris, 23 April 1910

While it is easy to criticise and make comments with the benefit of hindsight, what can actually be done to navigate our way through the current crisis and to prevent a recurrence? After looking into the different dynamics at play, both at a European level and globally, there are some surprisingly stark and straightforward implications for the key constituencies: the Greek government and society; the European Union; the banks; the financial services; and the economic management institutions, such as the IMF. The challenges stem not so much from technical complexity, but from the political and social dimension: can policymakers make sometimes courageous decisions, stick with them, and bring key constituencies alongside?

This chapter is an exercise in future gazing, with policy proposals. I do not intend to make predictions! Rather, the intention is to summarise the risks and potential scenarios that we should have confronted sooner, and must confront now – and to investigate how to confront them. Before setting out the priorities and policy options for the different constituencies, it might be worth summarising the context we are actually in, and how far removed it is from that imagined by policymakers and leading market participants. I began this book by noting how all key players – the European Union's leaders, Greek politicians and society, central banks, investment banks, international agencies – have been culpable for the crises of sovereign debt, economic imbalances and the euro. If there is a characteristic shared by these groups, it appears to be a belief in benign forces that tend towards convergence or equilibrium in deregulated markets or a single currency experiment. What begins as a policy objective becomes a desire, an expectation and then a prediction; all reinforced by *herd behaviour*, or *groupthink*, with its illusion of invulnerability, collective rationalisation, belief in inherent morality, stereotyping of outsiders, pressure on dissenters, self-censorship, illusion of unanimity and appointment of 'mind guards'. Whether it is belief in 'stable prices', the 'Great Moderation' or convergence of peripheral eurozone economies, there is a disinclination to look at the 'real' economy, or accept its unpredictable, non-linear properties.

The use of euphemisms is often a danger sign, examples including monetary union being referred to as a 'train' or a 'shield', debt being described as 'leverage' or 'fiscal stimulus', high-risk investments being relabelled as 'high yield', and the merging and slicing and dicing of high-risk with low-risk assets being branded as 'securitisation'. If the label on the tin does not state clearly what's inside, you need to understand the nature of the deception and the motivation that lies behind it.

Greece

For the short term, Greece should follow the IMF reform that it has begun: reform of the labour market, opening up closed shops, cutting waste in public sector procurement such as in hospitals, and so on. This has to be completed, irrespective of other developments. Even if Greece's debt were to vanish miraculously, the same reforms would still be needed to prevent a new fiscal problem from quickly reemerging.

The shrinking of the public sector will to some extent take care of the wastefulness. Obviously administrative inefficiency will have to be met with increasing productivity whilst the public sector is shrinking (i.e. a reduction of employees will have to be simultaneously fused with a reduction of waste to increase productivity). Digitalisation and IT investment in the public sector should be an impetus for this, given that Greece is currently vastly lagging behind other EU member states in this field. The government should use the troika (while it still can) – the IMF, European Commission and the European Central Bank – to push reforms through; they could be the lightening rod that absorbs the anger.

There are some promising signs: the refusal by the government to back down to the truck drivers in 2010 showed that the implicit threat of interest groups, which has held back reform for decades, may be much less of a threat these days than previously feared. This could in retrospect become a pivotal moment in moving the state away from clientelism, and be likened to the moment when President Ronald Reagan refused to back down during the air traffic controllers dispute in 1981, or Margaret Thatcher's 'the lady's not for turning' speech in 1980. However, the structural reforms will have to be equally and fairly administered across all special interest groups (treating alike pharmacists, lawyers, truck drivers etc.), without half-measures and endless delays.

End Immunity

Fairness is a deep-rooted, underlying fundamental human need. Few things outrage people in their relationships, jobs and in society overall as much as a lack of fairness. There is a long-established literature on justice, fairness and the social contract, based on reciprocity. This dates back to Enlightenment thinkers such as Jean-Jacques Rousseau and John Locke. One of the more recent thinkers, John Rawls, developed the useful notion of the 'veil of ignorance', in which individuals are encouraged to judge a situation as fair or otherwise without knowing in advance what social status they would have in any new arrangement. He offers a useful concept: 'Each person participating in a practice, or affected by it, has an equal right to the most extensive liberty compatible with a like liberty for all.'[1]

For Greece to adjust and reform there has to be a new constitutional settlement, with full independence of the judiciary and an end to immunity and special treatment for politicians. As a matter of urgency, there has to be a repeal of Article 62 of the Constitution, with politicians facing corruption charges in the regular courts, not special parliamentary committees. Accompanying this, the five-year Statute of Limitations must be repealed. These measures would allow any rifts and bitterness building up in Greece to subside. Furthermore, penalties for non-compliance in a fair society need to be much higher.

There also needs to be a better balance of powers throughout the state with more checks and balances, and proper separation of the judiciary, parliament and the executive.

While the Papandreou government has made progress on economic reforms, its blind spot is an inability to see the link between constitutional and economic reform; for as long as not a single senior individual has gone to jail over the Siemens scandal for instance, which has cost the Greek state millions of euros over many years, politicians will struggle to build the social consensus essential for economic and social reform. For example, there is a direct link between failure to uphold the law and difficulty in persuading more individuals and companies to pay tax. The process of the investigation into the Siemens case indicates that the political class still does not understand the seriousness of the accusations, and wants to live in its own little bubble (which has a forgiving criminal code). This expectation must end.

Reform of the judicial system will have to focus not just on the political class, but also on the local capitalist class that lived off the government spending works and effectively received a state amnesty for contract biddings, tax payment delays, labour law infringements, environmental and safety rule violations, and so on. So too must the general public's amnesty from its actions ('erasing' parking tickets, car licenses, building permit violations etc.) also be addressed and removed.

What is required is firstly to instill an acceptance of fairness, and simultaneously to boost both incentives to comply and penalties for breaching the law.

Transformation from a Low Tax Economy with Low Government Service to Higher Tax and Higher Government Service

There is no excuse for tax evasion; however tax reform must go hand-in-hand with all aspects of political reform that are inevitably interlinked. The Greek state has to tackle its lawless culture at all levels, preferably starting at the top, and hold people responsible for their actions. This, in combination with reducing grotesque waste in the public sector, should start creating incentives to increase the tax base. Fall short of this reform, and we will continue to consider that only the foolish or the unlucky pay their taxes in full.

Greece will not be transformed overnight from a low-tax, low-service society to a high-tax, high-service one like Sweden. There will be an inflection point, a dark moment before the dawn where taxes will have increased and services not improved. That will be a serious political testing point.

There is one silver lining: the fact that the Greek public sector is wasteful, the populace's tax payments irregular and the private sector uncompetitive means there is huge scope for improvement; even modest relative improvements could boost productivity significantly. The public sector needs to be made smaller, but also much more efficient and less corrupt. Outcomes on education, for example, lag behind other European economies. The public sector must become an efficient provider of services and not a means to employment for political favourites.

Practical Recommendations

Once the moral high ground on corruption, tax evasion, justice and fairness within the system has been ascertained again, numerous practical and efficient proposals to reduce waste and corruption might be implemented.

For example, see a recommendation from a report by three Greek professors of economics, Costas Meghir, Dimitri Vayanos and Nikos Vettas, published in August 2010.[2] In order to curb the culture of excessive bureaucracy and corruption, they propose to ensure that tax auditing is carried out in formal, written documents, and according to uniform standards, rather than via face-to-face meetings. This reduces opportunities for 'fakelaki' to exchange hands, and can help ensure a fair system in which penalties are proportionate to the offence. A written record increases transparency, and can facilitate appeals and so on.

Non-Practical Recommendations: Hiking VAT

Many of the IMF's measures are necessary. The austerity measures will create a dramatic fall in Greek GDP. If one were to conclude that most of the GDP growth from 2000 onwards was debt-induced, then the upcoming debt liquidation could erode a big chunk of the headline 'growth' in the coming years. Greece's adjustment process entails reducing the fiscal deficit by cutting spending, increasing tax receipts and restoring growth and competitiveness. As the GDP falls in the face of austerity – i.e. wage reductions and spending cuts that are GDP-negative – trying to raise tax collection as a percentage of the economy will at some point hit a wall. You can only milk the same cow so many times. As devaluation is currently not available, the increase in competitiveness will have to be created as a first stage from labour and product price decreases. However, the IMF's insistence on increasing VAT does not increase competitiveness; it decreases it, as the hikes directly increase both consumer prices and producer prices. It candidly admitted in a July 2010 interim report: 'The lack of evidence that any of the tax increases are being offset by narrower margins in prices points toward serious rigidities in the product markets'. Then in August they continued: 'It's true that inflation has been higher than originally expected – and we have revised our estimate for 2010 to 4.75 per cent. We underestimated the consequences of the higher indirect taxes'.[3]

Correct supply-side measures take years to filter through, while tax increases are felt immediately.

Tax Reform: Simplify the Tax Code

Tax reform would also help business survival rates. At the moment there is a vicious circle: a tenacious tax-gathering system applies a complex range of tax burdens to a few, while many pay little or no tax at all. This means that there is huge potential for a 'win-win' if the number of taxes were to be radically reduced and replaced by a simplified system based on moderate, typically flat rates. This would be more likely to be perceived as fair, and it would also be easier to enforce. Accompanying this should be a clampdown on evaders – already begun in 2010, to be fair – and the ushering in of a culture in which payment is expected and evaders are socially shunned. To this end, the proposed reduction of corporate income tax from 24 to 20 per cent in 2011, announced at the Thessaloniki International Exhibition in September 2010, is welcome – albeit not far-reaching enough. In addition, Papandreou proposed a final tax assessment, or 'closure', under which companies and individual professionals might pay a fee for the final closing of their books for the tax years 2000–09, in cases where ongoing disputes have not otherwise allowed for such closure.

The tax structure, non-wage cost burdens and administrative red-tape involved is currently a disincentive to the creation of new businesses. This will have to change to enable young entrepreneurs to step up in place of the shrinking public sector.

Restructure the (Odious) Debt

Having done all that, and given that Greece was one country which effectively lost out from all these capital flows, there should be a restructuring of the debt – because no matter how much fiscal tightening an economy attempts, all efforts will be futile and empty if it is supporting too much debt. Austerity will feed itself into repetitive GDP reductions, with debt simply growing on top of a shrinking economy. Precedents do not make comfortable reading. The only country that managed to do such a fiscal tightening was Romania under Ceauşescu. As Carmen Reinhart and Kenneth Rogoff recall in *This Time is Different*:

> In most instances, with enough pain and suffering, a determined debtor country can usually repay foreign creditors. The question most leaders face is where to draw the line. The decision is not always a completely rational one. Romanian dictator Nikolai Ceauşescu single-mindedly insisted on repaying, in the span of a few years, the debt of $9 billion owed by his poor nation to foreign banks during the 1980s debt crisis. Romanians were forced to live through cold winters with little or no heat, and factories were forced to cut back because of limited electricity.[4]

Asking Greece to pay foreign creditors 13 per cent of GDP per annum is too much. Meeting these demands at any costs will bleed the economy dry. Already there has been a huge exodus of Greek service companies, moving businesses to Cyprus, Bulgaria and so on. Any restructuring would involve a net essential value (NPV) reduction of Greek government debt. This would have to be conducted in a manner that Greek banks could cope with and would probably involve debt extensions and capital raisings of some sort.

Given the corrupt nature of the Greek political class and the complicity of the European Union and German and French banks, one could argue that Greece's excessive borrowing falls under the category of 'odious debt' – a long-established concept used to define a national debt accrued by a government that was used for ends that did not benefit the nation.

The concept of odious debts was first expressed in the post-World War I context by the jurist Alexander Nahun Sack in 1927. He wrote:

> ...if a despotic power incurs a debt not for the needs or in the interest of the State, but to strengthen its despotic regime, to repress its population that fights against it, etc., this debt is odious for the population of the State. The debt is not an obligation for the nation; it is a regime's debt, a personal debt of the power that has incurred it, consequently it falls within this power... The

reason these 'odious' debts cannot be considered to encumber the territory of the State, is that such debts do not fulfill one of the conditions that determines the legality of the debts of the State, that is: the debts of the State must be incurred and the funds from it employed for the needs and in the interest of the State. 'Odious' debts, incurred and used for ends which, to the knowledge of the creditors, are contrary to the interests of the nation, do not compromise the latter.[5]

In order for countries not to use this regime opportunistically he proposed the following:

(1) The new Government would have to prove and an international tribunal would have to ascertain the following:

(a) That the needs which the former Government claimed in order to contract the debt in question, were odious and clearly in contradiction to the interests of the people of the entirety of the former State or a part thereof, and:

(b) That the creditors, at the moment of paying out the loan, were aware of its odious purpose.

(2) Upon establishment of these two points, the creditors must then prove that the funds for this loan were not utilised for odious purposes – harming the people of the entire State or part of it – but for general or specific purposes of the state which do not have the character of being odious.[6]

Whilst it is a stretch to define all or most of Greece's debt as 'odious', given that there were elections during the period the debt accrued (the military government was fiscally responsible, interestingly enough), there has to be some discussion of reform, at an international level as well as within nations, of the ability of governments of small economies to borrow vast quantities of hard currency (as in the case of Greece) or to become exposed to a similar scale of liabilities through their banking systems (as in the cases of Iceland and Ireland).

Multiconstituent Involvement

Unborn taxpayers might end up paying off these vast debts, or suffering the effects of default. Thus a 'Sharing of Pain and Sacrifices Programme' under the guidance of fairness must be implemented. In order for

Greece's debt to be redirected to a sustainable path, not subject to future reneging and crisis, the costs of debt sustainability must be shared. All constituents must share the burden, namely: creditors, the bloated public sector, foreign multinationals, current and future taxpayers, and recipients of reduced public services. All must shoulder the burden – everyone already involved and potentially affected in future.

Once economic and constitutional reforms are in place, Greece will need a serious 'debt haircut'. It is not possible or necessary to give precise numbers here; suffice to say steps should be significant enough to put the country on a sustainable path without having to continually shrink the economy with increased taxes, forcing companies out of Greece. That of course is easier said than done. Greek politicians and EU representatives have frequently spelled out the negative consequences of default or restructure. They are not wrong in the narrow frame of reference they are working within, but this is really an inadequate policy response showing a lack of understanding of the negative consequences of *not* defaulting. It is typically assumed, for example, that a default means pariah status for many decades. In fact, the bond markets have short memories. Argentina is starting to function normally again, helped by economic development in the region.

Finally Develop a Country Business Model – and a Growth Engine

Day 1, post restructuring its debt and implementing supply-side reforms, Greece needs to have a business plan. This plan should not be the typical 'plan to get us through the next elections'.

Greece should focus on its comparative advantages. Its majestic natural beauty lends itself, for example, to focus on tourism. Its educated workforce could be a linchpin in becoming a research and development centre. Its numerous doctors could present an opportunity to become a centre for high-end hospital treatments. It could easily build on its historical cumulative advantage to become a world-class shipping training and management centre. Muddling along with a narrow parasitic capitalist class based on public spending and an economy based on consumption and imports will not suffice. The supply-side reform should allow unborn entrepreneurs eventually to take the place of the inefficient bloated public sector and the protected oligarchical businesses. Thus small businesses and entrepreneurs should be allowed to flourish, and not be strangled before birth by red-tape and closed professions that try to extract rents from them.

Washington Consensus

Capital transfers into smaller economies have spun out of control, in large part because of the excess credit growth, lack of regulations and the Darwinian opportunism of the banks. This pattern also exposes the limitations of the technocratic, optimistic but ultimately naive 'Washington Consensus' economic philosophy that has dominated policymaking in the West for the past three decades.

Simon Johnson, in his speech at the Peterson Institute in January 2009, summarised some of the dangers, and called on policymakers to identify 'the real structural problem that created the current situation and that has likely pushed the global economy into a new phase of instability'. He added:

> The global economic growth of the last several years was in reality a global, debt-financed boom... The US housing bubble was inflated by global capital flows... The European financial bubble, including massive lending to Eastern Europe and Latin America, occurred with zero net capital flows (the eurozone had a current account roughly in balance). China's export-driven manufacturing sector had a bubble of its own, in its case with net capital outflow (a current account surplus)...
>
> But these regional bubbles were amplified and connected by a global financial system that allowed capital to flow easily around the world. I am not saying that global capital flows are a bad thing; ordinarily, by delivering capital to the places where it is most useful, they promote economic growth, in particular in the developing world. But the global system also allows bubbles to feed on money raised from anywhere in the world, exacerbating global systemic risks.[7]

The free flow of capital into the small economies of Iceland, Ireland and Greece swamped them. The subsequent pulling out when deposits flee can be deeply destabilising, and governments feel obliged to intervene, causing their debt levels to rise – often during a recession. For the past two or three decades it has been assumed that zero control of capital flows is unquestionably a force for good in terms of efficient allocation of capital. In practice, we have seen extreme distortions, bubble economics and excessive levels of borrowing by governments of smaller countries that were opportunistic, corrupt or simply naively unaware of the risks being taken on.

Consideration has to be given to reintroducing capital controls, at least for those governments without the regulatory or constitutional infrastructure to cope with huge inflows.

What the credit crisis and sovereign debt crisis have also shown is that one element of the Washington Consensus can undermine another – they are not automatically self-supporting. In particular, market deregulation and liberalisation of capital made it easier for short-termist governments to abandon the principle of fiscal responsibility. Investment banks encouraged this development, and profited from it. The forces of global capital also caused huge, hidden liabilities in the banking system that have landed in the lap even of governments that had sought to be fiscally responsible, such as Ireland's. Investment banks have used the language of the Washington Consensus in their rent-seeking behaviour, but in many cases have undermined the principles of free markets, not least by tacitly expecting taxpayer support.

Deference to the investment banks is combined with an obsession on the part of policymakers with short-term monetary manipulations rather than long-term stewardship of the real economy. This is now exposed as a serious strategic weakness. There are compensatory factors for an advanced economy with huge debts, like the USA, compared with Greece, but these are factors that policymakers studiously overlook: high-tech, export-orientated business, top-class universities and so on.

The Washington Consensus and the emphasis of central banks on inflation targets appeared for many years to have created the 'Goldilocks' economy: non-inflationary, long-term growth, with policymakers dismissing those who pointed to the risks of growing trading imbalances and high public and private debts. The 'Goldilocks' claim was kind of true, but only with *narrow logic* and by ignoring the inevitable fallout – which is much like King Herod saying: 'But if you take the slaughter of the innocents out of the picture, you have to agree that my record on child protection bears comparison with any kingdom in the ancient world'.

The use of ratings agencies also requires reform. Overreliance on the Washington Consensus has led to excessive faith in economic data and ratings. The fault lies more with excessive reliance on superficial indicators than with the indicators themselves. Rating agencies overall have a good record; for example, all of the sovereign debts that have defaulted since 1975 received speculative-grade ratings one year ahead of their default. Just as the Washington Consensus should only be regarded as an outline for an economy's jurisdiction, so too should ratings only be regarded as a relative indicator. Neither should replace proper inquiry into the real economy and the real risk. As noted in chapter 9, too many investors have outsourced their risk assessment to the ratings agencies. A rating essentially provides a relative indication of credit risk. The 'smoothing' effect that ratings agencies have sought, in the understandable aim of avoiding frequent reratings, unfortunately means that there is a tendency for a 'cliff-like' plunge after undetected risk has built up and leads to overconfidence.

The Banks

Banks have become too big. In the deepest of ironies, the deregulation towards supposedly 'free market' economies over the past three decades has provided banks with the opportunity to behave like oligarchs. Those of us who have worked in emerging markets easily recognise the oligarchical behaviour of the Wall Street giants. They are out of control, lobbying to the extent that they have captured even the largest governments. They have become rent seekers: levying disproportionate amounts from the economy, benefiting from bail-outs and the implicit promise of bail-outs, and thus creating moral hazard on a potentially unmanageable scale.

There also has to be a reexamination of the excessive supply of credit, and a reexamination of the consensus of operating a fiat currency.

Since, the collapse of the Bretton Woods Agreement in 1971, money has been not backed by gold reserves, effectively putting no practical limit to the amount of the money and credit central banks and financial institutions can create.

This paved the way for the 'financialisation' of the global economy, whereby financial institutions progressively increased their dominance over the real economy, as unrestrained credit increased as a percentage of GDP over the last 30 years.

A contradiction in Western policy (pre-crisis that is) of the past two to three decades has been the emphasis upon tight control of a narrow money supply combined with loose control of credit supply – even though the latter can be more destabilising, especially where there are no capital controls and there are jurisdictions with insufficient capacity to handle large inflows. The banking sector has encouraged this: every time there is a financial or commercial transaction, they increase their revenues as the settlement of the flow of funds occurs through them. There is a short-term incentive for banks to encourage credit supply, and insufficient controls have been put in place by politicians. When a major deleveraging occurs following a credit boom, such as in the period from 2007 to 2010, the monetary tools used to counter a recession are useless, because the problem is of a lack of demand and overindebtedness relative to the productive capacity of the economy, not a lack of stimulus.[8] Simply put, once credit reaches a certain multiple of money and income, there is no room for further demand creation based on credit or monetary stimuli rather than productivity gains. Such debt cycles have existed for as long as there has been credit.

There have been some interesting contributions, from both fiscal conservatives and green economists, challenging the notion that the creation of credit should be profitable. Ron Paul, a Republican senator, is a long-standing critic of fiat currencies – that is, those not convertible into a commodity like gold. He claims that a fiat currency system is popular with economists, the business community, bankers and government officials, because it 'allows power and influence to fall into the hands of those who control the creation of new money, and to those who get to use the money or credit early in its circulation.'[9] The green economist James Robertson has questioned the degree to which money creation is interest-bearing credit creation by the banks. This encourages speculation in land and property, and the tendency towards boom and bust.[10]

There is increasing recognition that credit controls have been too weak. In November 2010, Andrew Haldane, executive director for financial stability at the Bank of England, gave a speech that used the metaphor of licensing controls and drunken behaviour. He noted that for the past three decades policymakers had assumed that moderating the business cycle was sufficient to hold credit in check, but that this had been ineffective, noting that the appearance of moderation fooled policymakers and regulators: 'In the UK, credit grew at three times the rate of money spending over that period, sowing the seeds of the credit crisis, while inflation and growth remained remarkably stable.' He suggested reorientating regulatory policy towards curbing the cycle in credit supply. One example would be increased regulatory requirements on banks to 'lean against' a credit boom. 'In the public houses for credit, intake would be monitored, opening hours restricted and the Happy

Hour abolished.'[11] Unfortunately, containing a credit boom, given the banks' lobbying power using the intellectual cloak of the 'efficient market' hypothesis would be not achievable for the powerless regulators.

The 'efficient market' hypotheses claimed that financial markets always correctly value asset prices given all available information at the time. The major regulators, including Alan Greenspan of the Federal Reserve, were long-term supporters of financial deregulation, believing that financial markets were best at pricing risk and efficiently allocating capital. With this backdrop there should be little surprise why credit growth was left unchecked and regulators left financial markets to their own devices. There are conceptual barriers to the right type of regulation, as too many key players still equate 'deregulation' with efficient markets.

Grotesque overlending (including to small and developing countries), is based on an outsized banking system. Debt has become commoditised. The brightest people have gone there, often draining more productive sectors of the economy. Rocket scientists better employed in aerospace have been producing dangerous financial products that their bosses do not understand.

In the US between 1973 and 1985, the financial sector earned less than 16 per cent of domestic corporate profits. By 1986, that figure reached had 19 per cent. In the 1990s, it oscillated between 21 per cent and 30 per cent, and by the 2000s it had reached 41 per cent.[12]

'Renting' is defined as the additional income that organisations can charge above the level that would be received in a competitive marketplace, owing to monopoly, secret price fixing or, in the case of the financial services, the ability to create complex products that even sophisticated customers do not understand. Thomas Philippon of New York University and Ariell Reshef of the University of Virginia have estimated that between 30 to 50 per cent of the extra pay bankers receive compared to similar professionals is attributable to rents.[13] The multiple bail-outs around the world since 2008, and quantitative easing, have allowed rent-seeking behaviour to continue.

In January 2009 Simon Johnson of the Peterson Institute for International Economics pointed to the 'deeper cause' of the crisis. The answer lies with the political economy of the US financial system, and in particular the lobbying power of the financial firms developing into an emerging market type of structure (see chapter 8).[14]

As this speech emphasises, the lobbying power of the big banks is too great and has been too effective – securing the repeal of Glass–Steagall, for example. The well-trodden path from the Goldman Sachs executive suite to the US Treasury is odious. Links with other governments have been too close: the massive debts imposed on unborn Greek and Argentinian taxpayers, by postponing and inflating already high levels of sovereign debt through *megacanje* and currency swaps, are a scandal.

As well as international rules that seek to curb the power of the big banks, individual nations should introduce constitutional checks and balances to prevent a single-term government devising plans with investment banks to secure cash for the next election by impoverishing the next generation. One such potential drastic reform hangs on the question as to whether (or not) foreigners should be allowed to buy domestic bonds. The idea of blocking foreign investment might sound a bit extreme, especially in the short term, but remember that eventually all borrowed monies must eventually be repaid. Any temporary benefits derived from living beyond your means must be weighed against the potential costs. Our reliance on foreign government borrowing exposes the country's finances to the fickle capital markets and the next global crisis.

Just to illustrate the power of banking, I have included a small example from the world of foreign exchange. Foreign exchange brokers allow private investors (read 'gamblers') to leverage their account up to 100 to 400 times. So lets say you go deposit US$ 100 in your foreign exchange account. You can trade US$ 40,000- worth in foreign exchange. With a 1 per cent currency move in your favour, you make US$ 400, or four times your initial capital. Pretty amazing! With a mere 0.25 per cent move the other way however, all your equity is wiped out. Why is this legal? What need is there for this to be possible in society? The answer is none. The higher transaction volumes this allows simply increases the amount of profits the banks make as 'market-makers' and is effectively a tax on society. If this occurred in a casino it would be purely illegal. The banking lobby still allows this sort of behaviour.

The banks' argument to each national government is that 'if you cut us down to size, we will go elsewhere and take our rent-seeking (but taxable) behaviour to another jurisdiction'. The bluff has to be called. This calls for bold, internationally coordinated leadership from governments. In the same way that the single market requires a strong anti-cartel commission, it is increasingly clear that globalised finance needs international rules backed by institutions that have real clout. Basel III is a modest step in this direction, aimed at forcing banks to boost capital reserves. What are also needed are clear, enforceable rules to prevent odious debt being created by governments and other toxic by-products by of the out-of-control investment banking industry. This is not impossible. Anti-cartel institutions in North America and Europe have had successes against corporations in non-financial sectors; similar resolve can and should be used against odious behaviour by the banks. A century ago, Theodore Roosevelt succeeded in breaking up industrial oligarchies with anti-trust measures. A similar historic challenge confronts the current generation of political leaders in the West: break up the financial oligarchies. So far, it is one that they seem to be ducking.

The GDP Fallacy

The intellectual backstop of the Washington Consensus – the naive belief that deregulation leads to free and efficient markets – when combined fatally with overreliance on GDP growth as an indicator, leads to the inability to distinguish between sustainable growth and a debt-fuelled consumption binge.

GDP is a measure of the flow of economic activity, not of the wealth of a nation. There are other measures of wealth, productive capacity and quantifying the sustainability of development. The net worth of a country equals its gross assets minus its liabilities. Borrowing to consume perishables that do not increase the capital stock of gross assets simply increases the GDP in the short run and flatters the ratios. Given that the liability-side also increases it may actually lead to a reduction in the net worth of country despite increased interim GDP.

In the USA, the growth figures looked promising throughout the 1990s and early 2000s whilst a complacent attitude let the twin deficits rise and rise. Growth, however, was most certainly elevated through a major misallocation of capital into, for example, the housing market. This however proved to be temporary (and essentially) non-productive growth which was borrowed from the future, its only lasting effect probably being in reducing the wealth of the US as these excesses are paid for.

The booms created by excess credit growth give the illusion of wealth creation, but the illusion of wealth creation is not sustainable. Over the longer term, the middle and lower income groups tend not to benefit.[15] This is politically dangerous. Historian Simon Schama has commented that: 'The stock epithet the French revolution gave to the financiers who were blamed for disaster, was "rich egoists". Our own plutocrats may not be headed for the tumbrils, but the fact that financial catastrophe, with its effect on the 'real' economy, came about through obscure transactions designed to do nothing except produce short-term profit aggravates a sense of social betrayal.'[16]

Economics is now convulsed by an intellectual crisis. The failure of intricate mathematical models, especially in the subprime crisis, has been followed by a debate over whether the discipline should be primarily quantitative, or follow a more qualitative approach, similar to historical analysis. This discussion is of interest, but runs the risk of becoming frivolous and partisan. A bigger risk than being 'too quant-' or 'too qual-' is to be too reliant on a single piece of supporting evidence and other traps of the familiar cognitive biases. Economics and policymaking need to be more inquiring, eclectic, sceptical; less certain or predictive. We need to look at fundamentals, not be misled by relative pricings or fads. We have to give up faith in the bogus guarantee, the supposedly protective effect of policy intention, marked by qualitative overexaggeration – 'Too big to fail', 'Too connected to fail', 'The euro train will not be allowed to crash', and so on.

European Welfare States?

For all their mutual hostility, European public sector trade unions and the investment banks are very similar: both are rent-seeking, insular and lacking any sense of responsibility towards the rest of society. As the Western economies of the world hit crisis and decline, they will seek to blame one another and shirk from any sense of culpability. Politically, they appear to be poles apart, but behaviourally they look and sound the same.

The out-of-control investment banks are unaffordable to any would-be rescuers; so are the European welfare states. A similar pattern is emerging in the USA and Japan also. Welfare states were only maintained at their generous levels in the early 2000s through borrowing – the demographic squeeze will add further pressure. Without reform, some Western states will simply become bankrupt; with a large pensions and healthcare liability with a small productive economy attached, some will be ripe for economic takeover as a colony of an Asian power. In order to reduce costs, especially of pension liabilities, some form of social cohesion is necessary. Letting the investment banks off the hook would make the equally necessary task of welfare state reform almost impossible; just as the culture of impunity for Greek politicians makes it difficult for society to accept the austerity measures.

More generally within Europe, we need to accept that we are going to get poorer in relative terms, and that emerging markets in Asia and Latin America are likely to become the future. Currencies are overdue a realignment in relative terms, and that realignment could be huge. A Greek builder can go to five-star hotel in Thailand, but the Thai doctor cannot afford a five-star holiday in Greece (neither can most law-abiding people for that matter, but I digress). This is not likely to prove sustainable over the longer term.

As and when the dollar and euro begin major depreciations against Asian currencies, the Asian middle class will have more purchasing power. There will be opportunities for competitive Western companies, provided their liabilities on tax, pensions contributions and healthcare are affordable.

Put simply, we are living beyond our means. Asians are living below their means. The currency peg of the euro has distorted matters, but this is unravelling. Within Europe, if Greece had stayed with the drachma it would have devalued; more Germans might have visited Greece on holiday, and there would be fewer purchases of German cars by Greece. If or when there is a global realignment, there is likely to be a major reshaping of relative living standards throughout the West and Asia. Why hasn't it happened already? Because China desires an export-led economy while incorporating rural workers into factory jobs – otherwise, unemployment would be higher. But the realignment is beginning: we can already observe demands for higher wages in China and the growth of the middle class. They will be able to spend more on Porsche Cayennes and (hopefully) holidays in the Aegean. Success breeds failure and failure breeds success.

Levels of debt in the West and our expensive ways of living are generally not sustainable. The dangers of drastic repayment over the very short term, Ceauşescu-style, have been well aired, but the dangers of inaction are also not well understood. The supposed Keynesian 'stimulus' effect of countercyclical borrowing might be overstated: the Ricardian equivalence theory states that deficit spending has no long-term impact on growth, as the private sector adjusts spending today to a reduced level, with the logical expectation that the additional government spending today implies compensating tax increases tomorrow. Indeed, while deficit spending can be helpful in stabilising demand during the initial stage of a downturn, it is not very efficient overall as a countercyclical policy tool. If governments try to stimulate growth and jobs today, no matter the cost, the impact on growth and jobs tomorrow will be even more severe.

Sovereign default has not occurred among 'advanced' economies since the West German default of 1948. It would be surprising if this long unbroken period did not create complacency. As a useful paper notes, sovereign default was actually quite common before the age of income tax and sales taxes, and we may be returning to an age in which it is common for the sovereign to have a lower credit rating than individuals and organisations in its jurisdiction, limiting its powers to tax such entities.[17]

Economic reform has to be fair. The European welfare states, propped up by borrowing, are unaffordable. But if they are cut down to an affordable size, while the investment banks continue to maintain their oligarchical grip on the throats of governments and the productive economy, awarding themselves massive, taxpayer-subsidised bonuses, the political risk will rise very sharply indeed.

The trust that is needed between citizens and state must be maintained as a part of the economic recovery plan; it's not an optional extra. As I have outlined earlier in this chapter, Greece needs to move substantially towards a culture of compliance, taxpaying, obeying the law (politicians included) and reduction in the scale of the informal economy. According to some studies, however, some advanced economies are moving in the opposite direction, not only in the rise of new oligarchies, but in the habit of avoiding tax and in the growth of an informal economy. This has been aided by the globalisation of finance.[18] So some of the lessons for Greece need to be heeded by other countries too, to prevent the slide from advanced to oligarchical practices.

In politically polarised countries, such as Greece or the USA, there is a risk of policy paralysis. The Left blames the banks; the Right blames government spending. The problem is that the costs that the oligarchical investment banks impose on the real economy, and the costs that the welfare state and pensions entitlements impose, do not cancel each other out. They add to one another, so both have to be tackled.

The Euro

The euro, and hence the European Union, is in crisis. It is being held together by a combination of borrowing, liquidity measures and a feverish desire that the periphery will catch up with the core, overseen by policymakers who ignored the fact that the opposite was occurring during the past decade.

This begs big questions: 'Is the European Union needed?' 'Is the euro needed?' The answer to the first is indisputably, yes. The establishment of the European Economic Community and creation of the single market were principal factors in the rebirth of Western Europe's economies after the Second World War, and demonstrated that free markets and democracies were vastly superior at generating better standards of living than the Communist dictatorships of Eastern Europe or the right-wing dictatorships of Greece and the Iberian peninsula.

The tragedy now is that the huge gains of the first few decades of the EEC/EU risk being squandered by errors in monetary union. The architects of the single currency ignored both theory and recent experience when deciding not to base euro membership on close adherence to the principles of the optimal currency area. They were warned both internally and externally.

The euro as currently configured stands little chance of survival: the austerity being asked of Greece is simply too much; the political risks on the periphery are likely to be too high and most importantly the economic fundamentals and structures of the economies of the countries too different.

Questions of public opinion and social consensus have been ignored. Practices such as effectively ignoring referendum defeats and treating the electorate in a patronising fashion must end. They have the perverse effect of encouraging the euroscepticism that the EU's leaders presumably want to counter. They were too keen to take credit for launching the euro and to make historic pronouncements at launch events, maximising the size of the eurozone rather than ensuring convergence. They need to apologise: for the dishonest threats to the 'out' countries; for the meaningless 'train' metaphor that insulted our intelligence and led their policymaking astray; for their negligence in failing to uphold the Stability and Growth Pact; and for letting debts rise uncontrollably.

They forgot that the concept of 'Europe' is actually quite young. It will take time to create an identity of being European. Greece only joined the EU in 1981; Spain and Portugal five years later. Over time, it will get politically and technically easier to arrange fiscal transfers and make monetary union work.

You could say 'everyone go back to their own currency', but there are benefits of monetary union, both for reduced transaction costs and exchange rate risks across the continent, and in competing against larger trading blocs. It may be that the eurozone will have to be smaller. Just as Greece will face a testing point where the effects of austerity are felt before the benefits, the same is likely to be the case for Europe as a whole. With the periphery mired in austerity measures and recession, there is talk of a 'two-tier' eurozone moving forward. The point here is that the 'out' countries suffered less than Greece or Ireland – the diametric opposite of the predictions made a decade earlier by euro enthusiasts encouraging Sweden, Denmark and the UK to join.

The leaders of the European Union still underestimate the requirements of a true monetary union, and lack the political will to make all the necessary reforms: fiscal union, labour market reform, the restructuring of Greek debts, policy coordination and reform of banking regulation. Moreover, this daunting policy challenge actually represents the *minimum* necessary for a fully functioning currency area. There is now open speculation about a reduction in the size of the eurozone to the central-northern core economies. Nicolas Sarkozy, the French president, has been reported as allowing his officials to explore such a proposal.[19]

This would have huge repercussions. Default on sovereign debt would be inevitable for Greece and likely for others. Another dimension is the question of how Ireland would respond. It might prefer to rejoin the sterling link, or have a floating currency before applying to join the 'northern' euro.

These stories of new regional currencies are speculations, though there is a similarity to the composition of the northern replacement for the euro in both stories, comprising countries that have similar profiles in their real economies. It is also similar to the optimum single currency area of the Greater D-Mark, identified by various studies cited by former ECB executive board member Otmar Issing, and confirmed by the study by Barclays Capital in 2010; an idea that was overlooked in the giddy rush to a large single currency area. What is remarkable is the way in which experience repeatedly indicates that the German-speaking countries plus Benelux and perhaps one or two other neighbours comprise the only truly converged optimal currency area in Europe. This was evident with the currency 'snake' in the 1970s, the collapse of the ERM in the 1990s, and the 'two-tier' nature of the single currency in 2010.

Where Now?

The single currency has not been the 'train' of its proponents' imagination, but it is a journey. This odyssey does not have a timetable or a track; it is marked by uncertainty and diversion, because that is the nature of real economies – this is the reason only true optimal currency areas can share the same coin. The convergence of participating economies did not occur, nor was it ever likely according to theory or the recent precedent of Argentina. Overconfidence in this expected convergence was shared by the European Union and the investment community alike. These institutions now have to unwind the thought patterns that fed this 'fingers-crossed' attitude. The fudging and amnesia that characterised the formation of monetary union illustrate a lack of understanding of the scale of the economic decisions being taken. In similar fashion, investors in the European convergence trade were indifferent or unaware of the instability generated by the mountain of sovereign debt they helped to accumulate. Trade unions are unconcerned about liabilities that build up in national pension schemes; IMF officials and central bankers have been content to issue Washington Consensus checklists or target inflation, or to issue communiqués that are exercises in understatement as speculative bubbles inflate and explode around them and odious debts grow uncontrollably. This collective indifference or unawareness of the scale of the economic dislocations in a world of globalised finance is dangerous. The only exit routes involve radical readjustments of policy and mindset, and will include short- to medium-term pain for which many in Europe are likely to be unaccustomed and unprepared.

Hold on for the ride.

NOTES

Chapter 1: From Buenos Aires to Athens

1 M. Kiguel and N. Liviatan, 'The Business Cycle Associated with Exchange Rate Based Stabilization', *World Bank Economic Review* 6, (1990): 279–305; also C. Vegh, 'Stopping High Inflation: An Analytical Overview', *IMF Staff Papers* 39, (1991): 626–95. A useful overview is Walter Molano's paper: 'Argentina: The Political Economy of Stabilization and Structural Reform', BCP Securities, January 2000. Online at: http://papers.ssrn.com/sol3/papers.cfm?abstract_id=203857 (accessed 16 March 2011).

2 From a conversation with a visitor to Chile during this month.

3 P. Blustein, *And the Money Kept Rolling In (And Out)* (New York: Public Affairs, 2005).

4 Information available at: http://en.wikipedia.org/wiki/Hyperinflation (accessed March 2011).

5 Quoted in Blustein, *And the Money Kept Rolling In (And Out)*.

6 E. Galeano, 'Las Venas Abiertas de America Latina', *Siglo Veintiuno Editores* (1971); 'The Open Veins of Latin America' (trans. Cedric Belfrage) (New York: Monthly Review Press, 1997).

7 Blustein, *And the Money Kept Rolling In (And Out)*.

8 UN data: http://data.un.org/CountryProfile.aspx?crName=Greece (accessed January 2000).

9 Organisation for Economic Co-operation and Development (OECD) data: http://stats.oecd.org/Index.aspx?DataSetCode=DECOMP (accessed January 2000).

10 Vito Tanzi, *Argentina: An Economic Chronicle* (New York: Jorge Pinto Books, 2007).

11 Molano, 'Argentina: The Political Economy of Stabilization and Structural Reform'.

12 Tanzi, *Argentina: An Economic Chronicle*.

13 Blustein, *And the Money Kept Rolling In (And Out)*.

14 'SEC Charges Siemens AG for Engaging in Worldwide Bribery', U.S. Securities and Exchange Commission press announcement no. 2008–294, 15 December 2008. Online at: http://www.sec.gov/news/press/pressarchive/2008press.shtml (accessed 17 March 2011).

15 J. Van Loo, *Political Clientelism and the Political Economy of Corruption in Transition Economies* (New York: Duke University, 2002).

16 M. Porter, *The Competitive Advantage of Nations* (2nd ed.) (Basingstoke: Palgrave Macmillan, 1998).

Chapter 2: Getting Lucky

1 The data on Greece has been subject to revision, and not all the various sources tally precisely with each other. In 2009 the Economic and Financial Affairs Council (Ecofin), the EU council of finance ministers, asked the European Commission to prepare a report on Greek fiscal statistics. This included a revision of the 2008 public sector deficit figure from 5 per cent of GDP to 7.7 per cent, and of the then projected 2009 figure from 3.7 per cent to 12.5 per cent. See the 'Report on Greek Government Deficit and Debt Statistics', European Commission, January 2010.

2 Information provided by the US State Department, online at: http://www.state. gov/r/pa/ei/bgn/26516.htm (accessed June 2010).

3 Data from the Argentine Ministry of Agriculture, online at: http://www. alimentosargentinos.gov.ar/0–3/olea/a_soja/aceite_soja.htm (accessed June 2010).

4 Encyclopedia of the Nations, online: http://www.nationsencyclopedia.com/ Americas/Argentina-AGRICULTURE.html#ixzz0yjsF14QU (accessed June 2010).

5 P. Blustein, *And the Money Kept Rolling In (And Out)* (New York: Public Affairs, 2005).

6 Vito Tanzi, *Argentina: An Economic Chronicle* (New York: Jorge Pinto Books, 2007).

7 D. Lachman, 'Greece Looks set to go the way of Argentina', *Financial Times*, 12 January 2010.

8 Blustein. *And the Money Kept Rolling In (And Out)*.

9 Paul Krugman, 'Greenspan and the bubble', *New York Times*, 29 August 2005.

10 From 'A Bravo New World', an internal report released by Goldman Sachs to its clients in 1996, as discussed in Blustein, *And the Money Kept Rolling In (And Out)*.

11 Walter Molano, 'Argentina: The Political Economy of Stabilization and Structural Reform', BCP Securities, January 2000. Online at: http://papers. ssrn.com/sol3/papers.cfm?abstract_id=203857 (accessed 16 March 2011).

12 Ibid.

13 'Lessons from the Crisis in Argentina', paper prepared by the Policy Development and Review Department of the International Monetary Fund, approved by Timothy Geithner, 8 October 2003. Online: http://www.imf.org/external/np/ pdr/lessons/100803.htm (accessed 7 March 2010).

14 Nikos Michaelian, 'Luxury Car Mania Grips Greece', *Kathimerini*, 11 November 2006.

15 'Δανειστήκαμε 8 δισ. ευρώ... για αγορά I.X.', Capital, online at: http://www. capital.gr/News.asp?id=1091873 (accessed 7 March 2011).

16 Reported by the Hellenic Resources Network. See entry no. 7 online at: http://www.hri.org/news/greek/apeen/2010/10–10–15.apeen.html (accessed 7 March 2011).

17 *Proto Thema*, 11 April 2010.

18 Kerin Hope, 'Forest fires point up challenges', *Financial Times*, 13 July 2007.

19 See note 1 in this chapter. Chapters 3 and 7 include discussion on how data on public deficits and debts seriously understated the real situation.

20 'Is Greece Heading for Default?', Oxford Economics, February 2010.

21 'Lessons from the Crisis in Argentina', Policy Development and Review Department of the International Monetary Fund.

Chapter 3: The Euro: Hard Sell, or Mis-Sell?

1 The text of Robert Schuman's famous speech can be found online at: http://www.schuman.info/9May1950.htm (accessed 16 March 2011).

2 'Functioning of EU product and capital markets – summary of European Commission report', European Commission memo no. 02/303, 23 December 2002.

3 European Union figures, online: http://europa.eu/abc/keyfigures/qualityoflife/wealthy/index_en.htm (accessed 7 March 2011).

4 Bernard Connolly, *The Rotten Heart of Europe* (London: Faber & Faber, 1995).

5 Ronald McKinnon, 'Optimal Currency Areas', *American Economic Review* 52, (1963): 717–25; also Robert Mundell, 'A Theory of Optimum Currency Areas', *American Economic Review* 51, (1961): 657–65.

6 Francesco Paolo Mongelli, 'New Views on the Optimum Currency Area: What is EMU Telling Us?', European Central Bank Working Paper 138 (2002). See also: Simon Tilford, 'Will the eurozone crack?', Centre for European Reform, September 2006.

7 Jeffrey A. Frankel and Andrew Rose, 'The Endogeneity of the Optimal Currency Area', *Economic Journal* 108, no. 449 (1997): 1009–25.

8 Mundell, 'A Theory of Optimum Currency Areas'.

9 Otmar Issing, *The Birth of the Euro* (Cambridge: Cambridge University Press, 2008).

10 'European Parliament Fact Sheet 5.2.0 – the EMS and the ECU'. European Parliament, 20 November 2000. Online at: http://www.europarl.europa.eu/factsheets/5_2_0_en.htm (accessed 16 March 2011).

11 See Roger Boyes, 'Eurosceptic legal challenge to stop Germany's Greek bailout', *Times*, 8 May 2010.

12 Quoted in Issing, *The Birth of the Euro*.

13 Connolly, *The Rotten Heart of Europe*.

14 Issing, *The Birth of the Euro*.

15 Reported online by the BBC: http://news.bbc.co.uk/1/hi/business/35886.stm (accessed 8 March 2011).

16 Issing, *The Birth of the Euro*.

17 European Central Bank computations on European Commission data; see also Table 7.2 in chapter 7 of this book.

18 See http://en.wikipedia.org/wiki/Goodhart's_law (accessed 16 March 2011).

19 'EU Bulletin 5', European Commission, 3 May 2000, points 1.3.4 and 1.3.5. Online at: http://ec.europa.eu/economy_finance/emu_history/legalaspects/part_c_1_i.htm (accessed 16 March 2011).

20 Eurostat rules described the 'Greek-type' swap in *Risk Magazine*, 18 February 2010.

21 'Status Report on Information Requirements in EMU', Ecofin 334, EFC, 28 October 2005.

Chapter 4: Western Branding, Eastern Legacy: A Country on a Fault Line

1 Percy Bysshe Shelley, 'Hellas' (1821–22), ll. 696–701.

2 'Greece and the Illusion of Europe', *Daily Telegraph*, 5 July 2010.

3 Robert Kaplan, 'A Family Portrait of a Greek Tragedy', *New York Times*, 25 April 2010.

4 A. E. Laiou and C. Morrisson, *The Byzantine Economy* (Cambridge Medieval Textbooks) (Cambridge: Cambridge University Press, 2007).

5 A list of quotes expressing admiration of Greek resistance, including Winston Churchill, Adolf Hitler, Albert Camus, Josef Stalin and others can be found online at: http://en.wikipedia.org/wiki/User:Hectorian#cite_note-4 (accessed 8 March 2011).

6 See http://en.wikipedia.org/wiki/Ottoman_Greece#Taxation_and_the_.22tribute_of_children.22 (accessed 8 March 2011).

7 Again, see http://en.wikipedia.org/wiki/Ottoman_Greece#Taxation_and_the_.22tribute_of_children.22, citing Stanford J. Shaw, *History of the Ottoman Empire and Modern Turkey* (vol. I) (Cambridge: Cambridge University Press, 1977).

8 Quote taken from Takis Michas, 'A cracked Greek vase' (2010), available online at: http://www.unfreemedia.com/manbitesdog/2010/05/a-cracked-greek-vase. html (accessed 8 March 2011). Michas is the author of *Putting Politics above Markets: a Greek Tragedy* (Washington D.C.: Cato Institute, 2010).

9 Chronis Polychroniou, 'Political culture and corruption in Greece: A synergistic relationship', Online Journal, 4 February 2008.

10 David H. Close, *Greece since 1945: A History* (Harlow: Longman, 2002).

11 Ibid.

12 Christos Lyrintzis, 'The Power of Populism: the Greek Case', *European Journal of Political Research* 15, (1987): 667–86.

13 Close, *Greece since 1945*.

14 Data provided by the CIA World Factbook, online at: https://www.cia.gov/library/publications/the-world-factbook/rankorder/2034rank.html (accessed 8 March 2011).

15 'Greece stresses Turk ship concern', *Kathimerini*, 19 July 2010.

16 'Turkey: the sentinel swivels', *Financial Times*, 20 July 2010.

17 'Greece and Turkey increasingly hostile over territory', BBC podcast, 14 May 2010. Online at: http://news.bbc.co.uk/1/hi/world/europe/8681835.stm (accessed 8 March 2011).

18 'Rafale International moves a step forward in Greece by reinforcing its presence in Athens', Dassult Aviation press release, 4 March 2008. Online at: http://www.dassault-aviation.com/en/aviation/press/press-kits/2008/rafale-international-moves-a-step-forward-in-greece-by-reinforcing-its-presence-in-athens.html?L=1 (accessed 17 March 2011).

19 'Trends in International Arms Transfers' SIPRI Fact Sheet, 15 March 2010. Online at: http://books.sipri.org/files/FS/SIPRIFS1003.pdf (accessed 16 March 2011).

20 *SIPRI Yearbook 2010: Armaments, Disarmaments and International Security* (Oxford: Oxford University Press, 2010).

21 'The Geopolitics of Greece: A Sea at its Heart', Stratfor, 28 June 2010. Online at: http://www.stratfor.com/memberships/166008/analysis/20100627_geopolitics_greece_sea_heart (accessed 16 March 2011).

22 Lyrintzis, 'The Power of Populism', *European Journal of Political Research* 15: 667–86.

23 T. Panagiotidis and A. Trampella, 'Central Bank Independence and Inflation: the Case of Greece', Discussion Paper No. 2005_7 (2005), Loughborough University Department of Economics.

24 Lyrintzis, 'The Power of Populism', *European Journal of Political Research* 15.

Chapter 5: The Looting of Greece: Scandals, Corruption and a Monstrous Public Sector

1   ''Ένας Έλληνας, ίσον έξι Βρετανοί', News 247, 3 July 2010. Online at: http://news247.gr/ellada/oi_aiwnovioi_ellhnes_syntaksioyxoi_einai_osoi_kai_oi_vretanoi.392726.html (accessed 16 March 2011).

2   Article 62 of the Constitution of Greece, in English, online at: http://www.hri.org/docs/syntagma/artcl80.html#A62 (accessed 8 March 2011).

3   Transparency International, *Global Corruption Report 2005* (London: Pluto Press, 2005). Online at: http://www.transparency.org/publications/gcr/gcr_2005#download (accessed 8 March 2011).

4   Benjamin Broome, *Exploring the Greek Mosaic: A Guide to Inter-cultural Communication in Greece* (London: Intercultural Press, 2000).

5   Christos Lyrintzis 'Political Parties in Post-Junta Greece: A Case of Bureaucratic Clientelism?', *West European Politics* 7, no. 2 (1984): 99–118.

6   Enet News report, 'Πάγκαλος: Φάγαμε σε διορισμούς τα λεφτά!', online at: http://www.enet.gr/?i=issue.el.home&date=22/09/2010&id=205496(accessed 8 March 2011).

7   Kerin Hope, 'Greece's economic burden', *Financial Times*, 2 December 2009.

8   Antonio Afonso, Ludger Schuknecht and Vito Tanzi, 'Public Sector Efficiency: An International Comparison', European Central Bank Working Paper 242, July 2003.

9   Michael Dragoumis, 'Greece on the Couch', a compendium of articles featured in the *Athens News*, 2004.

10 'Watchdog points to corrupt officials', *Kathimerini*, 2 July 2010.

11 Dragoumis, 'Greece on the Couch'.

12 David H. Close, *Greece since 1945: A History* (Harlow: Longman, 2002).

13 K. Tsoukalas, *Kratos, Koinonia, Ergasia (State, Society, Labour)* (Athens: Themelio, 1986).

14 Christos Lyrintzis, 'The Power of Populism: the Greek Case', *European Journal of Political Research* 15, (1987): 667–86.

15 'Country Briefing (Greece) from the Economist Intelligence Unit', EIU ViewsWire, 22 October 2008.

16 'Appointment of athlete "gardeners"', *Proto Thema*, 22 August 2010.

17 *Vima*, 30 August 2010.

18 'Civil service census starts shakily', *Kathimerini* online news, 13 July 2010.

19 C. Meghir, D. Vayanos and N. Vettas, 'The Economic Crisis in Greece: A Time of Reform and Opportunity', August 2010. Summary published by the *Financial Times*, 23 August 2010: 'Greek reforms can yet stave off default'.

20 Editorial in *Frankfurter Allgemeine Zeitung*, February 2010. Also quoted in 'Greek debt crisis: the view from Germany', *Guardian*, 11 February 2010.

21 Data available online at: http://www.businessinsider.com/greece-germany-pensions-2010-4#proportion-of-wages-as-pension-greece-80-germany-46-2#ixzz0yMWPE6Dy (accessed 8 March 2011).

22 'Five areas of Greek budget waste', Reuters, 28 April 2010, citing economics website www.capital.gr.

23 As revealed by PASOK deputy prime minister Theodoros Pangalos in July 2010. New Democracy did not deny the claim. Reported at: http://www.tovima.gr/default.asp?pid=2&ct=32&artId=341584&dt=06/07/2010#ixzz0sseih8eS (accessed July 2010).

24 Sotiropoulos Bourikos, 'Ministerial Elites in Greece, 1843–2001: A Synthesis of Old Sources and New Data', *South European Society & Politics* 7, no. 2 (2000): 200. Online at: http://www.ces.fas.harvard.edu/publications/docs/pdfs/SotiropoulosBourikos.pdf (accessed May 2010).

25 'Greece Offers EU500 Million Farm Package, Roadblocks Continue', Bloomberg, 23 January 2009.

26 *Kathimerini*, 31 January 2010.

27 'EC probes farmer cash: Government must recover last year's handouts if they turn out to be state subsidies', *Kathimerini*, 28 January 2010.

28 Close, *Greece since 1945*.

29 'Back down to earth with a bank', *Kathimerini*, 3 March 2010.

30 Dimitrios Vortelinos, 'Bureaucracy and Corruption', July 2010; research commissioned for this work.

31 Transparency International, *Global Corruption Report 2005* and *Global Corruption Report 2006*. Online at: http://www.transparency.org/publications/gcr (accessed 8 March 2011).

32 Transparency International, *Global Corruption Report 2009*. Online at: http://www.transparency.org/publications/gcr.

33 http://www.transparency.org/policy_research/surveys_indices/cpi/200.9/cpi_2009_table (accessed June 2010). See also Vortelinos, 'Bureaucracy and Corruption'.

34 Quoted in 'Tragic Flaw: Graft feeds Greek Crisis', *Wall Street Journal*, 15 April 2010. See also Daniel Kaufmann, 'Can Corruption Adversely Affect Public Finances in Industrialised Countries', online at: http://www.brookings.edu/opinions/2010/0419_corruption_kaufmann.aspx (accessed May 2010).

35 'Cabotage reaction costs keep growing', *Kathimerini*, 19 July 2010. Online at: http://archive.ekathimerini.com/4dcgi/_w_articles_economy_0_19/07/2010_118446 (accessed 16 March 2011).

36 *Proto Thema*, 25 August 2010.

37 'Closed professions to be opened', Anglo-Hellenic blogspot, September 2009. Online at: http://anglo-hellenic.blogspot.com/2009/09/closed-professions-to-be-opened-to-eu.html (accessed 16 March 2011).

38 'EU services directive a tough sell', *Athens News*, 27 July 2009.

39 'Kiosks and taxis in the grip of crisis', *Kathimerini*, 30 August 2010.

40 'No let-up in truck strike', *Kathimerini*, 28 July 2010.

41 News reports, including: 'Greek Truckers End Strike', *Wall Street Journal*, 2 August 2010.

42 Vortelinos, 'Bureaucracy and Corruption'.

43 *Kathimerini*, 19 May 2010.
44 *Kathimerini* and *Proto Thema* news reports, 25 August 2010.
45 'Cost of Athens 2004 Olympics', press statement from the American Embassy of Greece in Washington D.C., 13 November 2004. Online at: http://www. greekembassy.org/Embassy/content/en/Article.aspx?office=3&folder=200&a rticle=14269 (accessed 17 March 2011).
46 Statistics given in the Commission of Economics' official report on the Olympics, featured in news reports such as 'Now They're Sorry: Athens' Owe-lympics', AOL News, 24 May 2010.
47 Data online at: http://www.philip-atticus.com/2010/06/greeces-corruption-non-scandal.html (accessed September 2010).
48 'JP Morgan Offers to Buy Back Greek Bond After Pensions Probe', Bloomberg, 20 April 2007; 'JP Morgan Delays Greek Lawmaker Meeting on Bond Sale', Bloomberg, 22 May 2007; and 'JP Morgan Greek Tragedy Sets "Hero" Banker Against Old Bosses', Bloomberg, 26 October 2007.
49 Vortelinos, 'Bureaucracy and Corruption'.
50 'Tragic Flaw: Graft Feeds Greek Crisis', *Wall Street Journal*, 15 April 2010.
51 'Inside Bribery Probe of Siemens', *Wall Street Journal*, 28 December 2007.
52 'How German companies bribed their way to Greek deals', *Der Spiegel*, English-language edition 11 May 2010.
53 'Siemens suspects face detention', *Kathimerini*, 18 May 2009.
54 'Siemens Hit with $1.6 Billion Fine in Bribery Case', National Public Radio news website, online at: http://www.npr.org/templates/story/story.php?storyId= 98317332 (accessed August 2010).
55 'Former Siemens Manager given Suspended Sentence, Focus Says', Bloomberg, 4 March 2010, taken from 'Verfahren gegen Ex-Siemens-Manager eingestell', *Focus*, 3 March 2010.
56 '"No dawdling" in Siemens inquiry', *Kathimerini*, 10 September 2010.
57 'Calls for EU to Halt Corrupt Defense Deals', Bloomberg, 27 July 2010.
58 'German input sought in probes', *Kathimerini*, 11 June 2010.
59 'Greece set to probe Daimler', *Kathimerini*, 29 March 2010.
60 'How German companies bribed their way to Greek deals', *Der Spiegel*, English-language edition 11 May 2010.
61 'An orgy of waste', *Vima*, 10 April 2010.
62 'Γαλάζια ρουσφέτια στα Τουριστικά Ακίνητα', *Ta Nea*, 18 May 2010.
63 'Scandals The Looting of Greece', Robert Ajemian, *Time*. The website gives the date of 24 June 2001, but this appears to have been first published before Andreas Papandreou died in 1996.
64 'Greek Ex-Premier Not Guilty in Bank Scandal', New York Times, 17 January 1992. Online at: http://www.nytimes.com/1992/01/17/world/greek-ex-premier-not-guilty-in-bank-scandal.html (accessed September 2010).
65 'Cycladic ring exposed', *Kathimerini*, 30 August 2010.
66 '20 εκατομμύρια ευρώ για ροζ τηλέφωνα σε υπουργείο!', Astelor Angel blog, 20 May 2010. Online at: http://edo-makedonia.pblogs.gr/2010/05/627232.html (accessed August 2010).
67 'The "party" with the Procurement Contracts of Municalities', *Vima*, 8 August 2010, online at: http://www.tovima.gr/default.asp?pid=2&ct=32&artId=34755 4&dt=08/08/2010#ixzz0w6dWz5tf (accessed August 2010).

68 'The Unravelling of ERT has begun', *Vima*, 3 August 2010. Online at: http://www.tovima.gr/default.asp?pid=2&ct=1&artid=346653&dt=03/08/2010#ixz z0vY9MpEol (accessed August 2010).

69 'Grant of €8.5 million to a ghost company, via Mr Sioufas' hand', *Proto Thema*, 23 May 2010. *Vima* broke the story on 14 May 2010.

70 Jason Koutsoukis, 'Small-time corruption Greece's big problem', *Sydney Morning Herald*, 15 May 2010.

71 'Five areas of Greek budget waste', Reuters, 28 April 2010.

72 'Μαχαίρι στις "μαϊμούδες" αναπηρικές συντάξεις', *Proto Thema*, 27 September 2010, at: http://www.protothema.gr/economy/article/?aid=82703 (accessed September 2010).

73 Vortelinos, 'Bureaucracy and Corruption'.

74 '2,000 big depositors caught in Switzerland', *Proto Thema*, 22 August 2010.

75 'Greek taxpayers sense evasion crack-down', *Financial Times*, 16 April 2010.

76 'Super-wealthy investors move billions out of Greece', *Observer*, 7 February 2010.

77 Suzanne Daley, 'Greek Wealth is Everywhere but Tax Forms', *New York Times*, 1 May 2010.

78 'Super-wealthy investors move billions out of Greece', *Observer*, 7 February 2010.

79 '2,000 big depositors caught in Switzerland', *Proto Thema*, August 2010.

80 'Doctors probed', *Kathimerini*, 14 May 2010.

81 *Kathimerini*, August 2010.

82 BBC 'Today Programme', 30 April 2010.

Chapter 6: Getting Unlucky – It All Begins to Unravel

1 Nassim Nicholas Taleb, *The Black Swan: The Impact of the Highly Improbable* (London: Allen Lane, 2007).

2 'Economic survey of Greece 2007: Recent performance and key challenges', Organisation for Economic Co-operation and Development, 30 May 2007.

3 'Greece Country View', Economist Intelligence Unit, 22 October 2008.

4 Ben S. Bernanke, 'The Great Moderation', Federal Reserve Board, 20 February 2004. Online at: http://www.federalreserve.gov/BOARDDOCS/SPEECHES/2004/20040220/default.htm (accessed 9 March 2011).

5 'Is Greece Sustainable?', Bank of America Merrill Lynch, 21 April 2010.

6 Argentine competitiveness figure from: Peter Boone and Simon Johnson, 'What happened to the global economy and what can we do about it?', The Baseline Scenario, 11 March 2010. Online at: http://baselinescenario.com/2010/03/11/the-coming-greek-debt-bubble/#more-6757 (accessed 17 March 2011). The Greece figure of 20 per cent currency overvaluation from 'Is Greece Heading for Default?', Oxford Economics, February 2010.

7 C. Meghir, D. Vayanos and N. Vettas, 'The Economic Crisis in Greece: A Time of Reform and Opportunity', August 2010. Summary published by the *Financial Times*, 23 August 2010: 'Greek reforms can yet stave off default'.

8 Meghir et al., 'The Economic Crisis in Greece'; and Richard Koo, 'Learning the wrong lessons from the crisis in Greece', Nomura, 15 June 2010.

9 V. Rapanos, 'Μέγεθος και Εύρος Δραστηριοτήτων του Δημόσιου Τομέα', Foundation for Economic and Industrial Research (IOEB) Working Paper (2009).

10 Meghir et al., 'The Economic Crisis in Greece'.

11 Ibid.

12 Walter Molano in the *Latin American Adviser*, 15 December 2000, also quoted in P. Blustein, *And the Money Kept Rolling In (And Out)* (New York: Public Affairs, 2005).

13 'Lessons from the Crisis in Argentina', paper prepared by the Policy Development and Review Department of the International Monetary Fund, approved by Timothy Geithner, 8 October 2003. Online: http://www.imf.org/external/np/pdr/lessons/100803.htm (accessed 7 March 2010).

14 'IMF Country Report Number 09/244', IMF, August 2009.

15 'España paga seis veces más que Alemania por los intereses de su deuda a dos años', *El Pais*, 7 May 2010. Online at: http://www.elpais.com/articulo/economia/Espana/paga/veces/Alemania/intereses/deuda/anos/elpepieco/20100507elpepieco_1/Tes (accessed 17 March 2011).

16 'Brasil crece; la Argentina se achica', *La Nación* editorial, 29 May 2010.

17 Blustein, *And the Money Kept Rolling In (And Out)*.

18 Available at: http://www.youtube.com/watch?v=rH6_i8zuffs&feature=related (accessed 9 March 2011).

19 Walter Molano 'Addressing the symptoms and ignoring the causes: A view from Wall Street on dollarization', BCP Securities, March 2000.

Chapter 7: The Euro in Practice

1 'All Svilegkrant in Evros and Edirne', *Kathimerini*, 6 June 2010.

2 Francesco Paolo Mongelli, 'New Views on the Optimum Currency Area: What is EMU Telling Us?', European Central Bank Working Paper 138 (2002).

3 Richard Baldwin, Virginia DiNino, Lionel Fontagné, Robert A. De Santis and Daria Taglioni, 'Study on the Impact of the Euro on Trade and Foreign Direct Investment', European Commission Economic Paper 321, May 2008. Online at: http://ec.europa.eu/economy_finance/publications/publication12590_en.pdf (accessed 9 March 2011).

4 'A Special Report on the Euro', *Economist*, 13 June 2009.

5 'José Zapatero: No he traicionado mis principios con la reforma laboral', *El Pais*, 9 September 2010.

6 Speech by José Manuel González-Páramo, member of the executive board of the ECB conference on 'New Perspectives on Fiscal Sustainability', Frankfurt, 13 October 2005. Available from the ECB website at: http://www.ecb.int/press/key/date/2005/html/sp051013.en.html (accessed 9 March 2011).

7 Otmar Issing, *The Birth of the Euro* (Cambridge: Cambridge University Press, 2008).

8 Richard Koo, 'Learning wrong lessons form the crisis in Greece', Nomura research note, 15 June 2010.

9 'Recommendation for a Council Recommendation to Greece with a view to bringing an end to the situation of an excessive government deficit', Ref SEC (2009) 565/2, EU Commission, March 2009.

10 'Commission assesses Stability and Convergence Programmes of Ireland, Greece, Spain, France, Latvia and Malta; presents reports under excessive

deficit procedure', EU Commission statement, 18 February 2009. Online at: http://europa.eu/rapid/pressReleasesAction.do?reference=IP/09/274&format=HTML&aged=0&language=EN&guiLanguage=en (accessed July 2010).

11 'Euro Themes: Comparing euro area and US divergence', BarCap Economics Research, 22 September 2010.

12 Koo, 'Learning wrong lessons from the crisis in Greece'.

13 Zsolt Darvas, Jean Pisani-Ferry and André Sapir, 'A comprehensive approach to the euro-area debt crisis', Bruegel Policy Brief No. 2011/02, February 2011.

14 Josef Joffe, 'Germany won't let the Euro train be derailed', *Times*, 18 June 2010.

15 Nassim Nicholas Taleb, *Fooled by Randomness: The Hidden Role of Chance in Life and the Markets* (London: Texere, 2004).

16 Menzie Chinn and Jeffrey Frankel, 'The Euro may over the next 15 years surpass the dollar as leading international currency', *e21* 11, no. 1 (2008): 49–73.

17 Wolfgang Munchau, 'Why the Euro will soon replace the dollar as the world's reserve currency', *Eurointelligence*, 24 March 2008. Online at: http://www.eurointelligence.com/article/article/why-the-euro-will-soon-replace-the-dollar-as-the-worlds-reserve-currency.html?L=1&tx_ttnews%5BbackPid%5D=755&cHash=8378f09d14be5fde62de597c410e5c0e (accessed 17 March 2011).

18 'Decision not to join the euro was right, says Alexander', BBC online news, 21 September 2010.

19 'Wall St Helped to Mask Debt Fueling Europe's Crisis', *New York Times*, 13 February 2010.

20 'Monthly Update', Dromeus Global Opportunities Fund, April 2009.

21 'Greece: Selected Issues', IMF Country Report 07/27, January 2007.

22 Peter L. Bernstein, *Against the Gods: The Remarkable Story of Risk*, (New York: John Wiley, 1996).

23 Herman Van Rompuy, 'Summary of the opening address by Herman Van Rompuy, President of the European Council, to the Brussels Economic Forum 2010', 25 May 2010, online at: http://www.consilium.europa.eu/uedocs/cms_data/docs/pressdata/en/ec/114623.pdf (accessed 17 March 2011).

24 Simon Tilford, 'The Euro at Ten: is its future secure?', Centre for European Reform, January 2009.

25 Ibid.

Chapter 8: Liquidity Boom

1 Howard Marks, 'No Different this Time', memo to Oaktree clients, December 2007.

2 Nassim Nicholas Taleb, *Fooled by Randomness: The Hidden Role of Chance in Life and the Markets* (London: Texere, 2004).

3 There is a considerable amount of literature on Prospect Theory. The seminal work is Richard H. Thaler, Amos Tversky, Daniel Kahneman and Alan Schwartz, 'The Effect of Myopia and Loss Aversion on Risk Taking: An Experimental Test', *Quarterly Journal of Economics* 112, no. 2 (1997): 647–61. Also useful are James Montier, *The Little Book of Behavioral Investing* (Hoboken,

NJ: John Wiley & Sons, 2010), and Michael J. Mauboussin, *More than you Know* (New York: Columbia University Press, 2008).

4 Montier, *The Little Book of Behavioral Investing*.

5 Desmond Lachman, 'Chasing Yield', *International Economy*, Spring 2004.

6 Richard Koo, 'Does culpability for the latest Greek tragedy rest solely with Athens?', Nomura research note, 11 May 2010.

7 Montier, *The Little Book of Behavioral Investing*.

8 Paul Krugman, 'How did economists get it so wrong?', *New York Times*, 6 September 2009.

9 Ibid.

10 Montier, *The Little Book of Behavioral Investing*.

11 'The problem is not the shorts, but the longs', Buttonwood's blog, *Economist*, 10 June 2010.

12 Otmar Issing, *The Birth of the Euro* (Cambridge: Cambridge University Press, 2008).

13 Michael Mauboussin, *Think Twice: Harnessing the Power of Counterintuition* (Boston: Harvard Business Press, 2009); and Nassim Nicholas Taleb, *The Black Swan: The Impact of the Highly Improbable* (London: Allen Lane, 2007).

14 For an overview of the Washington Consensus, please see: http://en.wikipedia. org/wiki/Washington_Consensus (accessed 17 March 2011).

15 Simon Johnson, 'The Economic Crisis and the Crisis in Economics', presidential address to the Association for Comparative Economics, San Francisco, 4 January 2009. Online at: http://www.iie.com/publications/papers/paper. cfm?ResearchID=1090 (accessed June 2010).

16 Media reports including 'Tiger in a tailspin', *Der Spiegel* English-language edition, 27 September 2010.

17 'Ireland faces double dip, mulls restructuring of junior debt', *Daily Telegraph*, 23 September 2010.

18 Simon Johnson, 'The Quiet Coup', *Atlantic Magazine*, May 2009.

19 John Williamson, 'Did the Washington Consensus Fail?', speech made in Washington D.C. at the Center for Strategic and International Studies, 6 November 2002.

20 Joseph Stiglitz, 'More instruments and broader controls: moving towards the post-Washington Consensus', speech made in Helsinki to the World Bank Group, 7 January 1998.

21 Nancy Birdsall, Augusto de la Torre and Felipe Valencia Caicedo, 'The Washington Consensus: Assessing a Damaged Brand', Center for Global Development Working Paper 213, May 2010.

22 Carmen Reinhart and Vincent Reinhart, 'Capital Flow Bonanzas: An Encompassing View of the Past and Present', National Bureau of Economic Research Working Paper 14321, September 2008.

23 Paul A. Volcker, 'A perspective on financial crises', in Jane Sneddon Little and Giovanni P. Olivei (eds), *Rethinking the International Monetary System* (Conference Series 43) (Boston: Federal Reserve Bank of Boston, 1999).

24 Soyoung Kim and Doo Yong Yang, 'The Impact of Capital Inflows on Emerging East Asian Economies', Korea Institute for International Economic Policy, May 2008.

25 Richard Dobbs and Michael Spence, 'The era of cheap capital draws to a close', McKinsey Quarterly, February 2011. Online at: http://www.mckinseyquarterly. com/Economic_Studies/Productivity_Performance/The_era_of_cheap_ capital_draws_to_a_close_2741?gp=1 (accessed 9 March 2011).

Chapter 9: The Entertainers

1 Michael Mauboussin, *More than you know: Finding Financial Wisdom in Unconventional Places* (New York: Columbia University Press, 2008), and Nassim Nicholas Taleb, *The Black Swan: The Impact of the Highly Improbable* (London: Allen Lane, 2007).
2 'Reform of rating agencies poses dilemma', *Financial Times*, 10 June 2010.
3 Angela Monaghan, 'Pimco attacks ratings agencies over Greek crisis', *Daily Telegraph*, 6 May 2010.
4 'Credit Rating Agencies: Developments and Policy Issues', European Central Bank monthly bulletin, May 2009. Online: http://www.ecb.europa.eu/pub/ pdf/other/art3_mb200905_pp107-117en.pdf (accessed 10 March 2011).
5 Howard Marks, 'Now it's all bad?', Oaktree Capital memo to clients, September 2007.
6 Robert Cialdini, *Influence: Science and Practice* (4ᵗʰ ed.) (Boston: Allyn & Bacon, 2001).
7 There are concise summaries in James Montier, *The Little Book of Behavioral Investing* (Hoboken, NJ: John Wiley & Sons, 2010).
8 Bent Flyvbjerg, *Making Social Science Matter* (Cambridge: Cambridge University Press, 2001).
9 Quoted in Peter L. Bernstein, *Against the Gods: The Remarkable Story of Risk* (New York: John Wiley, 1996).
10 'Soros Speaks About Debt Crisis', Bloomberg, 14 June 2010.
11 'IMF Performance in the Run-Up to the Financial and Economic Crisis: IMF Surveillance in 2004–2007', Independent Evaluation Office of the International Monetary Fund, 10 January 2011.

Chapter 10: A Temporary Bail-Out? A Crisis Made Worse by Satisficing

1 D. Lachman, 'Greece Looks Set to Go the Way of Argentina,', *Financial Times*, 12 January 2010.
2 N. Roubini and A. Das, 'Medicine for Europe's Sinking South', *Financial Times*, 2 February 2010.
3 Wilhelm Hankel, Wilhelm Nölling, Karl Albrecht Schachtschneider and Joachim Starbatty, 'A Euro Exit is the Only Way Out for Greece', *Financial Times*, 26 March 2010.
4 Quoted in 'Soros Says Greek "Death Spiral" Risk Remains After Aid Package', Bloomberg, 12 April 2010.
5 'Greece Seeks to Sell China Banks €25 Billion Bonds', Dow Jones Newswire, 27 November 2009.
6 'China Shouldn't Rescue Greece by Buying Debt, Yu Says', Bloomberg, 28 January 2010.

7 Pierre-Henri Thomas, 'La Grèce, notre Argentine a Nous', *Le Soir*, 9 April 2010.
8 'Papandreou Prefers European Solution', *Financial Times*, 18 March 2010.
9 Nouriel Roubini, 'Crisis will Spread without a Plan B', *Financial Times*, 29 April 2010.
10 'Zapatero alega que España está en condiciones de prestar dinero a Atenas', *El Pais*, 26 March 2010.
11 'US Investors Cool on Greek Debt Sale Plans', *Financial Times*, 8 April 2010.
12 'José Luis Zapatero: Sarkozy amenazó con salirse del euro', *El Pais*, 14 May 2010.
13 'On the Secret Committee to Save the Euro, a Dangerous Divide', *Wall Street Journal*, 26 September 2010.
14 'ECB reveals €16.5 billion bond purchases', CNBC, 18 May 2010.
15 'La intervencion de Cajasur lleva al Ibex a caer mas que la majoria de las Bolsas europeas', *El Pais*, 24 May 2010.
16 W. Munchau, 'Europe risks failing the real test on banks', *Financial Times*, 4 July 2010.
17 'Staff Report on Request for Stand-by Arrangement', IMF report on Greece approved by Poul M. Thomsen and Martin Muhleisen, 5 May 2010.

Chapter 11: The Man in the Arena

1 John Rawls, 'Justice as Fairness', *Philosophical Review* 67, (1958).
2 C. Meghir, D. Vayanos and N. Vettas, 'The Economic Crisis in Greece: A Time of Reform and Opportunity', August 2010. Summary published by the *Financial Times*, 23 August 2010: 'Greek reforms can yet stave off default'.
3 Poul M. Tomsen, 'Greece Program on Track, but Challenges Ahead Interview Published', *Kathimerini* , 8 August 2010.
4 C. Reinhart and K. Rogoff, *This Time is Different: Eight Centuries of Financial Folly* (Princeton, NJ: Princeton University Press, 2009).
5 Alexander Nahun Sack, *Les Effets des Transformations des États sur Leurs Dettes Publiques et Autres Obligations Financiéres: Traité Juridique et Financier* (Paris: Recueil Sirey, 1927).
6 Ibid.
7 Simon Johnson, 'Economic Crisis and the Crisis in Economics', speech prepared for the presidential address to the Association for Comparative Economics, San Francisco, 4 January 2009.
8 Ray Dalio, 'A Template for Understanding What's Going On', updated version June 2010.
9 Ron Paul, 'Fiat Paper Money', 12 September 2003. Available online at the Ron Paul archive: http://www.lewrockwell.com/paul/paul125.html (accessed 17 March 2011).
10 James Robertson, 'Money from Nothing', *New Economy Magazine*, summer 2009.
11 Andrew Haldane, 'The Debt Hangover', speech to Professional Liverpool dinner, 27 January 2010. Online at: http://www.bankofengland.co.uk/publications/speeches/2010/speech422.pdf (accessed February 2011).
12 Simon Johnson, 'Quiet Coup', *Atlantic Magazine*, May 2009.

13 See 'Taxing spoils of the renting sector', Reuters blog, 22 April 2010.

14 Johnson, 'The Economic Crisis and the Crisis in Economics'.

15 Albert Edwards, 'Theft! Were the US and UK central banks complicit in robbing the middle classes?', Société Générale, 21 January 2010.

16 Simon Schama, 'The world teeters on the brink of a new age of rage', *Financial Times*, 22 May 2010.

17 'Is sovereign default "unnecessary, undesirable and unlikely" for all advanced economies?', *Global Economics View*, 16 September 2010.

18 'Is sovereign default "unnecessary, undesirable and unlikely" for all advanced economies?', *Global Economics View*, citing also F. Schneider and D. Enste, 'Shadow Economies and Corruption All Over the World: Revised Estimates for 120 Countries', Economics e-journal, October 2009.

19 'Germany and France examine "two-tier" euro', *Daily Telegraph*, 19 June 2010.

INDEX

ACKNOWLEDGEMENTS

To my parents, for their unconditional love and support, for being charismatic role models and for giving me a passion for books.

To Achilles Risvas, my business partner, for his patience whilst this book was being written and all the invigorating debates and market discussions.

To my close friends, who provided immense support and help by providing invaluable feedback and sound advice whilst reading draft manuscripts, brainstorming on cover designs, assisting in editing and collecting valuable data: Apostolos Mimikos, Christos Baltatzis, George Nowak, Kostas Togas, Nikos Passaris, Phillip Whiteley, Stephen Pinder and Yiannis Demopoulos.

To my academic and market peer reviewers, whose insightful and sharp comments assisted in making important improvements.

Finally, to Tej Sood and Janka Romero at Anthem Press, for their brilliant and smooth collaboration and for believing in me and my first book.

Lightning Source UK Ltd.
Milton Keynes UK
UKOW051158040112

184727UK00001B/17/P

9 780857 287717